Dewdroppers, Waldos, and Slackers

Dewdroppers, Waldos, and Slackers

A Decade-by-Decade Guide to the Vanishing Vocabulary of the Twentieth Century

Rosemarie Ostler

OXFORD
UNIVERSITY PRESS

OXFORD

UNIVERSITY PRESS

Oxford University Press, Inc., publishes works that further
Oxford University's objective of excellence
in research, scholarship, and education.

Oxford   New York
Auckland   Cape Town   Dar es Salaam   Hong Kong   Karachi
Kuala Lumpur   Madrid   Melbourne   Mexico City   Nairobi
New Delhi   Shanghai   Taipei   Toronto

With offices in
Argentina   Austria   Brazil   Chile   Czech Republic   France   Greece
Guatemala   Hungary   Italy   Japan   Poland   Portugal   Singapore
South Korea   Switzerland   Thailand   Turkey   Ukraine   Vietnam

Copyright © 2003 by Oxford University Press, Inc.

First published by Oxford University Press, Inc., 2003
198 Madison Avenue, New York, New York, 10016
www.oup.com

First issued as an Oxford University Press paperback, 2005
ISBN-13: 978-0-19-518254-5
ISBN-10: 0-19-518254-5

Oxford is a registered trademark of Oxford University Press

The Library of Congress has cataloged the hardcover edition as follows:
Ostler, Rosemarie.
Dewdroppers, waldos, and slackers : a decade-by-decade guide to the
vanishing vocabulary of the twentieth century / Rosemarie Ostler.
p. cm.
Includes bibliographical references (p.   ) and index.
ISBN-13: 978-0-19-516146-5
ISBN-10: 0-19-516146-7
1. English language—United States—Glossaries, vocabularies, etc.
2. English language—20th century—Glossaries, vocabularies, etc.
3. English language—United States—Slang—Dictionaries.
4. English language—20th century—Slang—Dictionaries.
5. English language—Obsolete words.
6. Americanisms.
I. Title: Decade-by-decade guide to the vanishing vocabulary of the twentieth century.
II. Title.
PE2838.O88 2003   428'.00973—dc21   2003008302

This book includes some words that are, or are asserted to be, proprietary
names or trademarks. Their inclusion does not imply that they have acquired
for legal purposes a nonproprietary or general significance, nor is any other
judgment implied concerning their legal status.

The publishers thank the American Safety Razor Company for permission
to reproduce Burma-Shave jingles. Burma-Shave is a trademark of
the American Safety Razor Company.

Designed by Mary-Neal Meador

1 3 5 7 9 8 6 4 2
Printed in the United States of America on acid-free paper

To my mother
Agnes R. Deep
and the memory of my father
Anthony P. Deep

Contents

Introduction   A Century's Worth of Old (and New) Words   ix

1900–1919   Modern Times   1

The Twenties   Flappers and Flaming Youth   25

The Thirties   Swinging Cats in Hooverville   47

The Forties   Rosie the Riveter and G.I. Joe   71

The Fifties   Hipsters in Squaresville   95

The Sixties   Getting With It   119

The Seventies   Pet Rocks and Plumbers   145

The Eighties   Tubular Times   169

The Nineties   Dot-Comming into Y2K   191

Afterword   Good-Bye to a Great Century   213

Bibliography   215

Index   223

Picture Credits   239

Introduction

A Century's Worth of Old (and New) Words

Ever encountered a **blatherskite?** How about a **darb?** When was the last time you got the **straight skinny** at a **rap session** or told someone to **keep on truckin'?** Played any hot **waxes** on the **Victrola** lately? How many once-popular American words aren't you using these days? Quite a few, if you're like most people.

Thousands of words and expressions entered American English between 1900 and 1999. Every era from the Roaring Twenties to the Me Decade brought its own fads and trends and the language to go with them—fresh youth slang, up-to-the-minute buzzwords, and colorful catch phrases. Most of this new vocabulary exploded into the vernacular, only to fizzle a few years later as trendier trends and more current events demanded new terminology. Even some relatively recent words like **tubular** and **Netizen** are starting to have an outdated ring.

This book gives yesterday's words another chance to sparkle before they retire to the archives for good. *Dewdroppers, Waldos, and Slackers* is not a comprehensive collection of every term that arrived and departed during the last century. Instead, it focuses on language that still resonates with the mood of its time. These are words that most Americans would once have recognized, if not actually used. I list vocabulary in the decade when it was most popular, rather than when it first appeared. Nothing says "sixties" like **groovy,** even though this resilient piece of slang was heard as early as the 1940s, was still around in the 1970s, and, amazingly, is making a twenty-first century comeback.

Specialized jargon is not included here, except on topics that were briefly popular with the general public—flying machines, hot rodding, and CB radios, for instance. I have also chosen to exclude obscenities and terms that denigrate certain groups, unless their absence would leave a noticeable gap (for example, **Okie** in the thirties chapter and **Charlie** in the sixties chapter).

The other criterion for the words in this book is that they are no longer current. A word isn't truly obsolete until everyone who knew its meaning is gone, but most of the vocabulary included here is now fairly obscure, or at least old-fashioned. Some words are as dead as the **hobble skirt, liberty dogs,** and **automobubbling.** Others are merely the sort of thing no one would say anymore except as a joke. You may have an idea what **hubba-hubba** means. You may even have said it—but not recently. If it's uttered at all now, it's always followed by a laugh.

All the obsolete language in this book was once excitingly new. Where did it all come from? Vocabulary arrives from many places. New inventions often contribute to the word hoard. In the early decades of the twentieth century, when the combustion engine was big news, everyone wanted to talk about the new fad. English rose to the challenge. Dozens of car-related terms entered the language around this time. Some stayed; others left after a brief visit.

The first question was what the new item should be called. **Horseless carriage** was outdated by the early 1900s. Hopeful word coiners provided such gems as *motocycle, petrocar, viamote, mocle, mobe* (pronounced 'MO-bee'), and *goalone.* Americans eventually settled on **automobile,** borrowed from the French. Another popular term was **motor car.** *Automobile* and *motor car* were both straightforwardly descriptive. Unlike *viamote,* people could easily guess what they meant.

Once *automobile* was part of the language, other derivations naturally followed. New *auto-* words included **automobilist, automobiling, autocamping, automobile depot,** and the joke word **automobubbling.** Since then, *-mobile* has been attached to other words to indicate the presence of a combustion engine, as in *bloodmobile* and *bookmobile. Motor* inspired *motor ambulance* and *motor truck,* among others. Some early auto terms were strictly descriptive—**electric self-starter,** for example—while others were metaphorical, like **breezer.** Still others, like **flivver,** were invented out of whole verbal cloth.

High-profile happenings are another fruitful source of new words. America's vocabulary has always swelled during wartime. A single event during World War II, the invasion of Italy's Anzio beachhead, resulted in four terms: **Anzio amble, Anzio foot, Anzio anxiety,** and **Anzio Annie.**

Names of people sometimes contribute to the vernacular as well. We still use the word **quisling** to mean a traitor, although many people no longer remember that the Norwegian fascist Vidkun Quisling encouraged the Nazis to invade his country during the Second World War.

Borrowing from other languages is another way to add to the word store. Soldiers often borrow words from the languages they come in contact with—**gohong, honcho, di dai,** and **choi oi** are some words from Korea and Vietnam. Occasionally, these make it into the civilian vocabulary, as the slang word **boonies** did after the Spanish–American War.

The miseries of combat call for many euphemisms, another excellent reason for word creation. At least two dozen labels existed for lice during World War I, including *galloping dandruff, flannel buzzards, pants rabbits, seam rats, shirt squirrels,* and *undershirt butterflies.* Expressions like **get it, go over the top,** and **buy a ticket west** obscured the brutal fact of getting killed during that same war.

The troops also alleviated their lot with their own private slang, featuring word play and humor. **Charlie** was the chaplain at a time when actor Charlie Chaplin was popular, **submarine chicken** was canned salmon, inexperienced new officers were called **Sears-Roebuck,** and the *Croix de Goof* was awarded for stupidity.

New words enter the language, at least temporarily, when the speech of closed groups spills over into the general conversation. Others who contributed their private vocabularies to the twentieth-century lexicon include jazz musicians, hoboes, computer experts, gangsters, truckers, and drug addicts. Some jargon becomes standard—the jazz word **hip,** for instance. The rest fades from the general consciousness when interest in the group fades. Hoboes are still with us (they even have a Web page), but middle-class people are not as fascinated with the hobo's lifestyle and language as they were during the Depression thirties.

When the populace buzzes about newsworthy events and trends, buzzwords come into general use. For a while, everyone is talking about **the long count** or **the sandwich generation.** Then they move to the next topic, and new expressions replace the old ones. Occasionally, buzzwords acquire a life of their own after the triggering event is all but forgotten. The meaning of the **-gate** ending on the nineties words *Monicagate* and **skategate** is clear, even to people who have no memory of the 1970s Watergate scandals.

Every era features nonsense words and phrases, coined out of sheer linguistic exuberance. **Twenty-three skiddoo,** found in the first chapter, is the grandparent of all frivolous catch phrases in the twentieth century.

Most "new" words are not completely original, but constructed out of already existing material. English speakers borrowed *automobile* from the French, and the French borrowed the parts that make it up. *Auto* means 'self' in Greek and *mobile* means 'movable' in Latin. (Greek and Latin are useful languages for aspiring word coiners, as scientists and product marketers have discovered.)

Insider slang and fringe-group jargon are usually in use for a while before they enter the linguistic mainstream. The word *geek,* as in **computer geek,** filtered into the general vocabulary around the 1980s, but was part of computer specialists' language long before that. And before hackers picked it up, *geek* was a carnival term for someone whose act consisted of biting the heads off live chickens and snakes. That usage probably comes from *geck,* an old word for a fool. Now that *geek* is part of the linguistic mainstream, its meaning has expanded to include specialists in subjects other than computers. It has also taken on positive overtones that were not part of its original sense. Meaning expansion and meaning change are two ways in which old words acquire a new gloss.

Yet another way that people shape the language is by assigning specialized meanings to words already in use. The words **curl, heavy,** and **hotdog** mean one thing to most of us, and something else to surfers. The words **squid, goose, bear, animal, doggy, roach, duck,** and **turkey** bring images of nonhumans, but they all had human counterparts in the youth slang of various decades.

Not all trends and historic happenings create vocabulary. The immigration surge that happened between 1900 and 1921 didn't trigger much word invention among people already living here, aside from ethnic nicknames. Although the millions who entered the country during those two decades powerfully shaped the era, Americans didn't invent new words to talk about their arrival. Maybe one reason is that the issues associated with early twentieth-century immigration were not new. They were the familiar ones of assimilation, poverty, and ethnic prejudice. These could be discussed with words that were already available. (Immigrants, however, did contribute to the language in another way—by introducing dozens of their native words into English.)

Just as words enter the language in many ways, they also exit for various reasons. The most straightforward one is that the object they referred to no longer exists. Few of us ever need to mention **kinetoscopes** nowadays, or **keypunch operators.** The latter were plentiful as late as the early eighties, but both are obsolete now. Words of this type can sometimes take a surprising amount of time to disappear. When refrigerators replaced iceboxes, diehards applied the old word to the new invention. Long after blocks of ice disappeared from food cooling units, *icebox* lingered on. It has a distinctly old-fashioned sound now, but it may take another generation or so to leave the language.

Some words don't exit the language, they just leave the mainstream. In the 1970s, thousands of drivers with new Citizens' Band radios started tossing around trucker jargon. **Breaker, breaker** and **ten-four** were as familiar as *hello* and *good-bye* to people who had never been closer to an eighteen-wheeler than the passing lane. Thirty years later, most people's CB radios are stashed at the back of the garage, but truck drivers are still using their own jargon. Much of it is different because slang is always evolving. On the other hand, some words are the same ones that were once well-known to the general public. They have returned to being the private language of long-haul truckers.

Other words die out for the same reason that **poodle haircuts** are no longer seen on movie stars. They simply become unfashionable and are replaced with something new and different. The language of young people is especially prone to this kind of cutthroat revision. For groups at the edges of society, such as drug users, slang is outdated and useless as soon as outsiders become aware of it. By the time the trendy words for marijuana have entered mainstream English, the drug subculture is calling it something else.

Although the words in this book are going or gone, they are not necessarily forgotten. Every reader will recognize at least a few, so dip into your favorite decade and indulge in some nostalgia. Older people can reminisce over the language that colored the Swing Era, the Cold War, or the Dust Bowl. Younger ones will recall the more recent past, when **hip-hop** was fresh and **soccer moms** were in the news. Readers of all ages can check out other generations' word lists and find out what they considered important enough to require special vocabulary. The twentieth century is over, but we can still appreciate the words we left behind.

Acknowledgments

Various people helped and encouraged me while I was writing this book. I am especially grateful to the members of the "Editorial Board," Deanna Larson, Mary-Kate Mackey, and Sally Sheklow. I read most of this book to them, four or five pages at a time. Their comments and suggestions have been invaluable. Elizabeth Lyon and John Reed also offered me helpful advice when my writing was at its beginning stages.

Thanks go to my agent, Sheree Bykofsky, and her associate, Janet Rosen. I appreciate their enthusiasm for this project, as well as their professional expertise.

I feel lucky to have drawn Erin McKean as my editor at Oxford University Press. Her commitment to the book, along with her friendly willingness to answer any question and sort out any difficulty, have made the publishing process amazingly smooth. Also at Oxford, I would like to thank Marina Padakis for her excellent copyediting and Ryan Sullivan for his help with technical questions. The two reviewers for the press, Allan Metcalf and Marilyn Motz, provided useful comments that helped shape the book.

I am grateful to my husband, Jeffrey Ostler, not only for his encouragement and support, but for his guidance through the thickets of American history.

Finally, I want to thank the American Dialect Society for their unflagging devotion to the American language. If not for Society members' collecting mania, thousands of twentieth-century words and expressions would have slipped away unnoticed. Anyone who checks the Bibliography will see that I have relied heavily on their journal, *American Speech*.

Drop into the automat for coffee and pie.

Modern Times

The twentieth century brought all sorts of modern inventions to make life more fun. Every parlor held at least one mechanical amusement. The family could wind up the **Victrola** and listen to Caruso records, or pop a self-playing music roll into the **player piano** for a little **ragtime.** Those who were not musical might spend an evening viewing beautiful three-dimensional landscapes through the **stereoscope,** or browsing through the pictures in the newspaper's **rotogravure** section. Or maybe they'd just curl up on the davenport with the latest **dime novel.** The adventures of schoolboy Frank Merriwell kept readers entertained for hours.

Folks who preferred to step out could head to the **penny arcade** for the latest in recorded **phonograph** music and **kinetoscope** pictures. **Nickelodeons,** also called *nickelettes* or *nickel theaters,* were another option. Enthralled customers could view exciting **photoplays** like *The Great Train Robbery,* complete with piano accompaniment, for only a nickel. What else could people get for a nickel? A ride on a **jitney bus,** a *five-cent cigar,* five pieces of *penny candy,* and, surprisingly, most dime novels.

If you weren't in the mood for a **gun opera,** you could always take in a vaudeville show. A hilarious **knockabout** act was just the right tonic when you were feeling **punk.** For the more genteel, a **tea dance** was a pleasant choice. Couples worked up an appetite for tea while doing the *bunny hop,* the *turkey trot,* the *kangaroo dip,* and the *Castle walk,* invented by famous dancing partners Vernon and Irene Castle. Hungry revelers who hadn't been to a tea dance could drop into the **automat** for a self-serve cup of coffee and a piece of pie.

Getting there was half the fun. The **trackless trolley** was the cheap way to go, but the twentieth-century way was to **motor** there in a **roadster.** Autos were known as the *playthings of the rich,* but even a **'Varsity man** could afford a cheap little **runabout.** Soon, Henry Ford brought out the **Tin Lizzie, everyman's car,** and **automobubbling** became the new sport. Adventurous ladies and gentlemen donned their **motor coats** to keep the dust off, and away they went to "see America first!"

Motor coats weren't the only innovative garments being worn in the century's first decades. In 1900, women's skirts swept the street (sometimes literally), undergirded with a chemise, a whalebone corset, and petticoats. The **New Woman** shed the layers in favor of simpler skirts and **shirtwaists.** The more daring wore **harem skirts** (practically

---

TWENTY-THREE SKIDDOO

This classic of popular slang came into vogue at the beginning of the twentieth century and is still remembered today. It was probably the first national catch phrase. Although **twenty-three skiddoo** (also spelled *skidoo*) is associated with the Roaring Twenties, it reached its peak of popularity around 1910. Pennants and armbands appeared at resorts and other public entertainment arenas with "23" or "skiddoo" printed on them. The expression usually meant 'go away', but it was also used as an exclamation of surprise, interest, or incredulity, or just an ebullient burst of nonsense.

Skiddoo is clearly a form of *skedaddle*, a Scots dialect word meaning 'to run away' or 'clear out'. But where did the *twenty-three* come from? Frank Parker Stockbridge, writing in the *Louisville Times,* claims that it came from the Broadway play *The Only Way,* a dramatization of Charles Dickens's *A Tale of Two Cities* that opened in 1899. In the last act, an old woman counts the victims of the guillotine, and hero Sydney Carton is number 23. According to Stockbridge, the exclamation "Twenty-three!" gained popularity. *Skiddoo* was added for the benefit of those who hadn't seen the play and didn't know what happened to Carton and his fellow victims. Other plays that have been mentioned as possibly having originated the phrase are *Little Johnny Jones* and *The Errand Boy,* which both opened in 1904. Since *twenty-three* was apparently in use by 1899, it's more likely that these plays incorporated a piece of slang that was already current.

An intriguing alternative suggestion is that the number 23 was part of a long-abandoned telegraph code, meaning something like 'away with you' or 'get off the line'. *Skiddoo* then emphasized the meaning of *twenty-three.*

H. L. Mencken, author of *The American Language,* and others attribute the phrase to T. A. (Tad) Dorgan. Dorgan was a cartoonist with a reputation for coining colorful expressions, although he may have merely popularized this one.

pants!), and the more fashionable **hobble skirts,** measuring only a yard around at the hem. The coolly elegant *Gibson Girl* exemplified the modern look, with her willowy figure and abundant hair swept up in a loose **pompadour.** Men wore loose-fitting *sack suits* or *frock coats* if they were going to the office, and tall silk hats.

More young people than ever were going to college at the beginning of the twentieth century. When not dashing around campus in their **flivvers,** they spent time **boning** so they'd have their studies **down chill.** Only the most **cork-headed** tried to **bull** their tests. A favorite leisure activity was attending a **hog wrastle,** and some young men **spiked** fraternities.

The good old days weren't always about fun. **Muckrakers** like Upton Sinclair and Ida M. Tarbell shocked the country with revelations of corruption in government and industry, while the **Wobblies** clamored for revolution. Teddy Roosevelt responded from his **bully pulpit** by promising workers and owners alike a **Square Deal.** It was still the age of conspicuous consumption, though. A **big noise** like Mrs. Cornelius Vanderbilt could spend thousands on exclusive little evening entertainments at her 70-room Newport cottage, "The Breakers." At least she could until the arrival of the income tax in 1913.

The era closed with the **war to end war.** American **doughboys** headed **over there,** and the watchword was **liberty**—not only *liberty bonds,* but **liberty cabbage** (sauerkraut), **liberty steaks** (hamburgers), and even **liberty pups** (dachshunds). **Aces** in their **flying machines** battled the Germans in dogfights over France, while **farmerettes** went to work on the land. Ordinary citizens conserved food by **Hooverizing,** voluntarily abstaining from pork on Thursday, wheat on Monday, and other foods on other days. When the **Great War** was over and **Armistice Day** finally arrived, the troops were ready for the Roaring Twenties. Modern times were here to stay.

LIFE'S A CAKEWALK

By 1910, many factory and office workers enjoyed a 50-hour week, giving them at least ten more free hours than their parents had. They didn't lack for ways to spend their newfound leisure time. They could take the **trackless trolley** out to the countryside and snap pictures of the scenery with their **box Brownies,** or they could stay home and listen to **phonograph** records. Those with the time and money could even hop into the **Pierce-Arrow** and **motor** to the 1904 Louisiana Purchase Exposition, popularly known as the St. Louis World's Fair. Life seemed like a **cakewalk** with so many novel amusements to try out.

➤ **automat:** a self-serve cafeteria where food was displayed in closed compartments. People would put a coin in a slot, open the see-through compartment door, and remove the dish of their choice. Automat employees replenished the compartments by pushing more food in from behind.

➤ **box Brownie:** the first widely used camera, manufactured by Kodak. A box camera was small enough to be conveniently portable, but its most innovative feature was removable film. Until that time film was sealed into the camera and the whole apparatus had to be sent away for film development. Box cameras are still the kind that most people use.

➤ **dime novel:** popular reading matter for the masses, about the length of a long short story, printed and bound like a magazine. In spite of the name, most cost only a nickel. Dime novels typically featured young male heroes who represented the ideal American type: healthy, athletic, idealistic, brave, handsome, and moral. One popular series described the adventures of schoolboy Frank Merriwell. The books usually had elaborate double titles like *His One Ambition, or Mishaps of a Boy Reporter* and *From Bootblack to Senator, or Bound to Make History.*

➤ **electric trolley car:** a streetcar running along metal tracks, powered by electricity from an overhead wire connected to the car by a pole. **Trackless trolleys** were not set on rails, but simply ran along the street. Certain interurban trolleys were highly luxurious. The "Berkshire Hills," which ran between Great Barrington, Massachusetts, and Bennington, Vermont, was painted white with buff trim and gold-leaf lettering. Its amenities included carpeting, wicker seats, and red brocade curtains, all for an extra 50 cents.

➤ **flying machine:** an early airplane. Although this method of travel remained highly exclusive until the 1950s, it got its start on December 17, 1903, with Orville and Wilbur Wright's first test flights at Kitty Hawk, North Carolina. Their longest flight lasted 59 seconds.

➤ **jitney bus:** a bus that carried passengers for a nickel; *jitney* was the slang term for that coin.

➤ **kinetoscope:** a box enclosing a film loop of photographs that passed in front of a peephole. The pictures passed by at the rate of 46 frames per second, giving the illusion of motion. The entire reel ran for about 90 seconds and usually showed pictures of moving people or animals.

➤ **penny arcade:** a brightly lit, open-fronted store where people could entertain themselves with various coin-operated listening and viewing machines. These included **cinematographs,** which projected moving pictures, and **gramophones,** a type of early record player.

➤ **phonograph parlor:** a version of a **penny arcade** that featured **phonographs,** machines that played sounds recorded on a wax cylinder. The customer dropped a coin into the cabinet holding the phonograph, and music or spoken words came out. Some phonograph parlors also boasted **kinetoscopes.**

➤ **player piano:** a piano that played automatically, using a perforated piano roll. As the piano roll rotated, air blew through the holes and worked the piano keys. Early player pianos were operated by pumping a treadle with the feet. Later, they ran on electricity.

➤ **ragtime:** a kind of music, usually played on the piano, characterized by a syncopated beat. Ragtime was a forerunner of jazz, reaching its greatest popularity between the beginning of the twentieth century and World War I. Its origins are in African-American folk music. Some popular composers were Scott Joplin, Thomas Turpin, James Scott, and Eubie Blake. Irving Berlin's 1911 hit song "Alexander's Ragtime Band" also contributed to the music's popularity. Ragtime was a popular type of music for **player pianos.**

CAKEWALK

In the early 1900s, the **cakewalk** was a dance based on strutting steps. *Cakewalk* was also slang for 'an easy task'. The word's history dates from the mid-nineteenth century, when cakewalks were walking competitions among African slaves. The walk itself was a kind of shuffle-glide step made with the back arched and the chest thrown out. Later, a high strutting step was added. Couples performed the cakewalk, with plantation owners judging the winners. The most stylish walk "took the cake," as an actual cake was awarded as the prize. Competitive cakewalks were so popular that top walkers often traveled from one plantation to another to compete.

The next incarnation of the cakewalk was as a minstrel show or vaudeville turn. From there, trendsetters adopted it as a fashionable dance. Fairs around this period featured *moving cakewalks,* platforms that rocked back and forth, so those standing on them had to take high steps to keep their balance.

Meanwhile, boxers began using the word for fights that were easy to win. Eventually, *cakewalk,* the dance, disappeared, and *cakewalk,* the easy fight, metamorphosed into a word meaning 'any task that is easy to accomplish'.

➤ **rotogravure:** a process by which pictures were printed from an engraved copper cylinder. The rotogravure section of the Sunday newspaper offered sepia-tinted pictures of newsworthy people and places.

➤ **stereoscope:** a hand-held picture viewer that showed a three-dimensional image, similar to the later *View-Master*.

➤ **tea dance:** an afternoon social event where couples practiced popular ballroom dances, then refreshed themselves with tea.

➤ **Victrola:** an early record player made by RCA Victor. The Victrola played when it was wound up with a handle, broadcasting sound through a large megaphone-type speaker. Although *Victrola* was a brand name, people used it to refer to any record player, sometimes spelling it with a small *v*. The term *record player* came into general use in the 1930s, but it first referred to a turntable that plugged into a radio and broadcast the record through the radio's speakers. This machine was also called a *radio gramophone*.

MOVING PICTURES

Thomas Edison and other inventors started capturing motion on film during the late nineteenth century, but moving pictures weren't big business until after the turn of the century. The first film with a sustained plot appeared in 1903: the 12-minute silent *The Great Train Robbery*. Suddenly, Americans had a new entertainment option—going to the **flickers.** It was the start of something big.

➤ **biograph:** an early type of moving picture similar to a **cinematograph.** *Biograph* was also the name of the movie studio founded by Edison's assistant, William Dickson. D. W. Griffith, sometimes called the Father of the Motion Picture, was the producer of the first full-length movie spectacular, *Birth of a Nation,* and made more than 450 short films (**one-reelers**) for Biograph.

➤ **cinematograph:** a machine that filmed and projected a series of instantaneous photographs of moving people, animals, or objects. The shots were projected onto a screen in rapid succession to give the illusion of movement. Early cinematograph films were very short and did not necessarily tell a story. The interest to viewers was in the machinery itself, not in the content of the film.

➤ **flickers:** a slang term for moving pictures, referring to their flickering visual quality. This was later shortened to *flicks*.

➤ **gun opera:** a cowboy movie, also known as a *horse opera*.

➤ **movie palace:** a building for viewing movies. Some early movie theaters really did resemble palaces, with elegant lobbies, crystal chandeliers, luxuriant carpets, and large orchestras to accompany the otherwise silent films.

➤ **nickelodeon:** a movie theater where the price of admission was a nickel. The word combines *nickel* and the Greek word for 'theater', *odeon.* Later, *nickelodeon* sometimes referred to a **penny arcade** because using the machines there actually cost a nickel, not a penny. Other names for the nickelodeon were *nickelette* or *nickel theater.* Early jukeboxes, which played a song for a nickel, were also called nickelodeons.

➤ **newsreel:** a short reel of film played before the main feature, showing news and interesting tidbits of high-life gossip.

➤ **one-reeler; two-reeler:** the length of early movies. Each reel held 12 to 14 minutes' worth of film. Most films were one-reelers, as two-reelers were considered almost too long to hold the audience's attention. Longer movies didn't become popular until D. W. Griffith made a splash in 1915 with *Birth of a Nation,* a three-hour-long drama about the Civil War.

➤ **photoplay:** an elegant alternative to the word *movie. Movie* was a widely used slang term among filmgoers, but the people making the films thought it sounded low-class, so in 1912 they sponsored a contest to find a new word. Musician Edgar Strakosch won $25 for thinking of *photoplay.* A compromise term was *movieplay.*

➤ **store theaters:** movie theaters set up in vacant storefronts.

FLASH ACTS

When the novelty of the movies palled, *stubholders* could enjoy 25 cents' worth of old-fashioned entertainment at the local *palace of variety.* Although vaudeville acts had been around since the late nineteenth century, they were most popular between 1900 and the First World War. The entertainment was truly varied, featuring every kind of act, from **crossover comedy** to **sister acts** to **ivory ticklers.** If a routine was on the **blue** side—unsuitable for families—performers might want to develop a **Boston version** so they could play the **Sunday school circuit.** A really **flash act** would get the whole audience cheering. It was **boffo!**

➤ **alley-oop:** an acrobatic act, from French *allez* ('go') and English *up.*

➤ **all wet:** a flop; a failure.

➤ **blue:** risqué or obscene.

➤ **boffo:** outstanding.

➤ **Boston version:** an edited version of an off-color routine, minus the dirty jokes. Performers needed a Boston version for family theaters. The word probably referred to the theaters owned by Benjamin Franklin Keith and Edward Franklin Albee, which advertised wholesome, family entertainment. Their original theater was the Colonial in Boston.

A big-time flash act! Alma Francis performing in *The Little Café,* 1913 or 1914.

➤ **brodie:** a serious flop, named for Steve Brodie, who claimed to have jumped off the Brooklyn Bridge on July 23, 1886. The term is still occasionally heard.

➤ **crossover:** a comedy act in which two performers entered from opposite sides of the stage, meeting in the middle for their dialogue.

➤ **crosstalk act:** an act consisting of snappy repartee between two comedians.

➤ **Death Trail:** a tour of small-town theaters stretching across the western states from Chicago to the West Coast. Neither performance schedules nor incomes were guaranteed. Small-timers working the Death Trail might perform in as many as 12 shows a day.

➤ **dumb act:** an act that didn't involve talking or singing, such as juggling, acrobatics, or animal acts. The first and last acts on the bill were usually dumb acts because a silent performance wasn't disturbed by audience members entering late or leaving early.

➤ **flash act:** a blockbuster act featuring a row of beautiful dancing girls, a stage full of trained tigers, or some other impressive spectacle.

THE BIG TIME

During vaudeville's heyday, "We've hit the big time" was more than just a metaphor. Big-time vaudeville meant big cities, big salaries, and only two shows a day. No more **Death Trail.** Schedules were guaranteed, and theaters were top-of-the-line. Certain popular performers, such as singer Lillian Russell, earned as much as $3,000 a week. Many comedians who later became famous in the movies or on television had their first success on the big-time circuit. Entertainers who fit this bill include W. C. Fields, Will Rogers, Jack Benny, Judy Garland, Milton Berle, Sammy Davis Jr., Bob Hope, Kate Smith, George Burns and Gracie Allen, and the Marx Brothers.

Although variety shows were fast-paced, the big time had a highly structured format. Typically, a show included eight acts, often beginning and ending with nonspeaking performances while the audience came and went. Song-and-dance or comedy routines filled the first part of the show. These were sometimes performed in front of the curtain while stagehands set the scene for more elaborate numbers to follow. The second half featured the headliners. Nobody appeared more than once during a show, no matter how famous or popular. Performers had 20 minutes or less for their one-shot opportunity to wow the audience.

➤ **freak act:** a novelty act, often presented by a celebrity or by people with physical deformities.

➤ **hoofers:** dancers.

➤ **hokum:** corny, old-fashioned jokes.

➤ **ivory tickler:** a piano player. Piano keys in those days were always made of ivory.

➤ **knockabout:** a comedy routine involving physical humor.

➤ **out of town:** any location other than New York City.

➤ **panic the house:** to be a huge success.

➤ **sister act:** an act featuring sisters, or two women pretending to be sisters. Sister acts were especially prevalent during World War I, when male performers were in the armed forces.

➤ **Sunday school circuit:** vaudevillians' way of referring to the Keith–Albee theaters (see **Boston version**).

➤ **terp team:** ballroom dancers; derived from Terpsichore, the muse of dance.

AUTOMOBUBBLING

The best new toy of all was the **motor car. Automobilists** had to be adventurous back then. Roads were mostly unpaved. None were numbered. Until the **electric self-starter** came along, people started their **Packards, Duesenbergs,** and **Model As** by turning a crank at the front and then leaping out of the way as the car began to move. The rules of the road were flexible—a magazine from the period offers this advice: try to drive on the right as much as possible.

Motorists were also their own mechanics. Blowouts or flats—two common problems in those days—necessitated pulling onto the grass and hauling out the tire repair kit. Toolboxes were stowed on the **running board,** along with extra cans of **gasolene.** How to tell when you were running low? Experts recommended poking a clean, straight stick into the tank.

In spite of the obstacles, Americans were soon in the midst of a full-fledged love affair with their **roadsters.** By 1920, more than 9 million people were registered as car owners. That number has been going up steadily ever since.

Among the most popular American songs in the first two decades of the twentieth century were "Toot Your Horn, Kid, You're in a Fog," "The Automobile Honeymoon," and "Henry's Made a Lady out of Lizzie," referring to Henry Ford's hot-selling **Model T,** or **Tin Lizzie.** To commemorate the first *auto tour* in 1905 (from Detroit to Portland,

Oregon), Gus Edwards and Vincent P. Bryan wrote "In My Merry Oldsmobile," featuring this immortal chorus:

> Come away with me, Lucile,
> In my merry Oldsmobile;
> Down the road of life we'll fly,
> Automobubbling, you and I.

➤ **autocamping:** camping along the roadside while on a long car trip. Early auto tourists couldn't expect to find conveniently located places to eat and sleep, so they usually provided for themselves.

➤ **automobile depot:** an early version of the public garage, where people could not only park their cars but have them serviced.

➤ **automobiling; automobilism:** driving and the cult of driving. These words were handy to distinguish car driving from the driving of other vehicles, like horse-drawn carts.

➤ **automobubble:** a popular joke pronunciation of *automobile*. It appears, among other places, in the hit 1905 song "In My Merry Oldsmobile."

TIN LIZZIE

The Ford Motor Company started producing the Model T in 1908. Known as the *universal car,* Model Ts were inexpensive enough to be purchased by those on a budget. They became even cheaper in 1914, when Ford started making them on an assembly line. Henry Ford, the company's owner, got to the heart of assembly-line philosophy with the famous words, "Any customer can have a car painted any color that he wants, so long as it is black."

These unpretentious little cars were known affectionately as **Tin Lizzies.** They inspired the invention of **Lizzie labels,** an early form of bumper sticker often seen pasted onto the cars of college students. Lizzie labels were usually self-mocking (or Lizzie-mocking): *Don't laugh, you may be old yourself some day*; *Runabout—run about a mile and stop*; *If we had milk and sugar, it would be a milkshake*; *Wreck? No just resting*; *Danger, 1000 jolts*; *I would have been a Lincoln but I was born too soon.* Some of Lizzie's myriad nicknames included **Detroit Disaster, Michigan Mistake, Bone Crusher, Rough Rider, Henry's First Go-cart, Blunder Buss, De Lapid 8, Little Bo Creep, Road Louse, Rolls Woise,** and **Ma Junk.**

Wreck? No, just resting.

⮞ **breezer:** an open car, the usual kind during this period.

⮞ **devil wagon:** an automobile from the perspective of the hapless pedestrian or horse driver.

⮞ **duster:** an ankle-length smock worn to keep clothes clean while driving. Since nearly all cars were roofless, drivers and passengers took their chances with wet weather and dusty roads.

⮞ **electric self-starter:** a device that started the car's engine without the need for cranking. Ignition keys were not yet in use.

⮞ **flivver:** a small, cheap car.

⮞ **gasolene:** an early spelling of *gasoline*.

⮞ **motor car:** another term for *automobile*.

⮞ **motor ambulance; motor truck:** a modern ambulance or truck, propelled by a combustion engine instead of being pulled by horses.

⮞ **motor chapeau:** a hat worn while motoring, from the French word for 'hat'. It featured a heavy veil to keep out the dust.

⮞ **motor coat:** another term for a **duster**.

⮞ **motoring goggles:** goggles worn to keep dust out of a driver's eyes.

⮞ **roadster:** a small, open car with one seat big enough for two or three people, and a large trunk.

▶ **rumble seat:** the trunk of a **roadster** or other car, the cover of which was hinged so that when opened it formed a narrow seat. The rumble was really meant for luggage, not people.

▶ **runabout:** another word for a small, cheap car. One early model was the Oldsmobile.

▶ **running board:** a wide footboard beneath the car's doors to help people get in and out.

▶ **shed:** a closed car.

▶ **Stanley Steamer:** a steam-powered car made by the Stanley Company. In 1906, a Steamer was clocked going at more than 125 miles per hour on the hard sand at Daytona Beach, Florida.

▶ **tonneau:** the interior of a car behind the front seat, a borrowing from French. Back seats were known as **tonneau seats**. **Tonneau covers** stretched across the back of the car to protect it from weather and dirt when not in use.

▶ **turn turtle:** to flip a car upside-down.

> ### SOME EARLY CAR MODELS
>
> **Peerless, Pierce-Arrow, Hispano-Suiza, Packard, Duesenberg, De Soto, Hudson, La Salle, Cadillac, the Black Crow, the Bugmobile, the Averageman's Car, the Dan Patch, the Royal Mail, the Lone Star, the Baby Grand, the Hupmobile, the Locomobile**

BABES AND BEARS

Full-fledged youth culture, and the language that goes with it, did not arrive until the 1920s. The beginning of the twentieth century saw a boom in college enrollment, however. By 1910, more than 1,000 colleges and universities had opened across the country. Naturally, all those **babes** and **bears** on campus needed a special vocabulary to **blurble** about their new experiences. Here are some of the words that colored the talk of Western Reserve (Case Western) University students. The first word on the list shows that college life hasn't changed that much.

▶ **aped:** drunk.

▶ **binger:** to prevent an activity by saying no to it, also known as **putting the binger on it.**

▶ **bull:** to plunge into a situation without preparation. Those who had to take a test they hadn't studied for just *bulled* along.

▶ **blub:** to complain.

▶ **blurble:** to express great enthusiasm.

▶ **bone:** to study. We now say *bone up.*

➤ **chill:** a variant of *cold* in the sense 'definite' or 'clear', as in *I had it down chill.*

➤ **cork-headed:** conceited.

➤ **crust:** aggressiveness.

➤ **dig:** to study.

➤ **dry out:** to inform the teacher at the beginning of class that you haven't prepared for the lesson.

➤ **flag rush:** an annual contest between freshmen and sophomores for possession of a flag.

➤ **flivver:** a hoax or a failure, possibly from the idea that **flivvers** were unsuccessful as cars.

➤ **hog wrastle:** a dance.

➤ **hump:** to study diligently.

➤ **meadow dressing:** nonsense; a reference to the ingredients found in fertilizer.

➤ **scurf:** to ridicule.

➤ **skin:** to hurry.

➤ **smear:** to make a high grade on a test without much work.

➤ **spike:** to pledge to a fraternity.

➤ **stick a button:** to induct a young man into a fraternity.

➤ **suck around:** to seek favor with a professor.

➤ **suds:** money.

CAMPUS DENIZENS

➤ **animal:** a young woman of questionable reputation.

➤ **babe:** a pretty girl, still more or less current.

➤ **bat:** a prostitute or someone given to carousing.

➤ **bear:** a young man who excelled at some activity, as in *He's a bear at games.* A professor who worked the students hard was also known as a *bear.*

➤ **blubber:** a chatterbox.

➤ **bug:** a specialist in some field of knowledge.

➤ **crib:** a cheater.

➤ **hairpin:** a girl.

➤ **key man:** a young man who wore a Phi Beta Kappa key, indicating that he was an exceptional student.

➤ **lexer:** a law school student.

➤ **parlor snake:** a young man who could be found visiting the ladies when he should have been studying.

➤ **red:** a freshman, from the red caps they wore.

➤ **suf:** a sophomore.

➤ **town man:** a student who hailed from the town where the school was located.

➤ **toy:** an eccentric or comical person.

➤ **'Varsity man:** a university student.

OH YOU KID

College students weren't the only ones who used slang. Their parents also had some special names for special people.

➤ **back number:** an elderly, out-of-date person; a reference to the *back numbers*—old copies—of magazines and newspapers. Human back numbers were also called *bottle noses*.

➤ **big noise:** an important or well-known person.

➤ **darb:** an excellent person or thing, still being used in the twenties. *Darb* could also be an adjective, said of a skilled or competent person.

➤ **kid:** a very popular way of addressing people, especially young women, although it also had the modern meaning of 'child' or 'young person'. A widely repeated catch phrase of the time was *I love my wife, but oh you kid!*

➤ **peacherino:** a pretty girl.

➤ **punk:** an adjective meaning 'low, worthless, or displeasing'. Later in the century the word became a noun and went through several meaning changes, although the negative sense remained. (See also the seventies chapter.)

➤ **some pumpkins** (or **punkins**): an important or impressive person, as in *he's some punkins!*

➤ **wind sucker:** a braggart.

THE GIBSON GIRL GETS DRESSED

Women's clothes were still all-enveloping and many-layered at the turn of the twentieth century, but by 1910 elaborate corsets and petticoats were on the way out. Clothes were plainer, and women wore more skirts and **shirtwaists.** Fashion still demanded sacrifice though, as any woman teetering along in a **hobble skirt** could tell you.

➤ **Alice blue:** a popular shade of light greenish-blue, named for Alice Roosevelt, the President's oldest daughter. The song "Alice-Blue Gown" by Joseph McCarthy and Henry Tierney celebrated this color choice.

➤ **harem skirt:** a daringly designed full skirt that gathered at the ankles to resemble Turkish pantaloons.

➤ **health skirt:** a skirt meant for walking in, with a hem that just hit the ankle—a shorter length than usual.

➤ **hobble skirt:** a skirt that tapered narrowly to the ankles, preventing the wearer from taking a full stride. Hobble skirts usually included a side slit, but, even so, some women tied their legs together loosely to prevent themselves from inadvertently taking a big step and ripping their skirts.

➤ **peg skirt:** a variation of the **hobble,** with a full pleated top and a narrow hem; also called a *peg-top skirt.*

➤ **pompadour:** a loosely upswept hairstyle, with the hair puffed out softly around the face and pinned into a bun in back. It was the invariable style of illustrator Charles Dana Gibson's *Gibson Girl,* an elegantly dressed woman with abundant hair. In the fifties, *pompadour* became the name of a men's hairstyle.

➤ **shirtwaist:** a shirt cut to look like a feminized version of a man's shirt, with a starched collar and small necktie. Shirtwaists were worn as early as the 1890s, but had their greatest popularity around 1910.

➤ **skirtless bathing suit:** a one-piece bathing suit that showed most of the legs, with no overlayer of skirt. Jantzen introduced the suit in 1913.

➤ **tea gown:** a loose, flowing gown meant to be worn at home in the afternoon.

THE WAR TO END WAR

On April 2, 1917, President Woodrow Wilson announced that the world had to be *made safe for democracy,* and the United States was plunged into *the Great War.* Europeans had been fighting since August 1914, when a Serbian nationalist assassinated the Austrian Archduke Franz Ferdinand. A complex entanglement of alliances pulled most of Europe, as well as Japan, into the imbroglio.

Although the United States was officially neutral, it did continue to ship food and supplies to Britain. Germany retaliated by torpedoing American ships, including some that carried civilians. The United States finally entered the fray on the side of Britain and France, and was at war until November 11, 1918, **Armistice Day.** The war brought a whole new vocabulary, familiar both on *the home front* and *over there.*

OVER THERE

➤ **ace:** a pilot who shot down at least five planes. Later, any exceptionally good pilot.

➤ **Armistice Day:** November 11, 1918, the day Germany signed an armistice treaty. The day was first commemorated in 1919 with church services, parades, and two minutes of silence at 11:00 A.M., the hour when the guns stopped firing. Armistice Day became *Veteran's Day* in 1954.

➤ **back-door furlough:** absence without leave, also called *AWOL*, as it is today. *Furlough* means 'a temporary leave' and was used at least through World War II.

➤ **barbed-wire undershirt:** a booby prize, generally awarded for clumsiness or stupidity.

➤ **Big Bertha:** a German long-range gun.

➤ **bird:** an airman.

➤ **bokoo:** a lot, from French *beaucoup*. The word was very popular with civilians as well as soldiers.

➤ **bowlegs:** cavalrymen.

➤ **brass:** officers. A **brass looie** was a lieutenant.

➤ **bunk fatigue:** time spent sleeping.

➤ **bunk lizard:** a soldier who tried to get a lot of sleep.

➤ **can:** an airplane.

➤ **canteen lizard:** a soldier who spent a lot of time lounging in the canteen.

➤ **Charlie:** an army chaplain (as in *Charlie Chaplin*).

➤ **civvies:** civilian clothes, also called *cits*.

➤ **cooler:** the guardhouse (military jail).

➤ **cot jockey:** a soldier who loafed in bed.

➤ **crock up:** to crash an airplane.

DOUGHBOY

Doughboy has been in use since the Mexican War of 1846, but it was probably most popular as a term for infantrymen during the First World War. Theories about its origin abound. George Armstrong Custer's wife, Elizabeth, wrote that doughboys were originally small, round doughnuts served to sailors. Since the round buttons on an infantryman's uniform resembled these doughnuts, they were known as doughboys. Another possibility is that infantrymen in the Mexican War were called *adobe boys* because they got covered with dust while marching, and that the term was later corrupted to *doughboys*. People have also suggested that the sucking noise made by infantry feet while marching through mud sounded like mixing dough, or that the word came from the doughlike pipe clay that soldiers cleaned their uniform belts with.

➤ **Croix de Chair:** a mock decoration for nonflying officers, a play on the French *Croix de Guerre,* or 'Cross of War', awarded for heroism. Other mock awards were the *Croix de Goof* for stupidity and the *Croix de Bois* ('Cross of Wood'), an ironic reference to gravesite markers.

➤ **Dead Man's Corner:** an area under constant enemy bombardment.

➤ **dog robber:** an enlisted man who acted as a servant to an officer, running errands and doing chores. As a reward, he was allowed to scrounge leftover food, castoff clothing, and whatever else was lying around. Dog robbers got the table scraps that would normally be tossed to a dog.

➤ **dreadnought:** a large, heavy battleship.

➤ **dugout hound:** a soldier who preferred the safety of the dugout to **going over the top,** where he would encounter enemy bullets.

➤ **echelon king:** someone who held a soft job in the rear echelon, rather than fighting at the front.

➤ **egg:** an inexperienced airman, not yet "hatched."

➤ **egg wagon:** a plane that dropped bombs.

➤ **farmerette:** a young woman who worked on the land during the war, replacing the men who had gone off to fight.

➤ **flat spin:** a state of confusion or distress. This term originally applied literally to pilots in flight, but came into general civilian use after the war.

➤ **foxhole:** a trench dug for protection from enemy fire.

➤ **fruit salad:** an easy target.

➤ **get it:** to be killed.

➤ **go over the hill:** to desert.

➤ **go over the top:** leave the **foxhole** and charge the enemy, at great risk of being killed by machine gun fire.

➤ **goldbrick:** an inexperienced lieutenant, not a career officer.

➤ **ground ace:** a nonflying officer.

➤ **groundhog day:** Armistice Day, when all the soldiers came out of their **(fox)holes.**

➤ **handshaker:** a soldier who tried to curry favor with the officers.

➤ **Hell's Half-acre:** an area of bloody fighting.

➤ **hitch:** a tour of duty.

➤ **Holy Joe:** an army chaplain.

➤ **Hooverizing:** a program of voluntary food rationing named after Herbert Hoover, the program's administrator. **Hooverizers** abstained from certain foods on one or two days of the week; for example, wheatless Mondays and porkless Thursdays and Saturdays.

➤ **huff:** to kill.

Hungry Lizzie: an airfield ambulance, a play on **Tin Lizzie.**

I'll tell the world: a strong affirmative, also used by the general public.

iodine brigade: a medical detachment.

Jerry: the Germans.

liberty: used to replace German words. **Liberty cabbage** was sauerkraut; **liberty steaks** were hamburgers; **liberty pups** were dachshunds.

liberty bonds: government bonds issued to help finance the war.

mad minute: one minute of rapid firing, not necessarily aimed at anything, with the goal of startling the enemy.

OD: olive drab, the regulation army color, meaning 'typically military'. Soldiers had to deal with *OD hash, OD haircuts, OD pills,* which were laxatives, and *OD water,* which was coffee. The use is similar to that of *G.I.* in World War II.

the old army game: a swindle or a passing of responsibility to others.

puttees: bandagelike cloth leggings worn by soldiers. These wrapped around the leg from ankle to knee.

NO-MAN'S LAND

Although now associated mainly with World War I, **no-man's land** was in use much earlier. In medieval London, No-Man's Land was a piece of land outside the city's north wall used for executions. More generally, it referred to the plots of waste ground, apparently belonging to no one, that always spring up here and there in cities. Both of these uses foreshadow the term's meaning during the war.

By the end of 1914, the French and the Germans had fought themselves to a standstill somewhere in the middle of France. Both sides then dug hundreds of miles of trenches (the Western Front), reinforced them with screens of barbed wire, and prepared to protect their lines. In between the lines of opposing forces lay no-man's land. At intervals, one side or the other would attempt to gain ground by streaming out of the trenches into this wasteland, where the enemy would mow them down or attack them with gas. Not surprisingly, the term has come to mean 'a place where it's hard to survive'.

Trench warfare also contributed some other vocabulary words: **trench fever,** caused by louse bites; **trench foot,** a type of frostbite due to prolonged exposure to cold and damp in the trenches; and **trench mouth,** ulcers of the mouth and throat caused by a bacterial infection.

➡ **Sears-Roebuck:** a new, green lieutenant.

➡ **short-timer:** an enlisted man nearing the end of his tour of duty. The term now means 'anyone at the end of a job', or 'someone about to move from one situation to another'.

➡ **sky pilot:** a chaplain.

➡ **strafe:** to reprimand harshly. The literal meaning of the word is 'to attack the ground from an airplane with machine-gun fire'.

➡ **submarine:** a bed pan.

➡ **swabbies:** sailors.

➡ **tea kettle:** a French locomotive.

➡ **ticket west:** a fatal wound.

➡ **war to end war:** an expression referring to World War I, probably suggested by H. G. Wells's 1914 book *The War That Will End War*. Another way people expressed it was *the war that will end all wars*.

➡ **Western Front:** a line of trenches separating the two sides that stretched across northeastern France from Switzerland to the English Channel. It was the front line in Western Europe.

➡ **whizz-bang:** a small, high-speed shell.

➡ **Zeppelin:** a giant airship that floated like a gas balloon, named after its designer, Count Ferdinand von Zeppelin.

THE ENLISTED MAN'S DIET

Doughboys had to get used to some unusual grub when they were over there. All too often, what the **belly robber** whipped up for the troops came out of a can. **Monkey meat** and **charlie horse** needed plenty of **red lead** to help them down. Even **OD water** didn't help **dum-dums** go down.

➡ **axle grease:** butter.

➡ **belly robber:** the cook, who was rumored to have kept all the best rations for himself.

➡ **bull meat:** corned beef, alias *embalmed mule* or *salt horse*. Corned beef hash went by *overseas chicken, canned willy, corned woolly,* and *bill*.

➡ **bullets:** beans.

➡ **charlie horse:** canned beef.

➡ **deep sea turkey:** canned salmon, also known as *goldfish, red mike, sewer carp,* and *submarine chicken*.

➡ **dog biscuit:** hard tack.

➡ **dum-dums:** beans. A dum-dum is a kind of bullet.

➡ **forty-fours:** beans.

➡ **gooey:** hash or stew.

- **goulash battery:** a field kitchen.
- **hard oil:** butter.
- **iron rations:** emergency rations.
- **jaw breakers:** hard tack.
- **kangaroo meat:** canned beef.
- **mongee:** food, or to eat, probably from the French *manger,* 'to eat'.
- **monkey meat:** tougher-than-usual beef.
- **native sons:** prunes.
- **red lead:** ketchup.
- **slum:** beef stew. **Slum with the tide in** was watery stew; **with the tide out** it was thick. **With an overcoat** meant that it sported a crust.

> **WORDS FOR UNWIELDY, SLOW, OR BADLY CONSTRUCTED AIRPLANES**
> **flying boxcar, flying chicken coop, flying bathtub, flying bedstead, galloping goose, orange crate**

- **stars and stripes:** beans and ham.
- **tin cow:** canned milk, also called *sixteen for one,* meaning sixteen men shared a can of it.

ARITHMETIC BUGS

Lice were called **arithmetic bugs** because they add to your troubles, subtract from your pleasure, divide your attention, and multiply like hell. They were really no joke, though, because they spread trench fever through their bites. Other words for these pesky creatures were **chemise lizards, circus bees, cooties, galloping dandruff, leaping dandruff, flannel buzzards, pants rabbits, seam rats, seam squirrels, shirt rabbits, shirt hounds, shirt squirrels, shirt rats,** and **undershirt butterflies.** Men who held a **cootie carnival** were searching for lice. They could also **be conducting a shirt hunt** or **reading their shirts.** Delousing stations were called **cootie casinos, cootie factories,** or **cootie mills.**

BUZZWORDS OF THE TIMES

You didn't have to study like a **bug** to be familiar with the following people and happenings during the first two decades of the twentieth century. They were widely discussed in magazines and newspapers, and across dinner tables.

- **bird of passage:** an immigrant, typically a man without his family, who later returned to his country of origin. The expression was used more generally to mean 'someone who doesn't stay long in one place'. The first part of the century saw an unprecedented flood of immigrants into the United States, mostly from Southern and Eastern Europe. Several million people crossed the border from 1900 until 1921, when the Immigration Act stemmed the flow.

Besides inspiring this term, newcomers contributed dozens of their own words to the American language. A few in use during the 'teens were Portuguese *cuspidor* (a pot for spitting tobacco juice into), Spanish-inspired *hoosegow* (jail, from *juzgado*, 'judged'), Yiddish *dokus* or *tuchus* (backside), and dozens of words ending in the German *-fest*, including *gabfest, smokefest, eatfest, sobfest, singfest, swatfest* (a golf or base-ball game), and *batfest* (a high-hitting baseball game).

➤ **muckraker:** a writer who exposed the social and political evils of the day. Theodore Roosevelt invented the word to express his dis-approval of so much concentration on dirt-digging. The public was fascinated with muckraking for a time, and eagerly read the latest scan-dalous installments in magazines like *Collier's* and *McClure's*. The most famous muckraking journalist was Upton Sinclair. His fictionalized indictment of the Chicago meatpacking industry, *The Jungle,* led to the Meat Inspection and Pure Food and Drug acts of 1906. Other well-known muckrakers were Ida M. Tarbell and Lincoln Steffens.

➤ **New Woman:** a modern woman. She was more independent than her mother, may have worked outside the home, and, if not, probably was a member of a **women's club.** Originally organized for the study of literature and art, women's clubs gradually transformed themselves into social-work organizations. Club women were a force in the tem-perance movement, and also concerned themselves with education and public health. Membership topped one million by 1912. If a New Woman had a job, she usually worked in a business office, store, fac-tory, or newspaper office.

➤ **Square Deal:** President Theodore Roosevelt's program of domestic reform. He encouraged Congress to pass laws that broke up or limited corporate monopolies on things like oil, beef, and railroads. Other parts of his program included establishing the National Conservation Commission and passing the Meat Inspection and Pure Food and Drug acts. Roosevelt declared that the White House was a **bully pulpit,** meaning an excellent or first-rate pulpit for expounding his reformist views.

➤ **suffragism:** the movement for **woman suffrage,** or the right of women to vote. The National American Woman Suffrage Association, along with the Women's Christian Temperance Union and other women's social-work organizations, mounted a major push for voting privileges during this era. The more radical marched, picketed, and chained themselves to the White House fence. When arrested, they went on hunger strikes. Although more than two dozen states had already granted women the right to vote in local elections, women were not universally enfranchised until the Nineteenth Amendment passed in 1920.

➤ **Wobblies:** the Industrial Workers of the World, formed in 1905. One of the most radical workers' movements of the age, the Wobblies wanted to abolish capitalism and the federal government. They relied on violence and industrial sabotage rather than mainstream political activity. They also staged several strikes. However, their membership never reached more than 100,000; it was not a large enough group to make a serious impact on the workings of the economy. The organization was weakened during the war, when several leaders were imprisoned for taking an antiwar position. Soon after the war, the organization dissolved.

Wobblies used an extensive jargon, although most of it never entered the mainstream. For example, **dehorn** meant 'lacking in class consciousness', from the literal dehorning of cattle to make them less dangerous. A **dehorn committee** was a group of Wobblies who policed taverns, houses of prostitution, and other distracting venues to keep members out of them during strikes. *Dehorn* took on the meaning 'adulterated alcohol' in the 1920s. **Scissorbills** referred to workers, especially rural people, who refused to join unions. The word could also mean 'foolish or incompetent people'. **Packing the rigging** meant 'carrying written propaganda for distribution'. **Boomers** were footloose workers who made the rounds of logging camps and construction sites, while **homeguards** were those who stayed in a steady job. **Brass check sheets** were mainstream newspapers, from Upton Sinclair's 1919 novel, *The Brass Check,* a sharp criticism of the journalism world.

The flapper—a smoking, drinking, kneecap-powdering red-hot mama!

The Twenties

Flappers and Flaming Youth

The **Jazz Age** belonged to the **flapper,** a smoking, drinking, kneecap-powdering, **red-hot mama** who caused preachers to predict the collapse of American civilization and her parents to throw up their hands in despair. She flung away her corset and rolled her stockings below the knee. She dolled up with plenty of makeup and short skirts that showed off her *gams.* She ran around with men and smoked *ciggies* in public. And she could look forward to voting when she reached the age of 21. The quintessential flapper was actress Clara Bow, **the It Girl.**

The stylish flapper *bobbed* her hair at the **bobatorium.** If her bob didn't wave naturally, she had it *marcelled.* Over her new cut she wore a **cloche hat,** a bell-shaped hat pulled low over the forehead. Cloche hats emphasized youthfulness and the possession of a slim, fresh face, because they looked terrible on everyone else. The flapper's male companion sported a new look, too. He wore **knickerbockers,** baggy pants gathered tightly below the knee, or **plus fours,** which were even baggier. For dressier occasions, he adopted **Oxford bags.** Tossed over it all was a **raccoon coat.**

The 1920s **ballyhooed** youth culture in a way that was virtually unknown earlier. *Flaming youth* were in revolt against their parents' stuffy moral codes. They were against **Prohibition** and in favor of greater freedom for women. They supported **Scopes** during the **Monkey Trial. Bolshevism** was out and cultural criticism was in. Those with intellectual pretensions read *The American Mercury,* H. L. Mencken's flamboyant magazine. *The American Mercury* lambasted **Babbitts,** Rotarians, Coolidge supporters, and other specimens of *homo boobiens.*

The less intellectual might go in for more physical pursuits, such as **flagpole sitting.** A record contender should expect to spend more than three weeks eating and sleeping on the pole. Athletic types could also participate in **bunion derbies,** running across the country to the detriment of their feet. In the evenings, the **Ouija boards** came out or the **mediumistic** Madame Sonja arrived to lead an hour or so of **table tipping.** Many **parapsychical** phenomena resulted from these exciting sessions. The **booboisie** viewed the antics of the **bright young things** with disapproval, but they still perused the gossip section of the paper for news of the sophisticated, the fashionable, and the notorious.

F. Scott Fitzgerald named the era with *Tales from the Jazz Age.* The music that defined the age wasn't new—African Americans had been inventing and playing jazz since the beginning of the century. To white Americans collecting **waxes** (as phonograph records were now being

---

JAS, JASS, JASZ, JASZZ, JAZZ

The word **jazz** is far from obsolete, but when it first came into wide use in the twenties, its meaning and spelling were much more fluid. No one is sure exactly where the word came from or how it got connected with the decade's most popular musical style. Etymologists can choose from a rich variety of possible origins.

One idea is that the word derives from a vaudeville term, **jazzbo** (also spelled *jazbo* or *jassbo*), meaning 'low comedy played for a quick laugh'. A shout from the wings of "jas it up" or "put in jas" advised a failing performer to add some comic antics before the tomatoes started flying. Composer John Philip Sousa believed that the word originally came from old-fashioned minstrel shows, where *jazzbo* meant 'to cut loose or ham it up'. He recalled that the grand finale of a vaudeville show, when all the acts appeared on stage together, was called a *jazzbo.* Black male performers were sometimes called *jazzbos,* implying that they were showy. The vaudevillian use of *jazzbo* may have grown out of the French Creole expression *chasse beau,* denoting 'a dandy' or 'a ladies' man'. This term was current in New Orleans when plantation cakewalks were popular. The male winner of the contest was dubbed "Mr. Jazzbo," or *chasse beau.*

Another French word, *jaser,* meaning 'to chatter or gossip', also has some supporters. When an editor of *Webster's New International Dictionary* tried to trace *jazz* in the late 1920s he found that it was a common Creole word meaning 'hurry up'. By stretching that meaning about as far as it will go without snapping, we can connect it to *chatter,* which is 'fast speech'.

Jazz fans tell the story of Jasbo Brown, the African-American musician who blew wild and crazy strains on his cornet. The audience loved it, and encouraged him with cries of "More, Jasbo!", sometimes shortened to the

called), it was still a fresh, hot sound. **Jazz babies** were **hipped on** Dixieland. Its syncopated beat and thrilling improvisations fit the mood of the times—lively, unconventional, exciting, and a little flashy. In **speakeasies** around the country, flappers and their dates strutted their stuff while **alligators** like "Satchmo" Armstrong laid down hot licks. The freewheeling *Charleston* and the even more daring *Black Bottom* were the latest dance crazes. If your partner could really *rag*, everything was *copacetic*.

Coolidge prosperity rolled on. Everyone was out for a good time. A **big butter-and-egg man** would take his **biscuit** to a swanky club for an

one important syllable, "Jas!" This remarkable performer's real name has been given as James, Jasper, Jess, Chaz, and Jack. Legend places him at music clubs in New Orleans, Chicago, Philadelphia, and Vicksburg. Sad to say, he probably never existed outside a musical folk tale. A similar story is told of Johnny Stein's Band, later renamed the Original Dixieland Jass Band. They say that during every performance, one of the band's most loyal fans would jump up, shouting "Jass it up, boys!" Whether this tale is true or not, bands did begin adding the word *Jass* or *Jazz* to their names around 1915.

The earliest appearance of *jazz* in print is in a series of 1913 baseball articles in the *San Francisco Bulletin*. The *Bulletin*'s sports writers used the word to mean 'pep' or 'energy'. This meaning would be a natural extension of the earlier vaudeville *jas*, if the two words are in fact connected. At some point, *jazz* also became a slang term for sexual activity. This usage is first recorded in 1918.

Some fans who knew about the naughty connotations of *jazz* were inspired to look for a more respectable name for their favorite musical style. One musician preferred to call it Modern Popular Music. Another aficionado urged, "Why not call it 'Ragtonia' or 'Calethumpia' or anything on earth to get away from the term 'Jazz'?" Concern about the word died down in the thirties, but in 1949 the music magazine *Down Beat* ran a contest for a new word to "describe the music of today." The $1,000 prize winner was the unlikely "Crewcut." Contenders included "Amerimusic," "Jarb," "Pulsemusic," "Le Hot," "Bix-E-Bop," "Swixibop," "Beatpoint," "Ameritonic," and "Syncorhythm." None, including the winner, ever caught on.

evening of **whoopee,** but a **flat wheeler** would escort her to an **egg harbor** where they could dance without paying admission. If a girl really **knew her oil,** her beau thought she was **the cat's whiskers, the duck's quack, the bee's knees, the snake's hips,** or **the flea's eyebrows.** She thought he was swell.

If the couple weren't headed for a dance, they might go to a movie theater to see a popular silent film like *The Sheik* or an exciting **talkie,** as the new movies with sound were called. Or maybe a friend would be throwing a **brawl,** also known to college students as a *rub,* a *work out,* or a *drag*—a *party,* to **Rock of Ages** types over 30. **Joe College** (or possibly *Joe Yale*) picked up his **heavy date** in the Stutz-Bearcat, which turned into a **struggle buggy** later in the evening, or, as the old folks claimed, *a bedroom on wheels.* The **rumble seats** in twenties *gas buggies* were perfect for **necking.** If he didn't have a car, he'd hail a **dim box,** the back seat of which was also a good spot for **flinging woo** while you were driven to your destination. *Hot diggity dog!*

SHEIKS AND VAMPS

During the twenties, jazz babies spent plenty of time out on the town. One of the biggest changes from previous eras was the new freedom of movement for young unmarried women. The gentle Gibson Girl gave way to the rebellious flapper, part of whose rebellion involved

SHEIK

When Rudolph Valentino appeared onscreen in the classic 1921 silent movie *The Sheik,* the word gained a new meaning overnight. A **sheik** went from being the chieftain of a desert tribe to any sexy, irresistible man. Valentino, born Rodolfo Guglielmi, was the heartthrob of the twenties. He immigrated to New York from his small Italian hometown in search of work and wound up in vaudeville as part of a dance team. Eventually he moved to California, where he first made a splash in *The Four Horsemen of the Apocalypse,* and later in *The Sheik* and other movies. Women were so thrilled by Valentino's dark, romantic looks that they fainted in the aisles during the exhibition showing of *The Sheik.* When Valentino died at the age of 31 from peritonitis brought on by a perforated ulcer, thousands of heartbroken women lined the streets of New York to view his coffin.

going out with men unchaperoned. Dating as we know it began during this decade. Naturally, young people had to invent some new terms to talk about this novel situation. Animal expressions were one trendy way to refer to your sweetheart. Some favorites were *bee's knees, cat's whiskers, clam's garters, duck's quack, flea's eyebrows, gnat's elbow,* and *snake's hips.* Both men and women also used various other words to describe their dates.

DATEABLE MEN

➤ **bell polisher:** a young man who lingered in the foyer after bringing his sweetheart home.

➤ **big butter-and-egg man:** a man with a healthy bank account, well able to provide his chosen with butter, eggs, and anything else her heart desired.

➤ **brush ape:** a young hayseed from the country.

➤ **cake-eater:** an impecunious youth who spent a lot of time at tea parties and other places where free food was on offer. Also called a *heavy-cake* or a *tea hound.*

➤ **candy leg:** a rich, popular young man.

➤ **cellar smeller:** a young man who knew where free drinks were to be had.

➤ **chair warmer:** a youth who preferred staying home with his sweetie to spending money on entertainment. This problematic beau was also known as a *porch warmer* or a *parlor leech.*

➤ **dewdropper:** a jobless youngster who slept all day.

➤ **drugstore cowboy:** a stylishly dressed fellow who loitered in public places, trying to pick up women.

➤ **egg:** someone who let his girl pay her own way at a dance. An **egg harbor** was a dance where no admission was charged, perfect for **eggs** and other cheapskates.

➤ **flat wheeler:** a thrifty young man who took his date to **egg harbors.**

➤ **goof:** a male sweetheart.

➤ **Joe Zilch:** a loser; a nobody.

➤ **lallygagger:** a **goof** who liked to kiss his sweetie in hallways.

➤ **lone nabisco:** a man who arrived at a party without a date, also called *chewing a lone nabisco* or *going stag,* still a fairly current term.

➤ **lounge lizard:** a ladies' man.

➤ **part-time papa:** a married man, especially a rich one.

➤ **snugglepup:** a young man who liked **petting.**

➤ **wally:** a smartly dressed man.

DATEABLE WOMEN

➤ **biscuit:** a young woman who liked to **neck.**

➤ **chunk of lead:** an unpopular young woman.

➤ **dumb dora:** a **flapper** with less than her fair share of brains; also spelled *dumdora.*

➤ **fire alarm:** a divorced woman.

➤ **flapper:** a modern young woman—unsentimental, lively, boyish, and frankly interested in sex. The word was used as early as the 1880s to mean 'a flighty or immoral girl', then 'an adolescent female'. It probably derives from the word for a young wild duck, called a "flapper" because it can't use its wings effectively yet. Many variants of *flapper* sprang up, including **flapperese** (the flapper's slang), **flapperology** (the study of flapper culture), and **flapperitis** (silliness), as well as *flapperdom, flapperhood,* and *flapperish.* A **flapper bracket** was the passenger seat on the back of a bicycle. In England, where women under 30 did not get the right to vote until 1928, that voting bloc was known as the **flapper vote.**

➤ **gold digger:** a young woman interested in **butter-and-egg men** and other rich dates.

➤ **heavy date:** someone who could be counted on for a little action after the dance.

VAMP

If women went wild for a sheik, men loved to be *vamped.* A **vamp** was a sultry, seductive woman, whose prototype was the actress Theda Bara. Bara played a vampire in the 1914 movie *A Fool There Was.* Her career as a femme fatale was launched with the famous line "Kiss me, my fool!" The Hollywood publicity machine took full advantage of Bara's exotic image, billing her as a mysterious creature from the Sahara. Bara (born Theodosia Goodman in Cincinnati) reveled in the image, wearing exotic eye makeup and granting interviews accompanied by a snake. Bara later went on to play Salome and Cleopatra, two well-known historical vamps.

An alternative source for the word is from the play *Upstairs and Down* by Fanny Locke Hatton and Frederic Hatton, produced in 1917. The play featured a character known as the **vampire baby,** a precursor to the flapper. The vampire baby was a fast young woman, a frequenter of wild parties who wore short skirts and flirted scandalously with married men. When the flapper later became a popular social type, the Hattons always insisted that their vampire baby was the first.

➤ **knows her oil:** said of a young woman who knows how to be entertaining on a date, also characterized as *full of vinegar* and *having a line.*

➤ **nonskid:** a young woman who was able to hold her liquor on a date.

➤ **red-hot mama:** a **flapper** who was always ready for a **petting party.**

➤ **sardine:** a girl, also called a *smelt.*

➤ **sheba:** the **sheik**'s female counterpart.

➤ **strike breaker:** a young woman who was ready to date her friend's beau when the couple was on the outs.

➤ **tomato:** an attractive young woman who enjoyed dancing, but didn't pet.

JUST PEOPLE, GOOD OR BAD

Besides romantic partners, a number of other twenties types frequented the social scene. Most were people you would just as soon avoid.

➤ **alligator:** at first, a **jazz** musician; later, anyone who appreciated the jazz sound.

➤ **big cheese:** an important person.

➤ **bright young thing:** one of the young, trendy set who was against anything old-fashioned or sentimental.

➤ **blatherskite:** a noisy, boastful person.

➤ **clothesline:** a gossip.

➤ **dudd:** a studious person.

➤ **Father Time:** any man over the age of 30.

➤ **finale hopper:** someone who arrived at a dance after the ticket takers went off duty.

➤ **flat tire:** a bore.

➤ **four flusher:** a show-off.

➤ **great on the shindig:** said of a very good dancer.

➤ **half portion:** a short person, usually female.

➤ **jazz hound:** someone who loved to dance.

➤ **jellybean:** an inferior type.

➤ **low lid:** the opposite of a highbrow or a **dudd.**

➤ **oil can:** a worthless or stupid person.

➤ **on the muscle:** description of an overbearing, pushy person who is ready to pick a fight.

➤ **pantywaist:** a weakling or sissy.

➤ **punch rustler:** a partygoer who hovered around the refreshment table.

➤ **Rock of Ages:** any woman over the age of 30.

➤ **thrill:** a popular companion.

➤ **wet sock:** a poor sport.

SKULLDRAGGERS

Most college slang in the twenties was just ordinary youth slang, but students did have a few terms for their own particular concerns:

➤ **brawl:** a party, also known as a *struggle, work out, rub,* or *drag.* To dance was to *rag, struggle, wrestle,* or *march.* Chaperones on these occasions were known as **alarm clocks.**

➤ **can:** a failing record. An admonishment to those who were reluctant to study was: *Come on peaches, here's your can.*

➤ **carrying nine hours and dragging six:** passing nine hours (usually three classes) and failing six.

➤ **doggy:** self-consciously well-dressed. **Joe Brooks** (as in Brooks Brothers) was the perfect example of dogginess.

➤ **grind:** a student who cares for nothing but studying.

➤ **house around:** to loaf around the dormitory.

➤ **huddle system:** cheating.

➤ **pipe:** an easy course. **Candidates for a plumber's degree** were students who registered for a lot of *pipes.*

➤ **prexy:** a university's president.

➤ **starvation hour:** the class immediately before lunch.

➤ **stay in the buggy:** to keep studying.

➤ **skulldragging:** hard studying.

➤ **wet:** someone who appeared ridiculous, unsophisticated, crude, or deficient in some other way. The word could be a noun or an adjective.

IT

It was sex appeal, and the girl who had it was Clara Bow, **the It Girl.** Born to a poverty-stricken Brooklyn family in 1905, Bow entered Hollywood by winning a movie magazine contest at the age of 17. She never looked back. In contrast to more ethereal stars like Mary Pickford, Bow played ordinary working women. She was a model flapper—youthful, vivacious, tomboyish, but sexy. When she starred in the film *It,* from the Elinor Glyn novel of that name, the label stuck, and Bow became the model for a generation of young female moviegoers. Bow was as hedonistic offscreen as on. Her private life was marked by scandal until she retired from films in her early thirties, married, and moved to Nevada.

PITCHING WOO

All of that unchaperoned togetherness, including driving around in cars, led to many opportunities for **pitching woo. Petting parties,** then as now, were excellent opportunities for **mushing.** A **snugglepup** might get carried away enough to **whip out a handcuff** and **speak his piece.** If the chosen one then **gave him the air,** he would sadly return to **lone nabisco** status, **carrying a torch** until he met another **red-hot mama.**

➤ **barneymugging:** kissing.
➤ **button shining:** close dancing.
➤ **carrying a torch:** suffering from unrequited love.

THE PRODUCTION CODE

Early in the century, movies were as freewheeling and uninhibited as the rest of society. Ads for forthcoming films promised scenes of "champagne baths, midnight revels, petting parties in the purple dawn," and other delights of twenties' high life. Sometimes the offscreen behavior of Tinseltown's vamps and sheiks almost matched their movies' publicity.

Public outcry against Hollywood's permissiveness reached a peak in 1921, when the well-known comic Roscoe "Fatty" Arbuckle was arrested and tried for the rape and killing of Virginia Rappe. The young starlet had died of internal injuries at the end of a long, drunken weekend party thrown by Arbuckle at the St. Francis Hotel in San Francisco. Arbuckle was acquitted, with his career in ruins, after a trial of unparalleled sensationalism. (Rappe's injuries apparently stemmed from some previous condition, possibly a botched abortion.)

Meanwhile, the Motion Picture Association of America hired former Postmaster General Will Hays to instill morals into the movies through self-censorship. In 1922, the **Production Code** came into being, although it was not seriously implemented until 1934. It required a morally uplifting ending to every film. Among forbidden screen behaviors were lustful kissing, suggestive postures, rude language, the shooting of police by criminals, excessive drinking, romance between people of different races, childbirth, adultery, and sexual relations between spouses. The Production Code is the reason Rhett Butler's immortal line "Frankly, my dear, I don't give a damn" was so shocking when *Gone With the Wind* was first released. It's also the reason why onscreen married couples slept in twin beds until the sixties.

- **dim box:** a taxi, where the lights were low.
- **flinging woo:** kissing and behaving romantically.
- **give the air:** to reject a marriage proposal.
- **give the ozone:** to brush off or dismiss curtly. This expression was also used for situations other than romantic ones. Another way to reject people was to give them *the icy mitt.*
- **handcuff:** an engagement ring.
- **making whoopee:** kissing and **necking.**
- **mushing:** same as **making whoopee.**
- **petting pantry:** a movie theater.
- **petting parties:** initially, parties where petting occurred, but eventually implying one couple only. **Petting** meant 'passionate kissing and fondling', but stopping short of sexual intercourse. **Necking** was similar, but with less groping.
- **pitching woo:** same as **flinging woo,** possibly with better aim.
- **rush:** to go steady with a young woman.
- **send to the showers:** to reject a marriage proposal. Also known as *showing the gate.*
- **speak his piece:** to propose.
- **stuck on each other:** in love.
- **struggle buggy:** an automobile where **petting parties** were held.

OXFORD BAGS AND APACHE SWEATERS

A radical new way of dressing was part of the flapper's rebelliousness. Her hair was short and so were her skirts. Her mother had aimed for a well-upholstered curvaceousness, but the modern girl went for the *garçonne* look, flat-chested and slim-hipped. (The word is based on the French *garçon* and translates to something like 'female boy'.) While women's clothes became more severe, men's outfits became softer. They traded the traditional stiff shirtfront required with evening clothes for softer shirt fabrics. During the day they wore flowing ties and **Oxford bags.**

Tutmania struck when British archaeologist Howard Carter discovered the tomb of Egyptian king Tutankhamen in 1922. All sorts of Egyptian-inspired accessories appeared, including combs, powder compacts, and cigarette cases decorated with Egyptian motifs or hieroglyphs, *Cleopatra earrings,* and beetle-shaped fake scarab pins. Popular colors were carnelian, Egyptian green, and mummy brown.

- **Apache sweater:** a casual sweater with Native American designs across the front, created by clothing designer Coco Chanel. Chanel was a pioneer of simplified, comfortable styles for women, and many of her daytime outfits featured cardigan sweaters.

➤ **bobatorium:** hair cutting emporium, also called the *bobber shop*.

➤ **cloche hat:** the hat of the decade, soft and bell-shaped, worn low over the forehead. Cloche hats were a symbol of modern dressing because they only fit properly if the wearer had short hair.

➤ **crossword puzzle stockings:** stockings patterned in squares reminiscent of a crossword puzzle.

➤ **Eton crop:** a very short, boyish women's haircut, named after the famous English boys' school.

➤ **knickerbockers:** baggy men's pants, gathered tightly below the knee. **Plus fours** were the same, but even baggier. Men wore these styles on casual occasions, such as when playing golf.

➤ **Oxford bags:** wide-legged men's trousers that pooled around the shoe.

➤ **raccoon coat:** a man's coat made of raccoon fur, associated mainly with fraternity members.

➤ **shingle:** a short, blunt haircut for women.

➤ **smoking suit:** a flowing trousers outfit, often worn with a turban, perfect for occasions when a modern woman wanted to try out the newly popular Egyptian or Turkish cigarettes.

WETS AND DRYS

Twenties sheiks and shebas fueled their frenetic nightlife with a bottomless reservoir of illegal alcohol. In the postwar enthusiasm for clean, healthy living, Americans quickly ratified the Eighteenth Amendment, forbidding the "manufacture, sale, or transportation of

THE NOBLE EXPERIMENT

Herbert Hoover, the dry Republican candidate for president, called Prohibition **the noble experiment.** Even he had to admit that the effectiveness of the Eighteenth Amendment didn't match its noble intent. When Hoover was elected in 1928, he established an 11-member commission, led by George Wickersham, to study problems of enforcement and other aspects of Prohibition law. The results were ambiguous. The lengthy report described in detail the utter failure of law enforcement to stop the flow of bootleg liquor. No one who wanted a drink went dry during the twenties. However, only two commission members favored the amendment's repeal. The majority recommended a further trial.

intoxicating liquors." In 1920 Congress passed the **Volstead Act** to enforce the amendment, and the United States embarked on Prohibition. Support for **the noble experiment,** as President Hoover called it, soon waned. By 1924, liquor smuggling was a $40,000,000-a-year business. Hundreds of **rum runners** ran **hooch** to shore from ships anchored 12 miles out in international waters. **Bootleggers** like Al Capone earned millions more from illegal **alky-cooking** operations.

Otherwise law-abiding citizens patronized **speakeasies** to funnel the *joy water.* In 1930, an estimated 35,000 of these **booze foundries** existed in New York City alone. People who preferred to do their *gin guzzling* at home bought **barrel goods** from their private **leggers** or made their own **bathtub gin.**

Wet and **dry** were relative terms in the twenties. Those in favor of Volstead repeal could be merely *dampish* or *wettish,* favoring limited prohibition of alcohol, or *sopping, soaking,* or *dripping wet,* or *as wet as the Atlantic Ocean.* If they believed in repeal, but didn't expect it, they were *pessimistically wet.* Dryness also came in varying degrees, from the cautiously *medium dryish* to the fervently *ultra, cracker,* or *bone dry,* or *most arid.* The well-organized *drymoderies* kept Prohibition on the books until 1933, but most of the country was *wet enough for rubber boots.*

SOMETHING ON THE HIP

Bootleg alcohol *lit you up like the sky, the commonwealth, a Christmas tree, a store window,* or *a church.* After the party was over, you might end up with *the jumps, the shakes, the zings, the heeby-jeebies, the screaming-meemies,* or *the whoops and jingles.*

➧ **alky-cooking:** illegal distilling.

➧ **bathtub gin:** homemade gin, usually made by the gallon and drunk with orange juice or another mixer to ease it down.

➧ **bootlegger:** a purveyor of illegal liquor. The word dates from Colonial times, when traders who sold alcohol illegally to Native Americans carried the bottles in their tall boot legs.

➧ **boozehister:** a **bootlegger.**

➧ **giggle water:** alcohol.

➧ **hooch:** alcohol, from the Native American language of Tlingit. *Hoochinoo* was the Tlingit way of referring to a kind of liquor made by the Hoochinoo Indians of Alaska.

➧ **jake:** a liquor made with Jamaica ginger. Also, a form of paralysis caused by drinking cheap, denatured alcohol. Paradoxically, the word *jake* could also mean 'fine', as in *All is jake.*

➧ **mickies:** liquor flasks.

➤ **nose paint:** alcohol.

➤ **pour-out man:** a **bootlegger.**

➤ **powder:** an alcoholic drink.

➤ **red ink:** homemade red wine. House-holders were legally allowed to make up to 200 gallons of wine a year for home consumption. If a few dozen bottles found their way into **speakeasies,** who was the wiser?

➤ **real McCoy:** good whiskey.

➤ **rum runners:** speedboats that brought liquor onshore from larger foreign vessels.

➤ **something on the hip:** liquor kept in a hip flask.

> ## WORDS FOR ILLEGAL DRINKING PLACES
>
> **blind pig, blind tiger, booze foundry, creep joint, gin mill, gin palace, jinny, moonlight inn, sample room, scatter, speakeasy, whoopee parlor.**

G-MEN AND GOONS

All that illegal alcohol had to be processed somehow. Gangsters like "Scarface" Al Capone took on the job. Alcohol-related racketeering flourished in Chicago and other large cities. Federal agents only succeeded in destroying a small percentage of bootlegged liquor, while gangs raked in unheard-of profits. In fact, unheard-of profits were Capone's eventual downfall. The Feds convicted him of tax evasion in 1931, and he spent the next several years in the *Big House.*

Here is a sample of 1920s gangster jargon:

BAD BEHAVIOR

➤ **belch:** a complaint.

➤ **bend:** to steal.

➤ **blot out:** to kill.

➤ **breeze:** to leave.

➤ **cold meat party:** a funeral.

➤ **creep joint:** a gambling den that moved nightly.

➤ **jolt:** a term in prison.

➤ **on ice:** locked up.

➤ **put the cross on:** to target someone for death.

➤ **rub out:** to kill.

➤ **slam off:** to die.

➤ **stiff racket:** the state of being dead.

➤ **take it on the lam:** to run away; escape.

➤ **whip over:** to smuggle liquor.

> ## WORDS FOR DRUNK
>
> **basted, boiled, bunned, elevated, embalmed, foxed, frazzled, fried, geezed, illuminated, jiggered, jingled, lit, lubricated, mellow, Methodist-conated, oiled, on the bus, organized, ossified, pifflicated, piped, potted, preserved, primed, rileyed, scrooched, seeing snakes, shellacked, snozzled, spifflicated, stinko, stuccoed, tanked, tuned, vulcanized.**

BAD GUYS AND THEIR WEAPONS

➤ **airedale:** someone employed on the docks by **bootleggers.**

➤ **chiseler:** a small-time operator; a petty thief.

➤ **copper-hearted:** likely to turn informer for the police.

➤ **Dinah:** nitroglycerine.

➤ **dropper:** a paid killer.

➤ **eight-minute egg:** an especially hard-boiled person.

➤ **fall guy:** a scapegoat.

➤ **fall money:** a crook's reserve fund for occasions when lawyers were necessary.

➤ **finger man:** someone who collected detailed information for his gang.

➤ **gat:** a revolver.

➤ **gat up:** to hold someone up with a revolver.

➤ **goon:** a hired thug.

➤ **grease:** protection money.

➤ **gun mob:** a criminal gang.

➤ **gun moll:** a female gangster.

➤ **heater:** a gun.

➤ **hot grease:** serious trouble.

➤ **ice:** jewelry.

➤ **lip:** a lawyer.

➤ **long rod:** a rifle.

➤ **Mickey Finn:** a drink, usually alcoholic, containing a knockout drug.

➤ **moll buzzer:** a pickpocket who specialized in women.

➤ **nose:** a police spy.

➤ **pineapple:** a bomb.

➤ **puller:** someone who smuggled liquor.

➤ **rod:** a gunman, also called a *skiboo*.

➤ **roscoe:** a hand gun.

➤ **skirt:** a woman.

➤ **slim:** a police spy.

➤ **Tommy guns:** Thompson submachine guns, the favorite weapon of Chicago gangs.

➤ **torpedo:** a gunman.

➤ **weak sister:** a sissy or coward.

➤ **wiper:** a killer.

AND A FEW GOOD GUYS

➤ **bull:** a policeman, borrowed from hobo slang.

➤ **buttons:** a uniformed police officer, also a *harness bull*.

➤ **flattie:** a policeman, presumably flat-footed from walking his beat.
➤ **fresh bull:** an incorruptible, energetic policeman, carrying the suggestion of someone new to the job.
➤ **G-man:** an FBI agent, short for *government man*.

WORDS FOR MONEY

➤ **two bits:** a quarter.
➤ **boffo:** a dollar.
➤ **finif:** five dollars, from German *fünf*, 'five'. Also called a *fin*.
➤ **sawbuck:** ten dollars. *Sawbuck* is another word for *sawhorse*, the X-shaped legs of which resemble the Roman numeral for ten. Naturally, a *double sawbuck* was twenty dollars. Later, *sawbuck* and *double sawbuck* could also mean a ten- or twenty-year prison sentence.
➤ **C-note:** one hundred dollars.

LOUSY AND SWELL

Twenties bright young things had strong opinions, and many ways to express them. They tried not to be **high hat,** but they knew **banana oil** when they heard it.
➤ **all wet:** wrong; mistaken.
➤ **applesauce:** nonsense.
➤ **baked wind:** bragging, idle talk, or, in other words, hot air. Also called *balloon juice.*
➤ **banana oil:** nonsense.
➤ **berries:** a wonderful person or thing.
➤ **big thing on ice:** an important event.
➤ **bull wool:** something shoddy or valueless.
➤ **high hat:** snobbish. Also used as a verb meaning 'to snub'.
➤ **hipped on:** enthusiastic about.
➤ **horsefeathers:** same as **applesauce** or **banana oil.**
➤ **hotsy-totsy:** pleasing; okay.
➤ **posolutely:** absolutely positively.
➤ **spiffy:** stylish.

LUCKY LINDY

One of the sensations of the age was Charles Lindbergh's solo flight from New York to Paris. Lindbergh's tiny 27-foot airplane, *The Spirit of St. Louis,* took off from Roosevelt Field on the morning of May 20, 1927. As Lindbergh began his lonely journey across the Atlantic, the whole population of the United States held its collective breath. Mass hysteria broke loose when he landed 33 hours later at Le Bourget airfield outside Paris. Most Americans seemed to agree with the *Evening World*'s extravagant statement that Lindy's achievement was "the greatest feat of a solitary man in the records of the human race." Humorist Will Rogers remarked that the flight proved that "someone could still make the front pages without murdering anybody," no small accomplishment in the age of **ballyhoo.**

Americans were familiar with airplanes from the daring flights of ace fighter pilots during the First World War. Flying and the language of flight now entered into the public consciousness. Besides inventing many flight words that are still current, twenties **barnstormers** had some slang of their own:

➤ **aerobat:** a stunt flyer.

➤ **airhog:** a pilot who loved to fly as often as possible and amass air time.

➤ **air-minded:** in sympathy with the idea of aviation.

➤ **barnstormer:** a stunt flyer who traveled around performing in exhibitions that sometimes included such daring feats as standing on the airplane's wings. The word is borrowed from the name for acting troupes that traveled around the countryside and often performed in barns.

➤ **big-boat pilot:** the aeronautic equivalent of a **big butter-and-egg**

BALLYHOO

Ballyhoo is boisterous sensationalism designed to attract a crowd. It originally referred to free performances given outside a circus or carnival tent as an enticement to passersby to go inside. Although the word was around by the late nineteenth century, the twenties are known as the *Age of Ballyhoo.* The search for sensation after the war helped turn events like the Scopes Monkey Trial and the Fatty Arbuckle rape case into public entertainments. This period also saw the beginning of aggressive commercial advertising, including promotional contests run by *ballyhoo artists.*

One theory of how the word originated is that it comes from the Irish town of Ballyhooly, known for being unusually raucous on Saturday nights. *Ballyhooly,* shortened to *ballyhoo,* might have been extended to mean any kind of uproar.

A more intriguing explanation is put forward by Charles Wolverton in a 1935 issue of the journal *American Speech.* Wolverton exchanged letters with one W. O. Taylor, an old-time showman, who related the story of his Mighty Midway exhibit at the 1893 Columbian Exposition. Taylor reminisced about one of his acts, a pair of Turkish whirling dervishes. When he fired them

man; a real sport. Literally, someone who specialized in flying big-boat seaplanes.

➤ **conk:** to break down or suddenly stop, said of the plane's motor. Now we would say *conk out.*

➤ **crab the wind:** to fly sideways into the wind as a way of counteracting the wind's velocity and heading the plane in the desired direction; from the sideways walk of crabs.

➤ **crate:** an old airplane, a word from World War I. A **peppy crate** was a plane in good flying condition.

➤ **high hat:** an expert stunt flyer.

➤ **jazz ride:** a pleasure flight, also called a *joyhop.*

➤ **kiwi:** a pilot who couldn't fly, named for the large, flightless New Zealand bird. The word could also refer to someone who worked on the ground at an airfield.

➤ **lindy:** to fly as a passenger, as in *I lindyed over here from Baltimore,* obviously from Lindbergh.

➤ **loop-the-loop:** to make a complete vertical loop with the plane.

➤ **night pilot:** a pilot who liked to sleep in the daytime and party at night.

for failing to draw a crowd, they stood outside the theater, performing their act for free. As they jumped and whirled, they cried "B'Allah hoo." (Wolverton derives this expression from Arabic *Allah hoo,* which he translates as 'God! He!'.) This remarkable performance was much more successful outside than onstage. It drew a large, potentially ticket-buying crowd. Thereafter, when Taylor wanted the Turks to repeat their act, he just shouted "Ballyhoo!"

As tempting as this etymology is, it can't be the whole story, because the word was in use much earlier. Herman Melville used the phrase *ballyhoo of blazes* in his 1847 novel *Omoo* to mean a slovenly, badly run ship. Rudyard Kipling also used the expression in *Captains Courageous.* The seafaring term apparently comes from the word *ballahou,* also spelled *ballyhoo,* a type of fast, two-masted vessel often used for sailing in the West Indies. How to make the connection between sea and carnival is unclear. Another option suggested by one etymologist is that the word comes from the Spanish name of a Caribbean garfish, *balao,* also spelled *ballaho* and *ballyhoo.* This fish was sometimes used as bait to catch larger fish. In this case, the analogy is obvious—carnival ballyhoo reeled 'em in.

➧ **pants leg:** a cloth cone indicating the wind's direction (a wind sock).

➧ **rubber cow:** an inferior type of aircraft kept aloft by gas, such as a balloon or a dirigible.

MESSAGES FROM THE OTHER SIDE

The modern spiritualist movement started in the nineteenth century, but **table turning, Ouija boards,** and other attempts to commune with the spirit world were popular activities during the 1920s. The writer Sir Arthur Conan Doyle, a fervent believer in spiritualism and psychic phenomena, helped bring the subject to the public's notice. The International Spiritualists' Federation was formed in 1923. Soon, society hostesses were hiring mediums for after-dinner séances, groups of young people were gathering in the dark for a spot of **table-tipping,** and sensitive young ladies were explaining to their friends that they were probably **mediumistic.** Although psychic research organizations that investigated spiritualist activities generally found fraud, dabbling in the unseen remained a popular pastime into the thirties.

➧ **automatic writing:** writing directed by a spirit or the unconscious mind. Words appeared on a blank page although the person holding the pen claimed that he or she didn't remember writing them. Whole books were advertised as having been composed by the spirits through automatic writing.

➧ **channeling:** entering a trancelike state for the purpose of conveying messages from the other side, usually achieved by professional mediums at séances. **New Agers** also talked about channeling in the 1980s, but eighties channeling did not typically involve séances.

➧ **hypnoid:** in a semi-hypnotized or hysterical state, during which the person had greater suggestibility than usual.

➧ **mediumistic:** sensitive to otherworldly influences; psychic.

➧ **Ouija board:** a small board on three legs that rests on a larger board marked with letters of the alphabet, "yes," "no," and "maybe." When participants asked the Ouija questions while touching the small board lightly with their fingertips, it skidded around the larger board, spelling out messages. To believers, the movement was obviously spirit-directed. The Ouija was first introduced in 1890 as a parlor game. The origins of the word *Ouija* are unclear. Some have suggested that it comes from the French and German terms for "yes"—*oui* and *ja*—or after the city of *Oudja* in Morocco. Periodically, it comes back into fashion.

➤ **parapsychical:** an adjective referring to supernatural phenomena like clairvoyance or telepathy.

➤ **planchette:** a small, heart-shaped board on casters with a pencil attached. When participants touched it lightly with their fingertips, it wrote clairvoyant or otherworld-directed messages. The **Ouija board** was an improvement over the planchette because it made a printed alphabet available.

➤ **table turning:** an activity where people sat around a table in the dark with their outspread fingertips touching. When the spirit arrived, the table would begin to rock. Participants asked questions and the spokesperson from the other side rapped answers on the table—three times for "yes," once for "no."

A planchette.

Since those around the table were touching fingers, the rocking and rapping were assumed to be caused by the visiting spirit. Also called *table tipping* or *table rapping*.

➤ **teleplasm:** an emanation from the body of a medium during a séance, supposedly a manifestation of the spirit that she was channeling.

➤ **telepsychy:** exerting psychic powers at a distance.

TWENTIES BUZZWORDS

Only **flat tires** and **dumb doras** didn't know the buzz on these twenties people and happenings.

➤ **Babbitt:** a small-town civic booster with conventional middle-class attitudes, a cultural philistine, joiner of the Rotary Club and the Masons. In the minds of tuned-in *American Mercury* readers, Babbitts held American civilization down to a crude level. The word is the title of Sinclair Lewis's satirical 1922 novel, featuring George F. Babbitt, real estate salesman. In the novel, Babbitt makes a halfhearted attempt to free himself from the narrowness of life in his hometown of Zenith, but fears being ostracized by fellow club members.

➤ **Black Thursday:** October 24, 1929, the day the stock market crashed. Financial speculation was rampant in the late twenties, a time when stock prices more than doubled. When prices suddenly dropped on Monday, October 21, insecurely margined traders were forced to dump thousands of shares. Stockholders everywhere panicked as they watched share values head toward the basement. The rush to trade peaked on Black Thursday with a record sale of 16,410,030 shares. Thousands of people who had been rich on paper were now poor. The Depression had arrived.

➤ **Bolshevists:** an early word for *communists,* later called *Bolsheviks.* The word comes from the Russian *bolshinstvo,* meaning 'majority'. After the Russian Revolution of 1917, Bolshevism was a popular topic among intellectuals of the smart set who were out of sync with the booming capitalism of the age. By the mid-1920s, the smart set had moved on to other cultural fascinations like modern literature, and the **Big Red Scare** had set in. Americans began to fear the spread of worldwide revolution. The Federal Bureau of Investigation was instituted under J. Edgar Hoover to combat the **Red Menace** at home. (This term reappeared in the fifties when communism was once again high on the public agenda.) Another popular term for communists, **pinko,** was also first heard around this time.

➤ **booboisie:** boobs, or idiots, belonging to the bourgeoisie, or middle class. H. L. Mencken invented the term, which he published as part of a list of related fantasy words in the February 15, 1922, Baltimore *Evening Sun.* These included *boobariat, booberati, boobarian, boobomaniac,* and *boobuli. Homo boobiens* was later added to the collection. *Booboisie* was the only one of these terms to achieve widespread use.

Mencken was a harsh critic of what he considered typical middle-class American culture. He frequently skewered the booboisie during the twenties in the magazine *The American Mercury,* which he edited. His most important linguistic contribution was a comprehensive study of American English called *The American Language,* which included many slang words. It was first published in 1919, with revised editions and supplements appearing until 1963.

➤ **long count:** a shining example of **ballyhoo,** occurring during the Jack Dempsey–Gene Tunney fight of 1927. Dempsey lost the heavyweight boxing title to Tunney in 1926. During their rematch a year later, Dempsey knocked Tunney down in the seventh round. The referee delayed starting the count until Dempsey moved to a neutral corner, giving Tunney extra seconds for recovery. He stood up on the count of nine, but it was actually thirteen or fourteen seconds after he was knocked down. Tunney went on to win the fight by a ten-round decision. Excitement reached such a peak during this episode that at least five people were reported to have dropped dead while listening to the fight on their radios.

➤ **Scopes Monkey Trial:** the trial of high school teacher John Thomas Scopes for exposing his Dayton, Tennessee, students to Darwin's theories of human evolution. Tennessee's recently passed Butler Act made such teaching illegal. The trial was actually a test case instigated by the American Civil Liberties Union. Scopes agreed to go along with it, and leading citizens of Dayton supported the idea as a way to put their small town on the map. They got their wish when dozens of reporters, including Mencken, crowded into town to record the verbal combat between famous defense lawyer Clarence Darrow and three-time presidential candidate William Jennings Bryan, who appeared for the prosecution as a biblical expert.

The trial took place over several sweltering days in July. Journalists and spectators packed the courtroom as Darrow cross-examined Bryan and proceeded to "make a monkey" of him. Darrow ultimately lost the case, but it was the anti-evolutionist Bryan who was ridiculed in newspapers across the country. He died less than a week after the trial ended. Scopes was fined $100, but the sentence was later overturned in a higher court.

➤ **Teapot Dome:** Historians agree that while President Warren Harding was honest himself, he was spectacularly inept at choosing upright associates. The most high-profile of the various scandals that troubled his administration was known as the Teapot Dome scandal. In 1922, Secretary of the Interior Albert Bacon Fall illegally leased naval oil reserves at Teapot Dome, Wyoming, and Elk Hills, California, to private oil companies. In return, he received an interest-free loan of $100,000 from the president of one company and more than $300,000 in cash from the president of the other. That was a lot of money at a time when the U.S. president's annual salary was $75,000. Many middle-class families lived on $3,000 or $4,000 a year. Harding was spared full knowledge of the situation, as Congress did not begin investigating it until 1923, two months after his death. Eventually, Fall served a year in prison for taking bribes.

Only someone who was dead between the ears didn't love to jitterbug.

The Thirties

Swinging Cats in Hooverville

The party that was the twenties crashed along with the stock market in 1929. *Coolidge prosperity* turned into the **Hoover Depression.** The newly unemployed stood in *breadlines* and slept on park benches under **Hoover blankets** made of newspaper. **Hoovervilles,** wretched shanty-towns where people lived when they weren't on the tramp looking for work, sprang up around the country. Even those who still had homes were throwing **rent parties** to avoid eviction.

In the cities, **Apple Annie** and hundreds like her loitered on every corner, hoping to earn a nickel or two selling surplus fruit. Meanwhile, decades of overfarming, combined with years of drought, brought **black blizzards** to the country's heartland. Destitute farmers fled the *Dust Bowl* to look for work in California. So many of these **gasoline gypsies** came from Oklahoma that all of them were sneeringly referred to as **Okies.** Not everyone was unemployed, of course. Movie stars, displaced aristocrats, and other members of **Café Society** still spent their evenings in speakeasies or, after the repeal of Prohibition in 1933, in elegant new restaurants. Columnist Walter Winchell publicized the exploits of these *celebutantes* in the paper and on the radio. Which **Glamor Girl** was planning a **Lohengrin March** with which *man about town*? Which couple was planning to **Reno-vate?** *Mr. and Mrs. America* were eager to know.

Young men who still had jobs took their **hot patooties** out to **drag a hoof** at popular swing clubs. Jazz in the thirties was hotter than ever. **Swinging cats** played **barrelhouse** or backed up golden-voiced **canaries.** Only someone who was **dead between the ears** didn't love to **cut the rug** to the **jitterbug. Hepcats** were **knocked out** by a good jam session. If you wanted to dance, but didn't have a date, you could go to a **taxi-dance hall,** or, as the band called it, **a dime-grind palace,** where professional **taxi dancers** would rhumba or samba with you for 10 cents a dance. Youngsters who went out jitterbugging could replenish their lost calories at the local soda fountain with a **black cow, dusty miller,** or other ice-cream treat.

Those who preferred to stay home could **listen in** to the radio. Although the **ether** provided hours of news and music, millions tuned in specially to hear their favorite serials. Mom, Dad, little brother, and sis gathered around the *squawk box* to follow such popular programs as *Amos 'n' Andy, The Lone Ranger, Fibber McGee and Molly, Dick Tracy,* and *Little Orphan Annie.* Kids, don't forget to send away for your secret decoder rings!

Democrat Franklin D. Roosevelt became president in 1932, pledging himself to a **New Deal** for the American people. Relying on the advisors in his **brains trust,** Roosevelt fought the Depression with a whole set of programs, always known by their initials—from **AAA** to **WPA.** He introduced these to the American people in a series of radio talks called **fireside chats.** Critics complained that Roosevelt's policies were too close to socialism, but he was confident that his government would do *the greatest good for the greatest number.*

Fashions followed the tone of the times. As the stock market came down, so did skirts, to within a foot of the ground. Eton-cropped former flappers let their hair grow, too. *Artificial silks* like rayon and nylon were popular, especially for soft, flowing outfits like *beach pajamas. Man-tailored* suits struck a severe note in keeping with the seriousness of the times, but *Eugenie hats,* worn tilted over one eye, introduced a little frivolity.

Stylish men copied the future king of England by wearing **Prince of Wales check,** a type of plaid. In the winter they donned **London cut** suits, featuring wide lapels, padded shoulders, and sleeves draped with extra fabric. In the summer they lightened up with *Palm Beach* suits, constructed of seersucker, linen, or shantung silk.

Those who wanted to get away from it all could hit the **high-gear road** in their **touring cars. Auto touring** was the new way to vacation. Often, **auto tourists** towed that popular recent invention, the trailer. Travelers who preferred to sleep indoors could stop at one of the many **cabin camps** that lined the road. If people wanted entertainment along the way, well, they were still motoring slowly enough to read the Burma-Shave signs.

FROM EASY STREET TO HOOVERVILLE

When the stock market began to plummet with the speed of a broken elevator, it took tens of thousands of investors down with it. By the time stocks hit the basement, many people who had been rich on paper were poor. This moment was the start of the **Great Depression.** In spite of President Hoover's assurances that *prosperity is just around the corner,* financial distress began to spread. Banks took holidays and companies laid off workers. At the Depression's height, about 25

HOOVERVILLE

Hooverville was not one place, but many. As the Depression deepened, clusters of tin and cardboard shacks mushroomed at the edge of every town. New York City had two Hoovervilles. For a while, Washington, D.C., had one that consisted of army veterans. These towns within towns became refuges for the burgeoning number of poor and homeless.

Why blame Hoover? Until 1930 he had been a popular president. When the stock market crashed he took quick action, trying to forestall disaster. He cut income taxes and lowered interest rates to encourage borrowing. In a move that Roosevelt would later follow he also initiated public works projects to reoccupy some of the unemployed. Hoover spent plenty of money on recovery projects, becoming the first president to run a federal deficit in peacetime. However, his principles kept him from one spending program that would have been much appreciated—monetary relief for those who had lost their jobs. The president believed that what he called *the dole* would ultimately damage society, creating a permanent underclass of unemployed. People whose children were weak from malnutrition bitterly resented this attitude. Hoover became known as the man who would pay for grain for starving farm animals, but not for food for starving humans. He added to his unpopularity by persistently expressing optimism about economic recovery. Statements like "the worst has passed" rang hollow when thousands were standing in breadlines. Many came to believe that President Hoover was either a fool or disingenuous.

Besides Hoovervilles, the poor attributed some of their other daily burdens to Hoover as well:

- **Hoover blankets:** newspapers used to keep warm while sleeping outdoors.
- **Hoover cars:** the bodies of broken-down cars pulled by mules, also known as *Hoover wagons.*
- **Hoover flags:** empty pockets turned inside out.
- **Hoover flush:** a "busted" or incomplete flush in poker, with only four cards of the same suit instead of the required five.
- **Hoover hogs:** wild rabbits that rural people caught for food.
- **Hoover shoes:** shoes with holes in the soles.

New York City had two Hoovervilles.

percent of the working population was unemployed. Life got a little better in 1933 with newly elected President Franklin D. Roosevelt's unprecedented flurry of recovery legislation. The economy didn't really improve, though, until the beginning of World War II.

Apple Annie: a woman who sold apples on the street to make ends meet, also called *Apple Mary*. Many men sold apples, too. This method of earning cash got its start in the fall of 1930, when the International Apple Shippers' Association discovered that it had a surplus. It sold its extra apples to the unemployed on credit, and they resold them at a nickel apiece.

bank holiday: a euphemism for the practice of closing a bank that was about to fail. The day after Roosevelt's inauguration, March 5, 1933, he declared a four-day national bank holiday while he and Congress worked to restore the country's financial system.

➤ **brains trust:** President Roosevelt's group of informal advisors before the 1932 election, composed mostly of college professors. Later shortened to *brain trust.*

➤ **fireside chat:** Roosevelt's radio talks, which he used to calm people's fears and garner support for his new programs. He gave 30 fireside chats during 12 years in office.

➤ **gasoline gypsies:** unemployed people who lived and traveled in their cars while looking for work.

➤ **Great Society:** Herbert Hoover's vision of a country without poverty, which included *two cars in every garage and a chicken in every pot.* President Lyndon Johnson used *Great Society* again in the 1960s to describe a similar idea.

➤ **New Deal:** President Roosevelt's package of recovery and relief programs. Roosevelt first used the term during his acceptance speech for the presidential nomination, promising the American people a "new deal" after years of depression.

➤ **rent parties:** gatherings where each guest donated $2 to help pay the rent.

➤ **tin can shows:** movies to which viewers brought cans of food for the needy.

BLACK BLIZZARDS

The farmers of the Great Plains endured a special misery during the Depression. In the late 1800s, grazing herds of cattle covered the plains, wearing down the area's protective wild grasses. Crops replaced cattle

SUITCASE FARMERS

Suitcase farmers were the rural version of stock market speculators. During the twenties, when mechanized farm equipment became widely available, many city people with extra cash invested in a parcel of land and a tractor. These urban farmers, who were businesspeople, teachers, or office workers in daily life, spent just enough time working on their property to produce a cash crop like wheat. Then they packed up their suitcases and went back to town. They plowed up large expanses of land that lay underdeveloped and nearly abandoned. When the winds came, the land blew away. Many suitcase farmers, like other speculators, eventually lost money on their venture. They also contributed mountains of dust to the Great Plains disaster.

When the winds came, the land blew away.

at the turn of the twentieth century and farmers plowed up whatever grass was left. When drought conditions arrived around 1931, these huge expanses of arid, unprotected soil turned into a giant *Dust Bowl*. Powerful dust storms reduced fields to deserts, while grit blew through every crevice of farmhouses. Gray layers of dust from the plains coated buildings as far away as the East Coast. Thousands of ruined farmers abandoned their worthless property and took to the road.

➤ **black blizzard:** a severe, sky-darkening dust storm, also called a *black roller.*

➤ **duster:** a shortened version of *dust storm.*

➤ **dust pneumonia:** lung trouble caused by inhaling dust-filled air.

➤ **Joad:** an itinerant farm worker, referring to the name of the displaced farm family portrayed in John Steinbeck's 1939 novel *The Grapes of Wrath.* The term was actually first used in 1940, and was typically plural, as in *a family of Joads.*

➤ **Okie:** an insulting name for a failed Dust Bowl farmer. Many farmers of the Oklahoma panhandle relocated to California, where they were considered a nuisance. Not only were there too many of them for the available work, but they demanded higher wages than usual and sometimes joined unions. One character offers this pithy definition in

The Grapes of Wrath: "Well, Okie use'ta mean you was from Oklahoma. But now it means you're a dirty son-of-a-bitch. Okie means you're scum." These days, the word is used to label any rootless, shiftless population. **Arkie,** also used derogatorily, referred to itinerant farmers from Arkansas, but was less widespread as a general term.

➤ **sand blows:** southwesterly winds that blew sandy soils into drifts; not as powerful as **black blizzards.**

➤ **tin-can tourists:** migrants from the Great Plains who arrived in other states by car. **Tin can** meant 'a dilapidated old car', yet another bow in the direction of **Tin Lizzie.**

NEW DEAL ALPHABET SOUP

Roosevelt's plethora of New Deal programs had everyone talking in abbreviations. Who could remember the full names of all those acts and administrations? Here are some of the more important ones:

➤ **AAA:** Agriculture Adjustment Act, a measure aimed at providing farm relief by raising commodity prices. The government paid farmers not to grow certain major crops, including wheat, corn, cotton, and dairy products.

➤ **CCC:** Civilian Conservation Corps, an employment program for young men, who were relocated from the cities to the national parks and forests. They planted trees, dug drainage ditches, and built firebreaks, bridges, and dams.

➤ **FCA:** Farm Credit Administration, an organization that refinanced farm mortgages.

➤ **NRA:** National Recovery Administration, regulators of wages and hours. The NRA was supposed to put people back to work, but big business and the unions alike were suspicious of the program. They agreed with the newspaper magnate William Randolph Hearst that the initials actually stood for "No Recovery Allowed."

➤ **NYA:** National Youth Administration, an early form of work-study program that provided part-time jobs around campuses to high school and college students.

➤ **PWA:** Public Works Administration, an organization that supervised and paid for large public projects, including roads and bridges.

➤ **REA:** Rural Electrification Administration, a program that brought electricity to rural areas.

➤ **TVA:** Tennessee Valley Authority, a large rural development program for the Tennessee River Valley. The TVA built dams, reclaimed and reforested land, and tried to reverse soil erosion.

➤ **WPA:** Works Progress Administration, one of the most famous programs, in which writers, musicians, and other artists produced various kinds of public art. Some of their efforts can still be seen, heard, or read today. Activities included collecting and recording folk songs, painting murals in post offices, train stations, and other public buildings, writing regional guide books, and performing with the Federal Theatre.

HOBOHEMIA

Men who wandered through the towns and countryside looking for work were nothing new, but in the 1930s their ranks swelled by thousands. Authors like Edward Dahlberg and John Dos Passos drew harrowing pictures of life on the road, while books by Box-Car Bertha and Dean Stiff offered the hobo's-eye view. Stay-at-home citizens absorbed some of the traditions, dangers, pleasures, and special vocabulary of the itinerant way of life. Hobo language is an unusual mix of underworld slang, traditional Romany (Gypsy) words, railroad and World War I terms, as well as the speakers' own inventions. Some hoboes were former **Wobblies** (see the "Modern Times"

HOBO, TRAMP, BUM

Everyone agrees that **hoboes, tramps,** and **bums** are three different types of drifters, but they argue about exactly what the distinction is among them. According to one widely accepted idea, hoboes work and travel (or travel for work), tramps travel but are idle, and bums are both stationary and idle. Dean Stiff, author of *The Milk and Honey Route* (1930), says that hoboes work and travel, tramps drift and dream, but bums are merely beggars, "too stupid or too ornery to dream." Another difference between hoboes and tramps is that the former travel by train whenever possible while the latter walk or hitchhike.

Some, like Dean Stiff, claim that hoboes are at the top of the vagabond hierarchy, essentially migratory workers, while tramps and bums are merely vagrants. Others argue the opposite, pointing out that traveling workers are often designated with the term *tramp*, as in **fruit tramp** (a migrant worker who harvests fruit). In this version, it is tramps who travel for work and hoboes who work in order to survive while traveling. However you shuffle this hierarchy, bums always come out on the bottom.

buzzwords), so Wobbly work camp slang also spilled over into hobo language.

➤ **ace note:** a one-dollar bill.

➤ **bazoo:** one's mouth, as in *Shut your bazoo!*

➤ **bindle stiff:** a hobo who carried his bedding, also called a *blanket stiff*. A **bindle** was a folded blanket or bedroll. The word **stiff** appears frequently in hobo slang and means 'the thing the hobo does, either habitually or for a living'.

➤ **blinds:** platform of a baggage car. **Jumping the blinds** meant 'catching a ride on this platform'.

➤ **bone polisher:** a vicious dog.

➤ **bumpers:** couplings between train cars. Although it was dangerous, hoboes would sometimes ride on these if they couldn't get into the cars.

➤ **calaboose:** the local jail, from a Spanish word for *dungeon*.

➤ **California blankets:** newspapers for sleeping on or under if the hobo was in a place like California, where it was warm enough to sleep outside.

➤ **cannon ball:** a fast train.

➤ **carry the banner:** to walk around all night to avoid vagrancy charges.

➤ **chuck a dummy:** to pretend to faint, a way of getting money from sympathetic bystanders.

➤ **crums:** lice.

➤ **deck:** the top of a passenger train.

➤ **drag:** a slow-moving freight train.

➤ **eat snowballs:** to stay in a cold climate during the winter rather than migrate south.

➤ **flip a rattler:** to jump onto a moving boxcar.

➤ **flop house:** a cheap place to sleep.

➤ **front:** a new outfit.

➤ **go by hand:** to walk. *By hand* may have referred to hitchhiking, or it could simply mean traveling the hard way. Hoboes always preferred to jump a train.

➤ **go with the birds:** to travel south for the winter.

➤ **high ball:** a whistle that blew when the train was pulling out of the station. Raising a ball at the side of the tracks was an early way of signaling the train to go ahead. Later, a *high ball* was a lantern waved in a high arc by the brakeman or conductor, meaning 'full speed ahead'.

➤ **Hobohemia:** the hobo's world. Sinclair Lewis uses the word **Hobohemian** in the 1915 novel *Trail of the Hawk* to mean 'an artistic type' (sometimes known as a *Bohemian*). The connection between the two usages is unclear. The first recorded use of *Hobohemia* to mean 'hobo territory' is from 1917.

➤ **house dog:** someone who offered to do chores for money.

➤ **hungry town:** a town that was known for being stingy with handouts.

➤ **jungle:** a rural gathering place for hoboes.

➤ **library birds:** those who took shelter by spending time at the public library.

➤ **Lizzie tramps:** out-of-work families traveling in their cars, and the hitchhikers who traveled with them. Sometimes also called *Lizzie stiffs.* Presumably, the term is based on **Tin Lizzie.**

➤ **main stem:** the street in town where hoboes usually congregated and panhandled.

➤ **mission stiff:** someone who turned up at a mission and allowed himself to be "saved" in exchange for food and a place to sleep.

➤ **nickel note:** a five-dollar bill.

➤ **on the thumb:** hitchhiking.

➤ **rattler:** a fast train.

➤ **reefer:** a refrigerator car.

➤ **remittance man:** someone who was paid by his family to stay away.

➤ **road sister:** a female hobo.

➤ **riding the cushions:** riding inside the train, on the cushioned seats.

➤ **sallies:** Salvation Army shelters, usually the hobo's last resort.

➤ **set-down:** to eat sitting down at a table.

➤ **shiv:** a razor or anything with a sharp cutting edge; a switchblade. From the Romany word *chiv,* filtered through British underworld slang.

➤ **side door Pullman:** a boxcar, where hoboes slept because they couldn't afford a bunk in a real Pullman car.

➤ **thin ones:** small coins.

➤ **turkey:** a bundle or canvas bag.

➤ **yegg:** a hobo criminal.

HOBO CHOW

Hoboes in the city took handouts or bought whatever food they could afford, but in the jungle they cooked over the campfire. Here are some typical dishes:

➤ **alligator bait:** fried liver, an expensive dish.

➤ **big four:** a duck-egg omelet, made with four eggs, four slices of bacon, and four sliced potatoes.

- **chicken in the clay:** a chicken with its feathers still on, rolled in clay and placed in the fire to cook.
- **combination stew:** meat and the usual vegetables.
- **potatoes and with-it:** boiled potatoes with milk gravy poured over them.
- **punk and gut:** bread and sausage. **Punk** was an old word for 'bread' among tramps and soldiers.
- **stack of bones:** boiled spareribs.
- **toppings:** dessert.

KICKING OUT

Daily life in the 1930s was not always miserable. Those with jobs, and even some without, found ways to entertain themselves. One popular pleasure for all ages and social levels was swing music. When Duke Ellington wrote "It don't mean a thing if it ain't got that swing," listeners young and old agreed. Youthful **jitterbuggers** loved their music **hot,** while their parents preferred a **sugar band.**

JITTERBUG

Jitterbug is a versatile word. In the 1930s, a *jitterbug* could be someone who played jazz or someone who loved to listen to jazz, but especially someone who engaged in a highly improvised, energetic form of swing dance, also called *jitterbug*.

Jitter meant 'to jump around or move in a nervous way'. The word may have descended from the British English dialect word *chitter,* meaning 'to tremble or shake'. In the late 1920s, the *jitters* began to replace the *heebie-jeebies* as a nervous twitch. The stock market crash was brought on by a major case of the jitters. *The jitters* could also refer to a jumpy state caused by drinking too much alcoholic *jittersauce.*

Jitterbug gained popularity in 1934 when musician Cab Calloway recorded "Jitter Bug," a song about a man who drinks a lot every night, then has the jitters every morning. A *jitterbug* started to mean any nervous person, not necessarily one with a hangover. The wild leaps and jumps of energetic swing dancing were a natural extension of the word's meaning. These days, the other meanings have dropped away and *jitterbug* is always a type of dance.

➤ **barrelhouse:** a playing style in which the whole band improvised.

➤ **canary:** a female vocalist.

➤ **cat:** a swing musician or anyone who loved swing. This word carried over into fifties beatnik slang.

➤ **corn:** unexciting old folks' music. Musicians who didn't play **hot** were **corny,** or **on the cob.**

➤ **cut the rug:** to dance to swing music. **Rug cut** was also an alternative term for the **lindy hop.**

➤ **dead between the ears:** what people were if they didn't appreciate swing.

➤ **go to town:** to play very intense music.

➤ **gutbucket:** music played **low down,** meaning 'slurred' or 'with heavy vibrato'.

➤ **hot plate:** a hot recording. **Hot** music made you want to tap your feet and dance.

➤ **ickie:** a person who was **dead between the ears.**

➤ **kick out:** to improvise.

➤ **lindy hop:** a type of **jitterbug** dance, invented at the Savoy Ballroom in New York, named after Charles Lindbergh.

➤ **long underwear:** conventionally played, boring music.

➤ **paper man:** a musician who played strictly by the notes, never improvising.

➤ **ricky tick:** heavy-duty **corn,** also called *rooty toot.*

➤ **shiners:** dancers who showed off for the crowd.

➤ **sugar band:** a band that played sweet, uninspired melodies with no improvisation.

➤ **swing out:** to spontaneously embellish a melody.

ON THE AIR

For those too old, too young, or too broke to go out dancing, **the wireless** was a popular form of entertainment. The thirties was the **Golden Age of Radio,** with a variety of programming throughout the day: breakfast chat shows, soap operas, advice for housewives, news, music, comedy, and drama. Most programs were broadcast live. By the end of the decade, at least 80 percent of Americans owned radio sets. President Roosevelt used radio to capture the attention of his constituents. Eleanor Roosevelt also gave a number of radio talks on social and women's issues. Radio was the best way for advertisers to connect with the public. Many shows were developed mainly as advertising vehicles, with names like "Campbell Playhouse," "Kraft Music Hall," "Lux Radio Theater," and "The Prudential Family Hour."

Radio buffs were fascinated by the inner workings of this new medium. Magazine articles began to appear with lists of radio slang. For example:

➤ **belly punch:** a joke that drew a belly laugh.

➤ **clambake:** a program that failed because of lack of rehearsal and resulting on-air mistakes.

➤ **cross-talk:** conversation picked up from an outside source; interference.

➤ **ether:** the radio waves.

➤ **listening in:** listening to the radio.

➤ **put in a wire:** to originate a broadcast from somewhere other than the station, for example, a ballroom; still reasonably current.

➤ **soso:** a joke rewarded by a smile, but not a laugh.

➤ **standby:** a program that could be used as a replacement if necessary.

➤ **stiff:** a terrible joke, rewarded only by silence.

➤ **wireless:** the radio, already becoming an outdated term by the thirties, pushed out by *radio,* which Americans started using around 1920.

STAND BY FOR THE ADENOID TENOR

Talking and singing filled the airwaves for much of the day. Frequent listeners would have been familiar with these performing types:

➤ **adenoid tenor:** a tenor with the pinched voice typical of someone with enlarged adenoids.

➤ **belcher:** a performer with a frog in the throat.

➤ **crawk:** an animal imitator.

➤ **gelatine tenor:** a tenor with a thin, wobbly voice.

➤ **Lady Macbeth:** an aging tragedienne.

➤ **Madame Cadenza:** a flighty female vocalist.

➤ **nervous baritone:** an overdramatic baritone.

➤ **old sexton:** a bass with a deep, sepulchral voice.

➤ **town crier:** a vocalist who sang too loud.

WINCHELLESE

"Good morning, Mr. and Mrs. North and South America and all the ships at sea. Let's go to press!" These words always opened the radio show of the decade's most popular gossip columnist, Walter Winchell. Winchell was a native New Yorker who began his career writing for *The Vaudeville News.* By the late twenties he wrote a syndicated column featuring show biz and celebrity gossip, as well as offering a daily 15-minute radio show.

Winchell catered to the public's fascination with the rich and famous, especially those in show business. He didn't settle for passing along the latest tidbits in ordinary English, though. When the subjects of his columns fell in love, they **sizzled for** each other and eventually **handcuffed.** When they fell out of love, they **abrogated.** They did it all under the influence of *whoopee water.* Winchell discovered all the good and bad news on *B'way,* also known as the *Main Stem, Gulch, Hardened Artery,* and *Grandest Canyon.* He also spent time there listening to *torch warblers* who sang *torch chunes* in *la-de-dah shows* or *revusicals.*

The spellings and abbreviations in Winchell's newspaper column had their own style. His days of the week included *Chewsdee, Wendsdee, Thursdee, Fridee,* and *Satdee.* *Ph-* replaced *f-* in *phavorite, phormer, phlicker,* and other words.

Mr. and Mrs. America couldn't get enough of Winchell's phractured phrases. At the peak of his influence, Walter Winchell was the most highly paid gossip columnist in the country, read by nearly five million people every day.

➤ **pashing it, sizzling for, that way for, uh-huh:** falling in love.
➤ **middle-aisle it, altar it, be handcuffed, Lohengrin it, Mendelssohn March it, merge:** get married.
➤ **baby-bound, stork'd, expecting a blessed event:** pregnant.
➤ **on the verge, have it abrogated, have it Reno-vated, have the seal shattered, be melted:** get divorced.

SODA FOUNTAIN TREATS

A small-town hero of the 1930s was the **soda jerk,** the kid who mixed everything from lemon Cokes to strawberry malteds. In those days, drinks didn't come in premixed bottles or cartons. When someone ordered a Coca-Cola, the **soda dispenser** behind the counter squirted some Coke syrup into a glass and filled it with carbonated water. A scoop of **hail** went in to keep it cold. For extra flavor, **jerkers** could *shoot one red* (cherry), *shoot one fresh yellow* (lemon), *shoot one fresh green* (lime), or *shoot a sissy* (vanilla).

Besides being quick lunch spots for office workers and shoppers, drugstore soda fountains were gathering places for the young. Soda jerks had to be quick on their feet to keep everyone served. Soda fountain lingo was colorful, clever, and easy to remember. It wasn't always faster than ordinary words, but it did make the job more fun. It could also serve as a code between the soda fountain worker in front and the short-order cook in back. The **soda clerk** could shout out **"Ninety-**

The soda jerk was a small-town hero in the 1930s.

eight!" to warn the other employees when the manager walked in, and only those in the know would be the wiser.

Drugstore dialect was often highly local. Sometimes the same words had different meanings in different places, or varying words and expressions were used to refer to the same thing. Some words were old hobo usages, just becoming mainstream. Here are some of the more ingenious names for soda-fountain treats:

- **barrel of black mud:** a chocolate milkshake.
- **barrel of red mud:** a strawberry milkshake.
- **black cow:** a root-beer float, still seen on ice-cream parlor menus.
- **black stick:** a chocolate ice-cream cone, also *mud stick.* A vanilla ice-cream cone was a **blond stick.**
- **Bossy in a bowl:** beef stew.
- **bovine extract:** milk.

➤ **cat beer:** milk.

➤ **chaser of Adam's ale:** a glass of water.

➤ **chewed fine with a breath:** a hamburger with onion.

➤ **chocolate dust:** a chocolate malted milkshake, from the dustlike appearance of the malt flavoring.

➤ **Coney Island chicken:** a hot dog. **Coney Island** is slang for 'a hot dog sandwich', usually including toppings like chili or sauerkraut, depending on where in the country you're eating it.

➤ **dog soup:** water.

➤ **dusty miller:** a chocolate sundae with malted milk.

➤ **eighty:** water, maybe short for H_2O. One glass would be **eighty-one** and a second glass **eighty-two.** This system could cause confusion for a large table because **eighty-six** also meant the kitchen was out of whatever had been ordered.

➤ **Eve with the lid on:** apple pie.

➤ **first lady:** spareribs, referring to Eve again, not to the president's wife.

➤ **graveyard stew:** milk toast, possibly so-named because it was a traditional food for invalids.

➤ **hounds on an island:** hot dogs and beans.

➤ **house boat:** a banana split.

➤ **knock off the horns and drive 'em in:** a colorful way to order rare steak.

➤ **lacey cup:** a cup of hot chocolate.

➤ **mug of murk:** coffee with no cream.

➤ **nervous pudding:** Jell-O.

➤ **Noah's boy with Murphy carrying a wreath:** ham and potatoes with cabbage, *Ham* being Noah's son and *Murphy* being any potato-loving Irishman.

➤ **pull one on the city:** a glass of water, freely provided by the city water system. Water was also *city juice* or *city cocktail.* The alternative names *Potomac phosphate* and *Hudson River ale* indicated its origin.

➤ **put out the lights and cry:** liver and onions. **Liver** and **lights** (an archaic word for *lungs*) are often paired in such expressions as *I'll have your liver and lights, you varmint!* or *You scared the liver and lights out of me!*

➤ **scandal soup:** tea, what ladies drank when they got together in the afternoon for tea and scandal.

➤ **splash of red noise:** a bowl of tomato soup.

➤ **tin roof:** water, because it's on the house.

➤ **yesterday, today, and forever:** hash, the final destination of leftovers.

COCA-COLA WITH A SPLASH

As long as the soda maker was mixing up a Coca-Cola (or **Coke,** to use the slang), why not splash in some extra flavor? And the flavors that some folks came up with were pretty surprising. No wonder two of the nicknames were **dilly** and **freak.** Note that neither caffeine-free nor diet is among the thirties options.

➤ **both barrels:** two plain Cokes. The slang directive for mixing one small Coke was **shoot one.**

➤ **freak:** an orange Coke.

➤ **frost one:** a Coca-Cola with a dab of ice cream.

➤ **gus:** a Coke flavored with Angostura bitters.

➤ **hang a dilly:** a large lime Coke. If the customer preferred a small drink, *hang* was replaced by *shoot* in the following orders.

➤ **hang a fresh:** large lemon Coke, also known as a *frown* (from the well-known pucker properties of lemon juice) or *hang a squeeze.*

➤ **hang an honest:** large cherry Coke, in honor of the country's first president, who could not tell a lie. Cherry Cokes were also known as *make it virtue,* referring in this case not to George Washington's virtue, but to that of young girls.

➤ **hang one:** a plain old large Coke.

➤ **hang a mud:** a large chocolate Coke.

➤ **hold the hail:** a Coca-Cola with no ice.

➤ **shoot one from the South:** a Coca-Cola with extra Coke syrup.

➤ **shoot a western:** a strongly chocolate-flavored Coke.

BIDDIES ON A RAFT

Cackle berries, more familiar to most of us as eggs, were a popular menu item at drugstore counters. Customers could order their **hen fruit** *sunny-side up, over easy,* or cooked in more mysterious ways:

➤ **Adam and Eve on a raft:** two fried or poached eggs on toast. This one had already been around for a while by the thirties, especially among hoboes.

➤ **biddies on a raft:** eggs any style on toast.

➤ **flop 'em:** eggs fried on both sides.

➤ **let the sun shine:** a fried egg with an unbroken yolk.

➤ **spoil 'em:** scrambled eggs. Also *wreck 'em.* A **wreck on a raft** was scrambled eggs on toast.

➤ **toast two on a slice of squeal:** ham and eggs.

MAGIC NUMBERS

When fountain employees wanted to communicate without shouting their business to the customers, they used their own code. Here are some popular numbers:

➤ **thirteen:** a boss is roaming around.

➤ **fourteen:** a special order.

➤ **eighty-six:** we're out of what was just ordered.

➤ **eighty-seven and a half:** a pretty woman just walked in.

➤ **ninety-five:** a customer is walking out without paying.

➤ **ninety-eight:** the manager is here.

BURMA-SHAVE

Before the advent of superhighways, motorists traveled the roads slowly enough to read signs placed along the shoulder. The **Burma-Shave Company,** along with many others, realized that highway billboards were a great way to advertise. What made Burma-Shave ads unique was that they consisted of a set of six signs, spaced so that travelers passing at a normal speed would have time to read and assimilate each one before reaching the next one. The final sign always said "Burma-Shave."

Burma-Shave was a shaving cream made mostly of ingredients from Burma and India. It could be applied without a brush, making it convenient for traveling salesmen and other men on the go. Early ads, beginning in 1927, were straightforward messages. Here is one of the first:

> Shave the modern way
> No brush No lather
> No rub-in
> Big tube
> 35 cents drug stores
> Burma-Shave

Later ads were jingles, using humor and whimsy to capture their audience. By the early 1930s, the company was running annual jingle contests, paying $100 for each one accepted. This tradition netted thousands of potential ads every year. Here is one winning jingle:

➤ **ninety-nine:** the head soda man is here.

AUTO TOURISTS

In 1925, the federal government instituted a highway numbering system, including standardized routes and road signs, and travel by car got easier. Trailers towed by automobile were another new invention to delight **motor gypsies. Cabin camps** lined the highways for those who preferred to sleep indoors, with *filling stations* springing up alongside. The Automobile Association of America and other *motor clubs* provided road maps and travel guides for motorists' convenience. Tourism boards across the country scrambled to advertise their state's unique attractions. The age of the driving vacation had arrived.

➤ **cabin camps:** clusters of roadside cabins, usually with plumbing

---

He had the ring
He had the flat
But she felt his chin
And that
Was that
Burma-Shave

Some verses addressed highway safety, with only the last line referring to the product:

Hardly a driver
Is now alive
Who passed
On hills
At 75
Burma-Shave

By the mid-1960s, times and traffic had changed enough to make the Burma-Shave signs less effective. The company decided to remove them and try different forms of advertising. Nonetheless, some claim to have spotted the signs since then, strung out along back roads as mementos of a more leisurely time.

and electricity, where auto tourists could stay. According to one magazine article, it was possible to find a comfortable cabin with its own bath and a shed for the car for as little as $1.50 per person per night. Cabin camps were also called *tourist courts, tourist camps, tourist apartments,* or *cottage camps.*

➤ **camp stores:** stores located near cabin camps, where the gullible or desperate tourist could buy everything from a loaf of bread to a decorated tire cover, with the emphasis on tacky souvenirs.

➤ **counting stand:** a stop designed to allow state travel bureaus to count the number of tourists driving through their area.

➤ **high-gear road:** a road that could be traveled at a steady speed.

➤ **motor court:** an early term for a motel.

➤ **motor gypsies:** people who sold their houses and traveled around, towing a trailer or *house-car* as their permanent abode.

➤ **touring car:** a car designed for long-distance travel, with plenty of room for people and luggage.

THIRTIES BUZZWORDS

During the thirties, serious topics competed with fads and gossip for news coverage. These are some of the wide-ranging topics that Mr. and Mrs. America read about in their morning or afternoon papers, or heard about on the radio news.

➤ **Abraham Lincoln Brigade:** a group of American volunteers who fought for the Republican cause during the Spanish Civil War. In 1936, the Fascist General Francisco Franco led an army coup against Spain's left-leaning Republican government. The Fascist leadership of Germany and Italy soon joined the fight on the side of Franco, while the Communist Soviet Union aided the Republicans. In 1937, the Communist International organized the Abraham Lincoln Brigade in the United States, which fought until the end of 1938. The Republicans lost the fight and Franco became the head of the Spanish government in 1939. He remained in power until his death in 1976.

The Abraham Lincoln Brigade numbered about 2,800 volunteers, 900 of whom were killed in action. The United States was officially neutral during the Spanish Civil War. Most Americans did not have strong feelings about the war's outcome.

➤ **Bonus Army:** a group of 15,000 or more unemployed World War I veterans who marched to Washington, D.C., to ask for immediate payment on their war bonus certificates, due in 1945. They also called themselves the *Bonus Expeditionary Force* after the American Expeditionary Forces of the First World War. While their leaders negotiated with the government, the vets camped out in shantytowns along the Potomac or squatted in abandoned buildings.

When Congress rejected the Bonus marchers' request, most went home. However, one or two thousand remained, a visible sign of the Depression and an embarrassment to President Hoover's administration. By the president's order, the army drove their former colleagues out of town using weapons, tanks, and tear gas. This incident was one more reason why voters overwhelmingly threw Hoover out of office in 1932.

➤ **Café Society:** the movie stars and idle rich who spent their evenings in cafés, speakeasies, or other amusing nightspots, in contrast to earlier times, when socialites entertained each other at home. Maury Paul, society editor of the *New York American,* coined the term. Paul provided high-life gossip under the byline of Cholly Knickerbocker. Other columnists adopted Paul's linguistic creation. *Café Society* also became the title of a movie starring Madeleine Carroll and the name of two New York City nightclubs. Paul also invented the term **Glamor Girl** (spelled without the *u*) to designate a high-profile society debutante.

➤ **dance marathon:** a dance contest in which contestants two-stepped around the floor for hours or days in hopes of profit or publicity. Dance marathons first became a craze in the twenties. In 1923, dance teacher Alma Cummings set the first American record of 27 hours. She exhausted six partners, all younger than she was. Couples were soon setting new records almost daily, tripping the light fantastic for 90 hours or more. By the 1930s, marathons were well-established as a cheap form of entertainment for the unemployed and a way of earning money for the participants. Standard rules were that couples must stay together (no partner replacements); they must take 10- or 15-minute breaks at regular intervals; they were not allowed to chew gum except late at night; men were not allowed to smoke on the floor and women were not allowed to smoke at all; women could wear trousers only late at night. Contestants used the breaks to dash to the bathroom, change shoes, swallow a snack, or catch a few minutes' sleep.

Inevitably, promoters began staging the competitions more rigidly with a view to keeping spectators entertained. Professional couples were paid to participate and to lose if necessary. **Sweetheart couples** got married on the floor. By the end of the decade, concerns about the safety of such a physically and mentally stressful ordeal, as well as pressure from movie theater owners, led many states to outlaw marathons. These contests were also called *dance derbies, danceathons,* and *jitterathons.*

➤ **sit-down strike:** tactic of downing tools but remaining at the work station. Sit-downs were also called *stay-in, crossed arms,* or *folded arms* strikes. Auto workers first used the sit-down strike in January 1937, at the Flint, Michigan, General Motors plant. Persistent efforts by the owners and the police to dislodge the strikers failed. When the company turned off the heat, the strikers built bonfires. When the police threw tear-gas bombs into the building, those inside broke windows to dissipate the fumes. The striking workers could have been starved out, but Democratic governor Frank Murphy refused to allow interference with food deliveries. After 44 days, General Motors capitulated and gave its employees the right to join the United Autoworkers Union. Sit-down strikes spread worldwide among all kinds of workers during the next few years. The Supreme Court ruled them against the law in the United States in 1939.

➤ *War of the Worlds:* a radio play narrated by Orson Welles based on H. G. Wells's 1898 novel, broadcast on Mercury Theater of the Air on the night of October 30, 1938. The memorable events of that night dramatically illustrate the power of radio in the thirties. *War of the Worlds* was the story of a Martian attack on the United States. To add realism, the actors presented it in the form of a radio news broadcast. The play began with a radio announcer introducing a dance music program. Music played for a minute or two. Then the frantic voice of the announcer broke in, exclaiming that Martians had landed in New Jersey, intent on conquering the United States.

Although the program broke four times to remind the audience that they were listening to fiction, thousands panicked. In one Newark neighborhood, twenty families rushed from their houses wearing wet towels over their faces, fleeing what they believed to be a gas raid. Hundreds of New Yorkers streamed out of their homes to congregate hysterically in parks or in the streets. Many packed their bags and clogged the highways trying to escape.

As the news spread, thousands called the police, newspaper offices, or radio stations for information and advice. *The New York Times* alone received nearly 900 calls. National Guardsmen jammed the phone lines calling headquarters about where to report for duty. One terrified man phoned the Bronx Police Headquarters with the news that Martians were bombing New Jersey.

"How do you know?" asked the puzzled telephone operator.

"I heard it on the radio!"

It seems remarkable now that so many people believed in a story of alien space invaders. However, the 1930s radio audience had heard programs interrupted for events that were almost as incredible, such as Hitler's invasion of the Rhineland. When war really did overwhelm the world barely a year later, it was the radio that broke that news to most Americans.

A former glamour boy wearing the canary.

The Forties

Rosie the Riveter and G.I. Joe

The year 1940 found Americans waiting for war. The **Axis** powers of Germany, Italy, and Japan had been on the move since the mid-1930s. Adolph Hitler's Nazis invaded the Rhineland in 1936, then annexed Austria. Fellow fascists in Italy under Benito Mussolini had already taken over Ethiopia. On the other side of the world, Japan waged war against China. After a 1938 meeting with Hitler, British Prime Minister Neville Chamberlain predicted *peace for our time,* but most people expected conflict. Barely a year later, it came. When Germany invaded Poland, Poland's **Allies,** France and Britain, declared war.

The first few quiet months seemed like a **phony war,** but the fighting turned real when the German **blitzkrieg** conquered most of Northern Europe and France. The neutral United States became an *arsenal of democracy* for struggling Great Britain, **lend-leasing** them war materials. Sometimes these were transported in newly built **liberty ships.**

American neutrality ended on December 7, 1941, a date that President Roosevelt declared *"will live in infamy,"* when Japan hurled a surprise attack against the Pearl Harbor naval base in Hawaii. Americans entered the new world war with *"Remember Pearl Harbor"* as their rallying cry. Soon **G.I. Joe** and **Rosie the Riveter** were at their posts, **going all out for America.**

Everyone did his or her part. Newly recruited **dogfaces** sailed away on *battlewagons* and, before they knew it, were busy **dawn patrolling** and saluting the **brass hats. Oh, my aching back!** Wives and mothers rationed with **red points** and dug **victory gardens,** or headed to the factories like Rosie, with **do-rags** tied around their hair. Young **victory girls,** also known as *patriotutes,* specialized in entertaining soldiers on leave, to the dismay of their parents and the police. Posters of **sweater girls** like Lana Turner cheered up the troops.

Most folks gave up good food for the duration. *Hashburners* in army kitchens kept **chow hounds** fed with such delicacies as **army**

strawberries (prunes) and **punk** with **salve** (bread and butter). Worst of all were **C-rations.** Biting down on the **dog biscuits** in the ration packet could give your teeth a **biscuit blast.** On the home front, **gazelleburgers** and **beaverburgers** became standard dishes, unless people patronized a **meatlegger** for more familiar ingredients.

Utility fashions were the favored war wear. **Convertible suits** were popular for women because the jackets could be removed for a dressier look at night. **Popover dresses** and **playsuits** saved valuable fabric, while **Eisenhower jackets** paid tribute to the Allied armies' supreme commander-in-chief. Long-haired women donated their hairpins to the war effort and lopped their tresses into **vingles,** shingles for victory. After the war, women were more than ready for the luxurious **New Look.**

Teenagers came into their own in the forties. The **bobbysox brigade** had its own outlook, its own pocket money, and its own vocabulary. *Junior debs* got a bang out of stunning the oldsters with expressions that were **burnt to a crisp.** Everyone except **mothballs** spent time dancing in **juke joints** or listening to **pancake turners** as they spun **bebop** records on the radio. Kids who were **in the groove** had **big eyes** for this musical craze.

After the war, former servicemen readjusted to civilian life with the help of the **G.I. Bill.** Nothing could help them get used to the snappy new postwar speech of ad men and radio announcers, whose **jokeroos** could be real **stinkeroos.** They were also *strictly nowhere* with younger college students, as the *vout* fad hit campus. **Voutians** and their **viddle vops** made the classrooms ring with their rhyming slang. *What's the deal, Macneal? Put it in your vest and let it rest!*

America's attention was still turned toward serious world events. As the **Berlin airlift** flew food to West Berliners, our former ally the Soviet Union drew an **iron curtain** across Eastern Europe. The **Atomic Age** had begun, with all its worries, and the fifties were almost here.

DAWN PATROL

Unlike World War I, the war of 1939 through 1945 was truly global. After the German army invaded Russia, the Soviets entered the fray as a major ally of the United States and Great Britain. Eventually, 50 nations in all joined the Allies, including such far-flung countries as Argentina, Egypt, India, Australia, Saudi Arabia, and Turkey. Axis countries included Bulgaria, Hungary, Romania, Albania, Finland, and Thailand, as well as Germany, Italy, and Japan.

G.I. Joes saw action in Western and Southern Europe, North Africa, Asia, and the Pacific. Some of their experiences, such as trench foot, renamed *fighting hole feet*, and the constant presence of *motorized freckles*, yet another term for lice, were familiar from the Great War. Some of the jargon was the same, too. In other ways, war in the 1940s had its own particular miseries. Dozens of new words crowded into the language to help the **blisterfeet** talk about their new situation until they could get *stateside* again.

Some of the places where they fought contributed memorable words and references that still resonate 60 years later.

➤ **Anzio:** the Anzio beachhead in Italy, scene of an Allied failure that gave rise to several expressions popularized by journalist Ernie Pyle in the New York *World-Telegram*. Troops landed on Anzio beach on January 22, 1944, hoping to panic the occupying Germans into pulling out. Instead, the Germans kept the area under constant fire. Some terms related to this fiasco include the **Anzio amble,** 'a quick move from one sheltered spot to the next to avoid being shot'; **Anzio anxiety,** 'stress caused from being in danger'; **Anzio foot,** 'swerving sideways when a screaming shell exploded'; **Anzio walk,** a version of the amble; and **Anzio Annie,** 'a long-range German gun'.

➤ **Battle of Britain:** the German bombing campaign against England that began in the summer of 1940. These attacks were also called the **Blitz,** from the German word *blitzkrieg*, meaning 'lightning-fast attack'. Hitler's *Luftwaffe*, or air force, first bombed British air bases, and then turned their attacks to English towns. The German goal was to debilitate the civilian population before invading across the English Channel. However, the Royal Air Force shot down enough German planes to make Hitler rethink his tactics. The planned invasion never took place.

➤ **Battle of the Bulge:** the Germans' westward push into Belgium and Luxembourg in December of 1944, causing a bulge of about 50 miles into the Allied front. The Allies had to fight fiercely to push the Germans back behind the original Allied front line. The Battle of the Bulge was the last hurrah for the Nazis, who were defeated soon after. The name has since become a joke term, usually referring to a bulge of fat.

➤ **D-Day:** code word for the date of a planned operation, used before its exact date was known. **H-Hour** was used to speak of an undetermined time. D-Day later referred specifically to June 6, 1944, the date of the Allied invasion of Normandy, France. The D-Day landing was the largest amphibian invasion in history, involving more than 60,000 men. D-Day is also called *the Longest Day*. The term *D-Day* is often used now to designate the day of any important planned event.

➤ **Leyte Gulf:** site of the largest naval battle in history, in October of 1944. The Gulf is the body of water surrounding Leyte Island in the Philippines. Americans first learned the word *kamikaze* during the battle of Leyte Gulf, a Japanese word meaning 'divine wind'. Kamikaze pilots, willing to die for the greater glory of Japan, crashed their obsolete, bomb-laden planes into American aircraft carriers.

COMRADES IN ARMS

As civilian **glamour boys** reported to base to start their new lives as soldiers, all the old army types were waiting to make their acquaintance. Some had new names, though.

➤ **bedpan commando:** a soldier in the medical corps.

➤ **big John:** a recruit.

➤ **big-time operator:** a prisoner of war who traded items until he ended up with more goods than he started with.

➤ **blisterfoot:** an infantryman.

➤ **brass hat:** a staff officer.

➤ **brownie:** a soldier-in-training who tried too hard to impress the instructor, staying after class and asking bright questions. Almost certainly derived from the term *brown nose.*

➤ **bunkie:** a friend; someone who bunked with you.

➤ **chow hound:** a fellow who was always at the head of the line in the mess hall.

➤ **coffee cooler:** a soldier who looked for easy jobs. This term was used in the army as early as 1876 to mean 'a loafer' or 'a straggler'. Soldiers in the West also applied it to Native Americans whom they deemed lazy or uncooperative.

➤ **dogface:** a soldier. After the war, this word could mean 'an unattractive boy'.

➤ **dog tags:** identification tags worn by **dogfaces,** so-named because they resembled the collar tags issued with dog licenses.

➤ **eight ball:** a soldier who got into trouble so often that the rest of his unit tried to avoid him. Presumably the term is from the eight ball in pool games, which the player avoids hitting until the very end—one who prematurely hits the eight ball into a pocket loses the game. Also, those **behind the eight ball** are in a difficult or problematic situation.

➤ **foot slogger:** an infantryman.

➤ **glamour boy:** a new draftee, whose civilian polish had not yet been completely buffed away.

➤ **gravel agitator:** an infantryman, scuffing up the gravel as he marched.

➤ **hedgehopper:** a careless pilot, also called a *flathatter.*

➤ **mitt flopper:** a soldier who saluted excessively; a yes-man.

➤ **sad sack:** a misfit, a civilian who had a hard time turning himself into a soldier. Sgt. George Baker popularized the term with his cartoon strip of that name, running in military newspapers. In the 1930s, *sad sack* was simply slang for 'an incompetent person'.

➤ **sky scout:** a chaplain.

➤ **yard bird:** a new recruit.

G.I.

The army used the abbreviation **G.I.** as early as the 1920s. It stood for *government issue,* or possibly *general issue,* and was stamped or stenciled on all army equipment. During World War II, G.I. started to refer to the soldiers themselves, although not to officers. It was only a matter of time before someone attached it to *Joe,* a common way of referring to a random male. The person who actually combined the two terms was Lt. Dave Berger, in his June 17, 1942, comic strip for the first issue of the military paper *Yank.*

The term *G.I.* took off. Soon it was attached to all sorts of military items, as well as to enlisted men. Here is a list of some of them:

➤ **G.I. cocktail:** a dose of epsom salts, used as a laxative.

➤ **G.I. haircut:** one inch all over.

➤ **G.I. hop:** a dance held on the base, also called a *G.I. struggle,* from earlier college slang.

➤ **G.I. Jane, Josephine,** or **Jill:** a member of the Women's Army Corps.

➤ **G.I. Moe:** an army mule.

➤ **G.I. party:** an organized cleanup before inspection.

➤ **G.I. turkey:** corned beef.

➤ **G.I. sky pilot:** another of the many terms for an army chaplain.

After the war, the **G.I. Bill** came into being, which provided federal money for education for veterans. Its official name was the Servicemen's Readjustment Act, but it is usually known as the **G.I. Bill of Rights.**

OH, MY ACHING BACK!

Yard birds were quickly introduced to a new slate of **daily details,** very different from the work they engaged in at home. The hardships and danger of war were part of it, but so were more mundane tasks like **bubble dancing.** If they complained about the work schedule, the brass hats informed them, **"You never had it so good!"**

➤ **AA:** anti-aircraft.

➤ **ack-ack:** a machine gun.

➤ **bubble dancing:** washing dishes.

➤ **captain of the head:** a latrine orderly on a ship.

➤ **crumb hunt:** a kitchen inspection.

➤ **daily details:** the daily work schedule.

➤ **dawn patrolling:** rising before dawn to start the day's work.

➤ **devil's piano:** a machine gun.

➤ **egg in your beer:** too much of a good thing. *What do you want, egg in your beer?* was a common retort to pointless or unjustified complaining, since in the wartime world either an egg or a glass of beer alone should have been a sufficient luxury for anybody.

➤ **flying boxcar:** a bomber.

➤ **flying the wet beam:** said of a pilot keeping on course by following the river.

➤ **galvanized gelding:** a tank. Another name for a tank was *iron horse.* For the first time, real horses were not a major part of the war effort, but their memory still lingered. Motorcycles were **iron ponies.**

➤ **geese:** bombers flying in formation.

➤ **gizmo:** anything that you don't know the name of, first used in the navy.

➤ **go over the hill:** to desert.

➤ **hell buggy:** a tank.

➤ **hit the silk:** to activate a parachute.

➤ **kite:** an airplane.

➤ **Maggie's drawers:** a flag used to indicate a miss on the rifle range, colored red like Maggie's flannel underwear.

➤ **milk run:** a routine mission, flown daily in a **kite.**

➤ **Molotov cocktail:** a bottle of gasoline with a fuse attached, first used in the fighting between the Russians and the Finns. Also spelled *Molotoff.* Later, **Molotov breadbaskets** (large bombs that exploded in midair, releasing dozens of smaller bombs) were developed. Vyacheslav Molotov was the minister of foreign affairs for the U.S.S.R. from 1939 until 1949.

oh, my aching back: a way of greeting the news that more work was on the horizon, or simply of expressing frustration over bad news in general.

pearl diving: washing dishes.

peep: a miniature jeep. The word *jeep* itself was introduced during this war. A few years earlier, cartoonist E. C. Segar had introduced the character Eugene the Jeep in his comic strip *Popeye*. Eugene was an unusual-looking animal that could perform almost any feat, all the while making a noise like "jeep, jeep." Although the official name of the army vehicle was *half-ton four-by-four command reconnaissance car,* or some piece of that, the nickname *jeep* made sense for the small but rugged car.

Quonset hut: a prefabricated metal building shaped like a half-circle, used for barracks, offices, machine shops, or any other necessary buildings. Named for Quonset Point, Rhode Island, where it was developed by the navy.

St. Vitus davenport: a tank. St. Vitus is the patron saint of those afflicted with chorea, a nervous-system disease that causes uncontrollable jerking movements. A tank that caused the same kinds of movements was his *davenport,* or couch.

see the chaplain: stop complaining.

toothpick village: wooden barracks used to house draftees.

Valley Forge: a cold-weather encampment of tents.

You never had it so good: the standard response to anyone ungrateful enough to complain about being in the military.

GERONIMO

"Geronimo!" was the favored shout of paratroopers as they leapt from airplanes. The word could also refer to the paratroopers themselves. Geronimo was the famous Apache chief who became the last Native American leader to surrender to the United States in 1886.

Although about 25,000 Native Americans served in the military during World War II, including some as paratroopers, the term probably did not originate with them. The most common explanation is that the men of the 505th Battalion, stationed at Fort Benning, Georgia, were the first to use it. On the evening before their first jump, they watched the 1939 movie, *Geronimo,* in which one character makes a daring leap. They must have been reminded of the movie when they were leaping the next day.

CHOWMOBILE

An army marches on its stomach, so words for chow are always important. In addition to the words listed here, young soldiers often used the soda fountain slang of happier times.

KILROY WAS HERE

Who was **Kilroy**? He was everywhere during World War II; a big-eyed, bulbous-nosed, hairless cartoon character peering over a fence. His image, accompanied by the words *Kilroy was here,* was rumored to have been spotted everywhere from the top of the Arc de Triomphe to the sides of enemy pillboxes. Legend has it that when the *Big Three*—President Roosevelt, Prime Minister Churchill, and Soviet Premier Joseph Stalin—met at Potsdam to discuss strategy, they had the use of a private outhouse. The first to enter it was Stalin. After he emerged, he leaned toward an aide and murmured, "Who is Kilroy?"

Many stories circulate about the origin of this piece of graffiti. Some claim that the original Kilroy was Sgt. Francis J. Kilroy Jr. His friend Sgt. James Maloney first wrote "Kilroy will be here next week" on a notice board at Boca Raton Field, Florida. Another story says that Kilroy was a wartime factory inspector in Braintree, Massachusetts. He supervised women who were paid for their work by the piece. At the end of each shift, he walked around the factory and drew a chalk line after the last completed item at each station on the assembly line. The women often tried to start a little ahead the next day by erasing Kilroy's chalk mark and drawing it a few places farther back on the line. Kilroy caught on. He responded by drawing hard-to-duplicate images and signing them.

The most common, and most likely, story concerns James J. Kilroy, a shipyard inspector. In order to save time when the proper papers were not available for him to sign, he would scrawl "Kilroy was here" in yellow chalk on the bulkhead of an inspected ship. After the war, several magazines ran pieces on the "real" Kilroy and the Transit Company of America sponsored a contest to find him. Dozens of men stepped forward, but the prize went to the former ship inspector James J. Kilroy. Shipyard officials and riveters supported his authenticity.

Kilroy was here usually signified that the U.S. armed forces had passed through, but it also became a popular scrawl on home-front fences.

➤ **albatross:** chicken.

➤ **armored cow:** canned milk.

➤ **army strawberries:** prunes.

➤ **battery acid:** coffee, sometimes taken **blond and sweet,** or with milk and sugar.

➤ **black strap:** coffee, dark as blackstrap molasses.

➤ **bean gun:** a field kitchen, which "shot" beans to the troops.

➤ **biscuit blast:** the damage caused to the teeth when biting down on a **dog biscuit,** the tough biscuit included in **C-rations.**

➤ **bootleg:** coffee, perhaps named while wistfully reminiscing about bootleg liquor.

➤ **bugs:** anything floating in soup.

➤ **C-rations:** subsistence rations, consisting of three cans of meat, one of powdered coffee and sugar, one of tough biscuits, and one of hard candy. Also called *K-rations.*

➤ **D-ration:** a chocolate bar mixed with oat flour to keep it from melting, to be eaten only in an emergency, which was probably the only time anyone would want to eat one.

➤ **grass:** salad.

➤ **jungle juice:** liquor made from the dried fruits contained in some rations.

➤ **punk:** bread, a word also used by hoboes.

➤ **salve:** butter.

➤ **serum:** an intoxicating beverage.

➤ **sewer trout:** any white fish.

➤ **side arms:** cream and sugar.

➤ **tiger meat:** beef.

➤ **the Waldorf:** the mess hall, named ironically after the New York temple of fine dining, the Waldorf-Astoria Hotel.

DOGFACES IN THE BOUDOIR

Even the army wasn't all work. Soldiers occasionally had time off for rest and relaxation, which they spent sending **behavior reports** stateside, or roaming the town on **skirt patrol.** If they were lucky, they might get an evening of song and dance from entertainers on the **foxhole circuit.**

➤ **behavior report:** a G.I.'s letter to his sweetheart.

➤ **blind flying:** going on a date with a young woman you have never met.

➤ **boudoir:** a squad tent.

➧ **delayed action bomb:** a young woman who was always late for a date.

➧ **foxhole circuit:** the touring route of entertainers who played for troops at the front.

➧ **skirt patrol:** going out on the town looking for women.

➧ **snore sack:** a sleeping bag.

➧ **sugar report:** a letter from the girl you left behind, hopefully not beginning with "Dear John."

KRIEGIES

Some men were unlucky enough to be captured by the enemy, and spent years trying to continue the struggle from behind barbed wire. They had a jargon of their own.

➧ **brew:** anything to drink, especially camp-brewed moonshine.

➧ **Dear Lootenant letter:** a prisoner of war's version of a "Dear John" letter, telling him that his girl had moved on to someone else.

➧ **glop:** any mixture of food, such as a stew.

➧ **goon:** a German guard.

➧ **goon up:** to watch out for guards.

➧ **in the bag:** captured.

➧ **Kriegie:** an abbreviation of *Kriegsgefangen,* which is German for 'prisoner of war'.

➧ **Krunchies:** toasted bits of bread crust, ironically named as if they were a breakfast cereal.

➧ **project:** an escape plan.

➧ **snoop tour:** a guard's rounds.

➧ **stooge:** a POW who would trail a guard at a distance as a low-level act of harassment. When the irritated guard ordered him away, another stooge would slip into his place.

➧ **tobacco:** a code word for 'news'.

➧ **weather:** a code word for 'news from a hidden radio set'.

➧ **wire fever:** depression, caused by being incarcerated behind barbed wire.

THE HOME FRONT

While America's fighting forces were stationed around the globe, folks at home were contributing to the war effort as well. Women got together to organize **Bundles for Britain,** schoolchildren practiced pulling their *dicky birds* over their faces at a moment's notice in case of gas attack, and teenagers chipped in by inventing the **bomb boogie.** The whole family helped dig the **victory garden.**

Everyone practiced rationing, although it was never popular. Respectable people tried their darnedest not to be **gas hogs,** but it wasn't easy at a ration of four, then three, gallons a week. Those with a sweet tooth suffered when sugar was limited to one cup per person per week. The coffee ration was one pound a week, the meat ration twenty-eight ounces, and the cheese ration four ounces. The government instituted a complicated point system, which assigned different point values to products, depending on their desirability. Every shopping trip was an exercise in math. As if Rosie wasn't busy enough riveting!

➤ **America Firsters:** an isolationist movement that included many fascist sympathizers. The America First Committee had about 60,000 members, including Alice Roosevelt Longworth and Charles Lindbergh. America Firsters believed that Hitler was unstoppable and that the United States should avoid challenging him. Increasingly, they were regarded as crackpots, especially after the Justice Department investigated accusations that the organization was spreading Nazi propaganda.

➤ **blacketeer:** a black market racketeer.

➤ **blue points:** the type of rationing coupon necessary to buy canned and processed foods.

➤ **bomb boogie:** a variety of the **jitterbug.**

➤ **Bundles for Britain:** an organization that sent relief packages to the United Kingdom. The British and other Europeans were far worse off than Americans in terms of essential consumer goods during the war.

➤ **canary:** a gas mask, also called a *dicky-bird* or *nose bag.* Gas masks were shaped with a large bulge to accommodate the nose, making wearers look as though they had beaks.

➤ **ersatz:** an inferior substitute for hard-to-get items, usually referring to artificial food ingredients or synthetic fabrics. Ironically, Americans borrowed the word from German.

➤ **foxhole house:** a temporary living space jerry-rigged by roofing over the excavated basement of an unbuilt house. Many houses were started near war-goods factories but never finished, usually due to lack of materials. Factory workers squatted in the unfinished structures to avoid a long daily commute.

➤ **gas hog:** someone who circumvented the gas rationing rules.

➤ **gazelleburgers, beaverburgers, caraburgers: ersatz** hamburgers. Unlike meat from domestic farm animals, game was not rationed.

➤ **interventionists:** those who wanted to enter the European war before the attack on Pearl Harbor.

V-J day in Times Square.

➧ **Lend-Lease Act:** the Lend-Lease Act of 1941 permitted the President to "lend or lease" weapons and other war supplies to countries whose safety was considered vital to the United States (in other words, the Allies). In return, those countries would eventually allow the establishment of U.S. army bases on their territories or offer some other advantage. Lending money outright to Britain and France was forbidden by neutrality laws.

➧ **liberty ship:** a standard cargo ship. Thousands of liberty ships were built in home-front shipyards during the war.

➧ **meatlegger:** seller of **bootlegged** meat.

➧ **Munichism:** an attitude of appeasement, a reference to the Munich conference of 1938 between British prime minister Neville Chamberlain and French premier Edouard Daladier, and fascist leaders Mussolini and Hitler. At this conference, Hitler agreed to refrain from claiming any more territory if the British and French would let him take Czechoslovakia's Sudetenland unchallenged. Chamberlain and Daladier acquiesced in return for what Chamberlain promised would be *"peace in our time."*

phony war: the period between Britain and France's declaration of war and the moment when actual fighting broke out, approximately from September 3, 1939, to the beginning of the German advance across Europe in the spring of 1940. There was a lull in the action at this time, prompting U.S. Senator William Borah to remark, "There's something phony about this war."

red points: the type of coupon necessary to buy meat, butter, and other fats.

Rosie the Riveter: an idealized version of a female factory worker. Rosie worked wearing overalls, with her hair tied in a scarf. She used her muscles. The most famous poster of Rosie shows her flexing a bicep, with the words "We can do it!" appearing in a balloon over her head. Redd Evans and John Jacob Loeb wrote a song about her in 1942.

victory garden: a vegetable garden. People helped the war effort by growing their own veggies, freeing more land for major crops like wheat and corn.

V-E Day: the day Germany unconditionally surrendered, May 8, 1945, ending the war in Europe.

V-girls: victory girls, also called *khaki wackies, patriotutes,* and *good-time Janes.* These were teenagers, sometimes quite young, who loitered around amusement arcades and other places where off-duty soldiers might go, because they were "wacky for khaki."

V-J Day: the day Japan unconditionally surrendered, August 14, 1945, or the date of formal surrender, September 2, 1945.

v-mail: letters written on small, preprinted forms, then shrunk on microfilm to be sent overseas. On arrival, they were enlarged again. The purpose of v-mail was to reduce the cargo space needed to ship the letters.

War Time: Daylight saving time, in effect year-round starting in February 1942.

"ENEMY EARS ARE LISTENING"

People buoyed their courage during the war with many slogans and catch phrases. These two warned employees of war-related industries not to talk about their work:

Enemy ears are listening

The slip of a lip may sink a ship

Other memorable slogans include:

Bye, bye—Buy bonds: the sign-off of Phil Baker's *Take It or Leave It* radio program, on the air Sunday nights from 1942 to 1945. Numerous slogans reminded people to invest in war bonds.

➤ **Do the job HE left behind:** a slogan urging women to take up war work.

➤ **Don't you know there's a war on?:** a stock phrase excusing poor service, shoddy workmanship, a shortage of some product, or anything else that seemed to need excusing during the war years.

➤ **Go all out for America:** a slogan using the popular term **all out,** which became widespread around 1940. It was usually used in a military context, such as *all-out assault*. It meant 'putting everything you had into a cause'. **All-outers** were advocates of fighting an all-out, total war.

➤ **Praise the Lord and pass the ammunition:** a phrase first uttered by Presbyterian naval chaplain Lt. Howell Forgy. It also became the title of a popular song by Frank Loesser.

➤ **Use it up, wear it out, make it do, or do without:** an encouragement to practice rationing.

FIFTH COLUMN

The **fifth column** of spies and enemy sympathizers was a matter of great concern for many people during the war. The term was a leftover from the Spanish Civil War, first used by rebel general Emilio Mola during a radio broadcast. He stated that he was counting on four columns of troops outside Madrid and another column of sympathizers inside the city, who would rise up when the troops marched in.

Ernest Hemingway adopted the expression as the title of a play, first produced on Broadway in 1939. Around the time the play was opening, Norway fell to the Nazis. A fifth column of Nazi supporters inside the country had made the German victory possible. Soon, newspapers were trumpeting the discoveries of fifth columns living secretly among the populations of France, Belgium, Britain, and even the United States.

The Nazi capture of Norway gave rise to a related word, *quisling,* still a common part of our vocabulary. Vidkun Quisling was the leader of the Norwegian Nazi party. He collaborated with the invading Germans and eventually became the head of occupied Norway's government. He was tried and executed after the war. Now **quisling** means 'any traitor who aids the invading enemy'.

UTILITY FASHIONS

In March 1942, the War Production Board began to regulate clothing production. Rules covered the amount of fabric that could be used for various types of clothing, and what kinds of decoration were allowable on *utility fashions*. Patch pockets, trim, and other "fabrics on fabric" were out. Dresses barely covered the knee and were cut close to the body. Women's suit jackets were 25 inches or less in length. Men's suits were also stripped to the bare seam, minus pocket flaps on the jackets and pleats and cuffs on the pants. Nylons were simply unobtainable. Stylish women who wanted to *put on the dog* drew lines up the backs of their bare legs with an eyebrow pencil to mimic stocking seams.

➡ **convertible suit:** a jacket, short skirt, and blouse ensemble, which could be converted to an evening look by removing the jacket.

➡ **do-rag:** a scarf wrapped around the head and knotted on top to keep a woman's hair out of the way while she worked.

➡ **Eisenhower jacket:** a short, fitted jacket, modeled after General Eisenhower's uniform jacket.

➡ **liberty cut:** a woman's haircut, styled so it only needed to be trimmed every three months. Short hair was patriotic because it saved on hairpins and was more suitable for factory workers.

➡ **New Look:** Christian Dior's postwar fashion vision, featuring long, full skirts, frilly blouses, and frivolously high heels. After the privations of war, women were ready to indulge in yards of fabric.

➡ **playsuit:** a fabric-saving, one-piece shorts outfit, often with an optional wraparound skirt.

➡ **popover dress:** a wraparound denim dress designed by Claire McCardell.

➡ **sloppy joe:** a bulky, oversized sweater, to be worn with baggy rolled-up jeans and saddle shoes. A teenage fashion, sloppy joes remained popular well into the fifties.

➡ **sweater girl:** a generously proportioned movie star who wore a tight-fitting sweater. The original sweater girl was Lana Turner, who wore such a garment in the 1937 movie *They Won't Forget*. Sweater girls were popular subjects of pinups in the barracks.

➡ **vingle:** a shingle haircut for victory.

SUBDEBS AND BOBBYSOXERS

Teenagers were a significant social group for the first time in the 1940s. After-school earnings that helped support the family during

Mellow men in zoot suits.

ZOOT SUIT

The **zoot suit** was one garment that fell far outside the Production Board's guidelines. Zoot suits, an outfit for men, featured knee-length draped jackets with high shoulder pads and wide lapels. The trousers were baggy in the leg, but tapered down to a narrow hem. A long chain attached to a watch or keys, a broad tie, a broad-brimmed hat, and pointed-toe shoes completed the ensemble.

Although young city dwellers of all ethnicities wore zoot suits, the look was especially favored by Mexican Americans and African Americans. Wearing the fabric-wasting suits was a slap to a larger culture that continued to exclude these two groups, even in wartime. Segregation still plagued African Americans, including those in the armed forces. Minorities were barred from most high-paying war work.

Tensions between zoot suiters and sailors based in southern California erupted into riots in June 1943. Sailors roamed the streets of Los Angeles, attacking young Mexican-American men and tearing off their zoot suits. Police looked the other way or arrested only the Mexican Americans. The violence didn't stop until the president of Mexico threatened to bar Mexicans from crossing the border to work.

the Depression now went into teenagers' pockets, making them a more important consumer group than ever before. Teens also made more of an effort to distinguish themselves as a separate social group. A big part of their self-identity depended on speaking a jargon incomprehensible to parents and other *fuddy-duddies*. It was colorful, clever, and fast-changing. Many words that were *on the beam* in 1942 were *positively nowhere* five years later. Here is a sampling of terms that were popular with *slick chicks* and *glad lads* for at least a year or two during the decade:

➤ **blitz the cold storage plant:** to raid the refrigerator.

➤ **bong!:** an approving response to some comment.

➤ **buggy:** irritated.

➤ **burnt to a crisp:** the latest thing.

➤ **collapse:** to sit down.

➤ **D.D.T.:** Drop dead twice, a short version of *Please do me the personal favor of dropping dead.*

➤ **F.F.F.F.T.O.Y.F.F.:** Fall fatally flat five times on your fat face.

➤ **giraffe party:** a necking party.

➤ **go quisling:** to be a teacher's pet, showing that teens, too, were paying attention to world events.

➤ **harvest it:** a response to a corny joke.

➤ **ice up:** to give someone the cold shoulder.

➤ **on the beam:** correct; in the know.

➤ **Jackson:** a name used to address anyone, but usually a smooth-looking boy.

➤ **juke joint:** an informal bar or roadhouse where people could eat, drink, listen to music, and dance. *Juke,* also spelled *jouk,* probably comes from the Sea Islands Creole (Gullah) word *jook* or *joog,* meaning 'wicked'. A **joog house** was a 'disorderly house' in this dialect. At first, **juke** was an African-American slang word denoting a certain type of jazz guitar playing. Then **juking it** started to mean dancing to jazz music, which people did at a juke joint. Of course, when they didn't have live music, dancers had to fall back on a *jukebox* or *juke organ.*

WORDS FOR ATTRACTIVE GIRLS

whistle bait, rare dish, solid sender, dilly, dream puss, zazz girl, destroyer, 20-20, drape shape, frame dame, wolfess, blackout girl, slick chick.

WORDS FOR ATTRACTIVE BOYS

drooly, heaven sent, swoony, mellow man, hunk of heartbreak, glad lad, twangie boy, go giver.

➤ **look that needs suspenders:** a very interested glance at a young woman by a young man. The suspenders were needed to keep his eyeballs attached to their sockets.

➤ **mothball:** serious student with no time to get *on the beam.*

➤ **murder:** wonderful.

➤ **oogley:** good.

➤ **pancake turner:** a disk jockey.

➤ **Pierre:** an unfashionable male.

➤ **the real Bikini:** an exciting happening, a reference to Bikini Island in the South Pacific, where the United States began testing atomic bombs in July 1946.

➤ **rusty hen:** an unattractive girl.

➤ **shove in your clutch:** to get going.

➤ **Step up closer to the mike:** I didn't hear you—could you repeat that?

➤ **subdeb:** a young adolescent female, short for *subdebutante.* Subdebs lived at a high emotional pitch. Life was either *simply too perfect* or *utterly loathsome.* The activities of subdebs were briefly of some interest to adults. Articles with titles like "Meet a Subdeb" appeared for a few years in popular magazines.

➤ **sub-zero:** terrible.

➤ **toujours la clinch:** said of a girl who was enthusiastic about necking, also known as a *necker-chief* or a *chin-up girl.*

➤ **upper plate:** an older person.

BOBBYSOX

With stockings almost unobtainable, teenage girls chose socks as a comfortable alternative. **Bobbysox,** or *bobby socks,* were short ankle socks, usually white, worn pushed down sloppily around the top of the shoe. **Bobbysoxers,** also called *bobby sockers,* wore this stylish footwear with skirts or rolled-up pants. The term may come from the verb *bob,* meaning 'to cut short', as in 'bob a horse's tail' or 'bob the hair'.

Tame as this style now seems, some adults considered the wearing of bobbysox a sign of rebellion. Police dubbed youthful *victory girls* the **bobbysox brigade,** and the term stretched to include female juvenile delinquents. Another characteristic of bobbysoxers was their adoration for that *hunk of heartbreak,* crooner Frank Sinatra.

➤ **void coupon:** an unattractive guy.
➤ **You shred it, wheat:** You figure it out.

JUMPIN' TO JIVE

Jazz continued to be very popular through the forties, but the big band sound was gradually being replaced by something more radical. *Cool daddies* were digging **bebop.** Jazz great Dizzy Gillespie invented the term one night while trying to explain to a bass player how two notes should sound. He finally demonstrated by singing, "Be-bop! Be-bop!"

The music itself was a reaction by young black musicians against a jazz sound that they felt had become too mainstream. They referred to the music as modern, or progressive, jazz. It wasn't for everyone, but those who were **hep to the jive** couldn't get enough. Here is a sample of insider lingo, characterized by rhyming slang and wordplay, and including many words related to romance. Both musicians and their fans talked jive, so it sometimes overlapped with more general teenage slang. It also influenced a later group of slangsters, the Beats.

➤ **Able Grable:** a sexy woman, probably an allusion to the movie star Betty Grable.
➤ **Alan Laddy:** the male version, a reference to actor Alan Ladd.
➤ **alreet:** swell.
➤ **Bells, man!:** a bop expression of approval.
➤ **bopera:** a nightclub featuring **bebop** music and dancing.
➤ **brush mush:** a man with a moustache.
➤ **chuckle chick:** a giggly girl.
➤ **cooking with gas:** doing very well; strutting your best stuff.
➤ **date bait:** an **alreet** young woman.
➤ **folding lettuce:** paper money, also sometimes called *silent money*.
➤ **good Joe:** a nice guy.
➤ **have eyes for:** the beboppers' way of saying they want something, as in *Have you eyes for a sandwich?* To want or like something a lot was to **have big eyes** for it.
➤ **Hello sugar, are you rationed?:** Do you have a boyfriend?

> **SOME JIVE WAYS TO SAY *HELLO* AND *GOOD-BYE*:**
>
> Hello sweet, you look neat.
> Hi good lookin', what's cookin'?
> Hi Joe, what do you know?
> What's buzzin', cousin?
> What's knittin', kitten?
> What's your story, morning glory?
> Sal-loon, goon, alcohol you!
> So long, mater, see you later.

➤ **hep to the jive:** to be up on the trends; an insider. *Hep* and its twin, *hip,* first appeared in forties jive talk. They are still going strong, although *hip* is the usual variant of choice these days.

➤ **hot gingerbread:** an attractive woman.

➤ **jerk of all trades:** someone you really don't want to know.

➤ **kick:** the thing you're good at or love to do. **Bebop** was Dizzy Gillespie's kick.

➤ **king size:** terrific.

➤ **latch your lashes:** to take a look.

➤ **out of this atmosphere:** describing an exceptionally attractive woman.

➤ **pretty pigeon:** a pretty girl.

➤ **rebop:** another way of saying **bebop.**

➤ **righteous:** an adjective for a good-looking woman.

➤ **sassy chassis:** woman with a **righteous** figure.

➤ **shooting the Ferdinand:** exaggerating; a fancy way of shooting the bull (*Ferdinand* being the name of a bull in a popular children's story).

➤ **super-solid:** excellent.

➤ **tall, dark, and handy:** a male heartthrob of the moment.

➤ **wolf in Jeep's clothing:** a soldier on the lookout for dateable women.

VOUTIAN VOCABULARY

Jazz musician Slim Gaillard, composer of the one-time hits "Flatfoot Floogie With a Floy Floy" and "A-Reet-a-Voutie," invented a variant of jive talk known as **Voutian.** This language (pronounced 'VOW-shun') relied heavily on jive-type rhymes, as well as the endings *-reety, -oreety,* and *-oroony* to express approval or strength of feeling. A really good hamburger was a **hamburgeroroony.** A young man's girlfriend was a **routie-voutie** or a **viddle vop.** Other examples of the talk are **blink-o-roony** (sleepy), **mello-reeny** (wonderful), and **drug-o-reeny** (sad). The *vout-o-reeny* fad was predictably short-lived, but while it lasted, it attracted a fair amount of attention. Here is a scene from a Voutian college-student *Romeo and Juliet,* as quoted in a 1947 issue of *Life.* Notice the use of the word *groovy,* a trendy term coined by hipsters about twenty-five years before the rest of us heard it.

> Romeo: *But soft, what's your story, morning glory?*
> Juliet: *Got no tale, nightingale.*

Romeo: *What's your pleasure, treasure? You snap the whip, I'll take the trip.*

Juliet: *That sounds as groovy as a ten-cent movie.*

TALK WITH A SNAPPEROO

One linguistic trend of the 1940s was the tendency to add endings to words for emphasis. A more common ending than *-oroony* or *-oreeny* was *-eroo.* Everyone who wanted to add the old *ziperoo* to their talk, from advertising people to radio announcers to sports writers, tacked *-eroo* onto the nouns of their choice. The following are some of the more typical *-eroo* words from the many collected in *American Speech:*

➤ **brusheroo:** the brush-off.

➤ **checkeroo:** the bill, or check, at a restaurant or nightclub.

➤ **crusheroo:** a major crush on someone.

➤ **flopperoo:** a disastrous failure, often used for a stage show, but also for other failed experiments. According to one newspaper, "Hollywood divides the failures into three subdivisions: flop, flopperoo, and kerplunk."

➤ **jokeroo:** a good joke.

➤ **kisseroo:** the old kisser, but more so.

➤ **sapperoo:** a remarkably gullible person.

➤ **smackeroo:** money, otherwise known as *smackers.*

➤ **snapperoo:** the punch line.

➤ **snoozemarooed:** pretty drunk.

➤ **stinkeroo:** a very bad person or thing.

➤ **ziperoo:** having plenty of energy.

FORTIES BUZZWORDS

With one frivolous exception, these Forties buzzwords are all fairly somber, referring to the war or its aftermath.

➤ **Berlin airlift:** Anglo-American-sponsored cargo planes that delivered food and other necessities to West Berlin during an 11-month period between 1948 and 1949. After Germany's defeat, the Union of Soviet Socialist Republics, Great Britain, France, and the United States each occupied different sections of Germany. They also shared control of Berlin, with the Western powers in charge of the west side of the city and Soviet Russia controlling the east side. When the British, French, and Americans made plans to consolidate their zones of control, the Soviets responded by shutting down all transportation access to West Berlin. The airlift was a way of defeating Russia's bid for control of the city. The Russians called off the blockade after 324 days.

➤ **hubba-hubba:** a popular exclamation of enthusiasm or support. Like all catch words, this one seems to have sprung up everywhere at once during the mid-1940s. Many G.I.s claimed to have heard it first at their training camps, where it was used during drills to mean 'pep it up'. When one squadron was put at rest, allowing the soldiers to talk, they invariably responded with some ear-splitting hubba-hubbas. Others first heard the word as "chatter" on the baseball field. It was also sometimes spoken to create crowd noise on the radio or in movies, replacing that old favorite, *rhubarb-rhubarb*. During the height of its popularity, *hubba-hubba* was the expression that came to a man's lips when he caught sight of an appealing woman. That's how most people remember it today. Later it became an adjective, as in *hubba-hubba girl*.

➤ **iron curtain:** a widely used derogatory metaphor for the Soviet Union's isolation from the West after World War II. Originally, an *iron curtain* was a fireproof theater curtain, but the expression had been used to mean 'a hostile barrier' since the 1920s. Winston Churchill popularized the term in a 1946 speech in Fulton, Missouri. He said, "From Stettin in the Baltic to Trieste in the Adriatic, an iron curtain has descended across the continent." It inspired the invention of a number of other metaphorical "curtains." The **paper curtain** was Soviet magazine propaganda, and later South African censorship practices. **Uranium curtain** was used by the Soviet Union to refer to **the Bomb,** America's protective "barrier." The **bamboo curtain** referred to the postwar closing of communist China.

➤ **Manhattan Project:** the secret wartime project that developed the atomic bomb. The Corps of Engineers' Manhattan Engineer District was in charge of producing the bomb, although the work took place far from Manhattan. Research locations included Chicago, Illinois; Oak Ridge, Tennessee; Hanford, Washington; and Los Alamos, New Mexico. The **Atomic Age** arrived on July 16, 1945, when the first-ever atomic bomb was detonated in the desert near Alamogordo, New Mexico.

Americans became aware of the Atomic Age on August 6, 1945, when the United States dropped an atomic bomb on Hiroshima, Japan, and three days later, on Nagasaki. People were soon calling this weapon the **A-bomb** or simply **the Bomb.**

➤ **Marshall Plan:** a popular name for Secretary of State George Catlett Marshall's European Recovery Program. Marshall proposed the program partly to forestall economic collapse and the threat of starvation in Western Europe, and partly to ensure that Soviet Russia wouldn't gain influence in the area. The Plan spent more than $13 billion on European aid.

Too much television turns you into a vidiot.

The Fifties

Hipsters in Squaresville

The country took it easy during the Eisenhower years, at least as much as it could in the shadow of the *A-bomb* and the **H-bomb.** Americans *liked Ike*. Former G.I. Joes traded their uniforms for gray flannel suits, while former Rosies changed from their overalls into **can-can petticoats.** Together they moved to suburban **Levittowns** and started families. Babies were really booming in the fifties.

Some of those new houses out in suburbia featured *bomb shelters* or **life safes,** cozy holes in the back yard complete with carpet and three-way radios. With the newspapers talking about **nuclear piles** and **megadeath,** who knew what might happen? Some member of the **nuclear club** might decide to drop its own small **kitten bomb** in the near future. Kids at school were taught to **duck and cover,** so if the big one blew during class hours they'd be protected under their desks.

In the 1950s, red was America's unfavorite color. **Red China** appeared on the map in 1949, and the same color covered Soviet Russia and much of Eastern Europe. Before long, **McCarthyites** were looking for **Reds under the bed** at home. The Cold War was raging. The United States had to practice **brinkmanship** to keep even more countries from falling to the communists like dominoes.

Reds were not only under the bed, but up in the sky when the Soviets launched the first *Sputnik* satellite in 1957. Although Americans were concerned about Reds in outer space, they were charmed by the Russian word ending *-nik*. Magazines and newspapers broke out in a flurry of *spoofniks, Yankniks, whatniks, muttniks,* and other *-niks,* and are still inventing new ones today.

People can't stay worried all the time, especially teenagers. **Cool dads** and their **dollies** had fun watching movies while sitting in their cars at the local **passion pit.** In bad weather, they moved to the top balcony at a **hardtop** theater for the latest *hecklethon*. **Deepies,** which required special *3-D* glasses, were the coolest kind of movies. Sitting around the **quirt counter** drinking Cokes was fun, as was **cramming** the nearest phone booth. And what about that new rock 'n' roll music? Really **George!** Only **scurves** and **egg heads** spent their after-school hours **cemetery working** to get good grades.

The younger set had fun too, the boys wearing coonskin caps in honor of Davy Crockett and the girls swaying around the yard, trying to keep their plastic hula hoops on their hips. If Mom and Dad were out in the yard, Mom would be wearing **pedal pushers** or **clam diggers** and Dad a Hawaiian shirt made of *Dacron*. If the weather was foul, the family stayed inside watching the *idiot box* (in black and white, of course). Occasionally, someone would get up and adjust the antenna on top of the set, known as *rabbit ears*. Everyone wanted good reception for tonight's quiz show. Who would win the prize money? That was the **$64,000 Question.** The kids weren't allowed to watch too much television, though. They might turn into *vidiots* (or *videots*).

The biggest fad for older boys was **hot rodding.** They drove customized **bombs, raked** in the front and sporting **frenched** headlights. If a boy's **machine** was really hot, he painted flames on the sides. Out at the **drag strip,** he could race that rod for **five dollars a gear,** especially if he could **lay a cool shift** and **tromp it.** If it was just a **bucket of bolts** that **chattered** when he tried to **herd** it, maybe a trip to the **speed shop** was in order. For the less serious hot rodder, **necker's knobs** could be installed on the steering wheel, leaving the driver's right arm free when he was out with his **Sophie.**

Not everyone was satisfied with life in **Squaresville.** A new generation of **hipsters fell in** at their favorite **beanery** to drink espresso and hear some far-out **cat** read poetry. **Lay it on me, Daddy-O,** that Kerouac is like **Flipsville, man, real gone.** Of course **schmos from Kokomo** and other **cubistic** types didn't really **dig** the **Beat** scene. Hearing about parties where **subterraneans** turned on with **dexies** and **bennies** made the older generation **go rotary.** But **beatniks** didn't care—they knew they were **straight from the fridge**. When the counterculture arrived in the 1960s, the Beats were already there. **So long pal, stay pure.**

DUCK AND COVER

What made the bomb so scary was the fact that the communists had it too. The Soviet Union detonated an atomic bomb in the autumn of 1949, and the nuclear arms race was on. Suddenly the threat of war gained a terrifying new dimension. Americans heard the ticking of the *Doomsday Clock* and rushed to build **life safes,** more commonly known as *bomb shelters,* behind their houses. (The federal government eventually built some public *fallout shelters,* but not until 1961.)

The government offered information on how to survive the blast in pamphlets like "You Can Survive." The 1948 educational film *Duck and Cover* taught children to duck under a table and cover their heads with their arms if they suspected that a nuclear explosion was imminent. Even with these precautions, the specter of **megadeath** was ever-present during the fifties.

➤ **baby bomb:** an atomic bomb small enough to be carried by an ordinary jet bomber rather than the heavier, more unwieldy B-29, but with the same amount of explosive power as a larger bomb.

➤ **"Better Red than dead":** a slogan of nuclear disarmament groups in the 1950s. Opponents of communism would sometimes retort with **"Better dead than Red."**

➤ **clean bomb:** a hydrogen bomb that supposedly did not create widespread nuclear fallout.

➤ **fail-safe:** the precautions taken against the possibility of a bomb exploding accidentally or being triggered by the wrong person. These included automatic shut-down devices and the need for direct instructions from a specific person before the bomb could be detonated. The goal was to make the bomb fail in a safe rather than a disastrous way.

➤ **H-bomb:** a nickname for the hydrogen bomb, also called the *superbomb* because it was hundreds of times more powerful than the original atomic bombs. President Truman established an accelerated program of H-bomb research after the Soviets developed their own atomic weapon.

➤ **kitten bomb:** a small, "baby-size" atomic bomb.

➤ **life safe:** a euphemistic term for what was usually known as a *bomb shelter* or *fallout shelter.* It was mostly used by advertisers who wanted to sell prefabricated versions to the nervous public. Fallout shelters were a popular status symbol in the early 1950s. Architectural plans were frequently printed in magazines and were also available from the government. The cost of building and stocking one could run into thousands of dollars. Although most shelters were small and cavelike, some came equipped with toilets, telephones, carpets, and other amenities. And until they were needed for survival, they were great places to store extra canned goods.

➤ **megadeath:** one million deaths, a way of calculating a nuclear weapon's potential for annihilation. The Atomic Age first familiarized Americans with the prefix *mega-,* meaning one million. The explosive force of atomic bombs was measured in **megatons,** equal to one million tons of TNT. Later *mega-* words include *megabucks, megadose,* and *megabyte.*

➤ **mutual assured destruction:** the notion that if the United States and the Soviet Union had enough nuclear weapons to destroy the other, the situation would be a deterrent to an actual nuclear war since the stakes would be too high for either side. This idea also went by the variant *mutually assured destruction* and the apt acronym *MAD.*

➤ **nuclear club:** the group of countries that possessed nuclear weapons.

➤ **nuclear furnace:** an early term for a nuclear reactor. Other temporary terms were *atomic furnace, atomic energy machine,* and *nuclear pile,* the last of which is still sometimes used. University of Chicago scientist Enrico Fermi coined the term **nuclear pile** because the layers of graphite and uranium that produce the chain reaction form a big pile.

COMMIES

The alliance between the United States and the Union of Soviet Socialist Republics barely lasted until the end of the Second World War. The United States, ten Western European countries, and Canada formed the North Atlantic Treaty Organization (NATO), while the Soviets took political control of Eastern Europe. At the same time communist troops under Mao Zedong drove out the Chinese Nationalist government, and China went red behind the bamboo curtain.

MINUTES TO MIDNIGHT

In 1947, the *Doomsday Clock* first appeared on the cover of the *Bulletin of the Atomic Scientists.* The picture showed the fourth quadrant of a clock with the hands pointing to seven minutes before twelve. An artist named Martyl, the wife of a nuclear physicist, designed the clock as a symbol of the threat of nuclear disaster. Over the years, the clock's minute hand has moved away from or closer to midnight, depending on the world political situation. It displayed three minutes to midnight after the Soviets tested their first atomic weapon. In 1953, the minute hand came its closest to midnight—two minutes before the hour—when the United States and then Russia successfully exploded H-bombs. It moved the farthest away, seventeen minutes to midnight, in 1991, when the two major nuclear powers signed the Strategic Arms Reduction Treaty. The minute hand crept forward again when India, Pakistan, and other countries started stockpiling their own atomic arsenals.

US vice-president Richard Nixon and Soviet premier and brinkman Nikita Khrushchev in their famous "kitchen debate" at the American National Exhibit in Moscow, 1959.

Cold War battle lines were drawn. American politicians began to speak of containment of the communist threat and to search for **fellow travelers** in the State Department. The word **brinkmanship,** the art of going to the brink of war without engaging in actual fighting, first came into use during the fifties. Newspapers often reported on the activities of *brinkmen* on both sides, such as Soviet premier Nikita Khrushchev and Secretary of State John Foster Dulles.

Fear of the spread of communism led to the invention of some serious new vocabulary words:

➤ **deviationism:** swerving from the main line of communist thought.

➤ **domino theory:** the belief that if a communist government took over one country, nearby countries would also fall to communism like a row of dominoes. President Eisenhower was among the first to use the term.

➤ **fellow traveler:** someone who was not a member of the Communist Party, but nonetheless felt some sympathy with its aims. Many Americans during this period were worried about fellow travelers in the government who might try to turn the country toward socialism.

➤ **Free World:** the part of the world not under communist influence.

➤ **massive retaliation:** the plan of responding to communist incursions with nuclear weapons.

➤ **missile gap:** the perceived gap between American and Russian missile-launching capabilities after the U.S.S.R.'s successful launch of the *Sputnik* satellite. In reality the Russians lagged behind, but no one realized that until decades later.

➤ **New Look:** not a reference to full skirts during this decade, but the Republican foreign policy plan during Eisenhower's presidency. The New Look relied on the threat of nuclear weapons and **massive retaliation** rather than a traditional military response to keep the Soviet Union from invading other countries. Part of its purpose was to save money by reducing the amount spent on conventional arms and soldiers.

➤ **Red China:** mainland China after the communists came to power in

---

SPUTNIK

One of the shocks that Americans sustained during the 1950s was Russia's successful launching of the ***Sputnik*** satellite. The original *Sputnik,* which means 'traveling companion' in Russian, was sent into outer space on October 4, 1957. It weighed about 183 pounds and took 98 minutes to orbit the earth. A month later, while the United States was still scrambling to develop a similar satellite, the Soviets sent up the much larger *Sputnik II,* complete with a canine passenger named Laika. This achievement seemed to prove that the Soviet Union was capable of aiming and launching things other than satellites, like intercontinental ballistic missiles.

The Defense Department shifted into high gear when Soviet leader Nikita Khrushchev told alarmed Americans, "We will bury you." The government approved increased funding for satellite projects and, on October 1, 1958, created the National Aeronautics and Space Administration (NASA). By that time, American scientists had already sent up a small satellite of their own, but surpassing the Soviets was still a major priority. Eventually, this commitment led to the space program of the 1960s.

Meanwhile, Americans had been introduced to the beguiling word ending *-nik.* The first coinages to appear were *muttnik, poochnik, woofnik,* and *pupnik,* following the *Sputnik II* launching. Failed American launchings were dubbed *pfuttnik, dudnik, sputternik, goofnik,* and *kaputnik* (combining

1949. Communists had been known as *Reds* since before the 1917 Russian revolution, when the international communist movement flew a red flag.

➤ **red marketeer:** not a widespread term, but a good example of how Americans used *red* during the fifties. A steel industry magnate coined the expression during a speech in which he stigmatized anyone in the industry who was stockpiling steel as a *red marketeer.* He argued that this practice drove prices up and encouraged the government to take greater control of the industry. Hoarders, in his opinion, might as well "ship the steel to Stalin himself."

➤ **Red Menace:** the threat of communist world domination, a term left over from the twenties Red Scare.

➤ **Reds under the bed:** an expression of fear that certain people, possibly in the government, had hidden connections with Red friends or secret communist sympathies.

---

two foreign languages, German and Russian). Magazines and newspapers started firing off *-niks* at a quick rate. Here are a few:

➤ **Bronxnik:** a flying manhole cover spotted in the Bronx.

➤ **mousenik:** a homemade rocket that made the news when two schoolboys tried to launch it with a mouse as passenger.

➤ **oatnik:** a picture of a race horse wearing fake antennae.

➤ **spoofnik:** the caption for a trick photograph of what looked like a space man, but was in fact a hat on top of a Pontiac taillight.

➤ **sputnikburger:** a hamburger served with Russian dressing, garnished with a cocktail hot dog and an olive "satellite" pierced with toothpick antennae.

➤ **whatnik:** a questionable spaceship sighting reported in newspapers shortly after the *Sputnik* orbit.

➤ **Yanknik:** a name for the first American satellite while it was being built.

The Yiddish word *nudnik,* meaning 'a tiresome pest', didn't arise from *Sputnik.* It was in use in English as early as the twenties. After the 1950s *-nik* remained a popular ending in words like *draftnik, peacenik, no-goodnik, neatnik,* and, of course, *beatnik.* In recent decades a number of *-nik* words have appeared one time in print, but the only recent invention to gain widespread currency is *refusenik,* a word for Israeli soldiers who refuse to fight in the Occupied Territories.

➤ **third force:** a country that was balanced politically between the United States and the Soviet Union, for example, many of the countries of Western Europe. Generally it meant someone who was middle of the road.

WORDS FROM THE FORGOTTEN WAR

At the end of World War II, the Soviets and the Americans shared occupation of Korea, with the Soviets above the 38th parallel and the Americans below it. After the war, Korea remained divided into a communist North and a capitalist South. When the North invaded the South on June 25, 1950, President Truman decided to send troops. Although General Douglas MacArthur told Truman he would *have the boys home by Christmas,* the conflict lasted three years. The two sides reached an armistice in July 1953. Korea remained divided at the 38th parallel. Just north and south of this dividing line was a no-man's land called the *demilitarized zone,* or *DMZ,* a term also used later in Vietnam.

The Korean conflict is often called *the forgotten war* because it didn't make much of a lasting impact on the public consciousness. Likewise, Korean War words are much less plentiful than words from any other twentieth-century war. Part of the reason is that many words from World War II were still current in the military of 1950. New words that did appear often reflected the soldiers' contact with a new culture, as well as new technology.

➤ **bed-check Charlie:** a night-bombing enemy aircraft.

➤ **big pickle:** the atomic bomb, also known as the *gadget.*

➤ **blast furnace:** a jet plane. The Korean War was the first to use jet aircraft extensively, and soldiers invented many words to refer to jets' unique properties. Other nicknames included *blowtorch, firecan, flame thrower, pipe, speed burner,* and *squirt.* Jet pilots were **pipe jockeys** or **jet jockeys. Jetwash** was the backwash of air from a jet engine.

➤ **bug out:** to leave in a hurry or desert. The term was used as both a verb and a noun. A *bug out* not only meant 'a quick leave-taking', but could also refer to a rear exit from the trenches.

➤ **Chicom:** a Chinese communist, especially one fighting alongside the North Koreans.

➤ **chop-chop:** usually 'hurry up', but in Korea, also 'to eat'. It's unclear exactly how the word acquired this double meaning. Soldiers and sailors had been using *chop-chop,* a pidginized version of a Chinese word meaning 'hurry' or 'fast', since at least World War II. *Chop* was also a well-established slang word for 'food' in English. As early as the seventeenth century, British seamen were calling Chinese eating utensils *chopsticks*. Possibly the meaning of 'food' drifted from the single *chop* to the double *chop-chop*.

➤ **cowboy-and-Indian tactics:** hand-to-hand combat, an expression reflecting the stateside popularity of Westerns.

➤ **demoth:** to take military equipment from World War II out of mothballs.

➤ **die for a tie:** an expression indicating the sense that the American military was fighting for a stalemate rather than a win. It is often attributed to General MacArthur, who did say (in a speech to Congress) that "in war, there is no substitute for victory."

➤ **dough:** a short form of the World War I term **doughboy,** used in phrases like *a squad of doughs*.

➤ **egg beater:** a helicopter, also called a *whirlybird* or a *windmill*.

➤ **friendlies:** South Korean troops.

➤ **gohong:** food, based on a Korean word for 'rice'.

➤ **helitrooper:** a soldier who parachuted into battle from a helicopter.

➤ **honcho:** the man in charge, from the Japanese for 'squad leader'. The word is still sometimes used, especially in the phrase *head honcho*.

➤ **hoochie:** a living place, often the home of a Korean woman living with an American man, although it could also refer to any kind of makeshift structure, like a dugout or a tent. It comes from the Japanese word for 'house'. Sometimes the word was shortened to *hooch,* but it's not connected with the slang term for 'liquor', which derives from the Native American language Tlingit. American servicemen often adopted Japanese words, both because they were common in Korea and because soldiers spent much of their leave time in Japan.

➤ **jaypee:** jet propulsion.

➤ **K-day:** the first day of fighting in the war.

➤ **MiG Alley:** a section of airspace over North Korea where Soviet-made MiG-15 jet fighters frequently intercepted American jets.

➤ **Mister Truman's War:** the Korean War, so called by those who felt skeptical of Truman's motives, also known more harshly as *Truman's Folly*.

➤ **moose:** a Korean girlfriend, from the Japanese word for 'girl' (*musumi*).

➤ **ride the pipe:** to pilot a jet plane after the engine died.

➤ **ROK:** the Republic of Korea (South Korea), pronounced either 'rock' or 'rook'.

➤ **skoshi:** 'small' or 'a little bit' in Japanese-Korean pidgin. The word was later shortened to *skosh* and used widely by soldiers and civilians in expressions like *Just a skosh more*.

CLAMS, DUCKS, AND POODLES

After World War II, the look for women turned soft and sexy. Fifties suits featured close-fitting **pencil skirts.** They were worn with stiletto heels, tiny veiled hats, and gloves. Pants were form-fitting too, and nearly always had side zippers. Front zippers were considered a bit daring. Teenage girls favored the feminine look too. A typical outfit was a **poodle skirt** worn over a stiff, bouffant petticoat, a tucked-in blouse with a **peter pan collar,** and flat shoes. Synthetic fabrics like *Orlon* and *Dacron,* manufactured by DuPont, were popular because they made permanently pleated skirts possible.

Fashion changes for men were less striking. Most traded one uniform for another—the ubiquitous *gray flannel suit* became a metaphor for fifties conformity. Sometimes Dad broke out over the weekend though, wearing Bermuda shorts and a colorful Hawaiian shirt.

➤ **Apache:** a short-lived hair style for young men, with close-cropped sides and a shaved center strip, almost a reverse Mohawk.

➤ **can-can petticoat:** half slip made of stiff nylon net, worn to pouf out full skirts. Petticoats were a dressy look, worn both by young girls in party dresses and grown women in knee-length, full-skirted *cocktail dresses.*

➤ **cat-eye glasses:** eyeglasses with frames that slanted up from the bridge of the nose to form a point where the frame connected to the earpiece. The frames were often decorated with rhinestones or fancy metallic designs.

➤ **clam diggers:** women's pants that hit below the knee and could be rolled up to a long shorts length.

➤ **duck tail:** popular young man's haircut, with the sides of the hair brushed back until they met behind the head and the back hair flipped up like a duck's tail. Also called a *duck's ass* or *D.A.* by the less refined.

➤ **frontier pants:** women's pants, so narrowly tapered that they required ankle slits or ankle zippers, also called *fireside pants* or *slim jims.*

➤ **pedal pushers:** mid-calf-length women's pants, usually featuring a cuff.

➤ **pencil skirt:** a narrow, form-fitting skirt that fell just below the knee.

➤ **peter pan collar:** a round collar that buttoned at the throat, popular for girls' and women's blouses. The collar was named for J. M. Barrie's character Peter Pan, who wore a typical Victorian boy's outfit featuring such a collar. Later Walt Disney put the character in a more modern V-necked shirt.

➤ **pompadour:** a men's hair style that featured flat sides and hair swept up high over the forehead and held in place with pomade. The flashiness of young men's hair styles was balanced by the relative plainness of their clothes.

> **poodle cut:** a popular women's haircut, very short and curly, exposing the forehead and ears. Many Hollywood actresses sported a poodle cut for a year or two. It was a difficult look for anyone whose features were less than Hollywood-perfect.

> **poodle skirt:** a full skirt, often made of a felt circle, with a poodle appliquéd on the front. Sometimes the poodle was attached to a sewn-on leash.

> **rudder pouf:** shirred layers of fabric that cascaded down the sides of a narrow underskirt.

> **sack dress:** an exception to the close-fitting styles of the fifties, a loose-fitting dress that skimmed over the waist and hips. Designed by Givenchy, it was also spelled *sacque dress.*

> **scatter pins:** miniature jeweled pins worn clustered on sweaters or blouses.

THE SILENT GENERATION SPEAKS

Fifties teens were dubbed the **Silent Generation** because they tended to be conventional and apolitical. More young people than ever before were attending college but while there they concentrated on career preparation. Teen slang of this decade was neither as colorful nor as plentiful as earlier versions. In spite of occasional borrowings from the beatnik world, most of it concerned innocuous topics like dating and school.

> **big tickle:** something very funny; a joke.
> **black time's here, termite:** sadly, we must part.
> **blast off:** please go away.
> **book gook:** a studious person.
> **cemetery work:** serious studying.
> **clanked:** rejected by one's love interest.
> **cool dad:** a well-dressed, popular young man, also called a *cool head, cool Jonah,* or a *hard cat,* clearly beatnik-influenced terms.
> **cramming:** a college fad of squeezing as many people as possible into a small space, such as a public telephone booth or a tiny Volkswagen Beetle.
> **curve killer:** a straight-A student.
> **cut the gas:** be quiet.
> **D.D.P.:** damn door pusher, a young woman who sat at the extreme right of a car's front seat.
> **deck of ready-rolls:** a pack of cigarettes.

➤ **dirty bop:** a slow version of the **jitterbug** with suggestive hip movements, also called the *dirty boogie.* Two alternative jitterbugs were the *Shag,* with smooth, languid movements, popular in the South, and the *Fish,* the dance of New York gangs, with virtually no foot movement but a grinding hip action.

➤ **dolly:** a cute girl

➤ **egg head:** a smart person, although not necessarily as smart as a **curve killer.**

➤ **exotically Edgar:** exceptionally good.

➤ **frampton:** extremely cool.

➤ **fuzzy duck:** a young woman with a short haircut.

➤ **geetafrate:** the cost of something, from bebop **geets,** meaning 'money'.

➤ **George:** excellent; very positive. *That's George, really George* was a frequently heard expression in the early 1950s, said of people, things, and events. Eventually, *George*'s opposite, **Tom,** arrived on the scene.

➤ **give me a bell:** call me.

➤ **go à la bois:** to park a car for romantic purposes. *À la bois* means 'to the woods' in French.

PASSION PITS

Car culture really took hold after the war, and *drive-in* businesses proliferated. Americans drove in to restaurants (where they were sometimes served by *car hops* wearing roller skates), pharmacies, funeral parlors, wedding parlors, and open-air church services that included uplifting color slides flashed across giant screens. Most popular of all were drive-in movies, also known as **passion pits** or *ozoners.*

Although only a few hundred drive-in movie theaters existed in the late 1940s, by 1955 more than 4,000 had sprung up around the country. Rows of parking spaces were lined up in front of a large outdoor screen. Each space was equipped with a small speaker that hooked to the door on the driver's side, providing the passengers with sound. Some theaters had room for up to 2,000 automobiles.

At first, drive-ins really were *passion pits,* appealing mainly to young people who sat in the car's back seat. They could hardly have named which movie was playing. Most showings were of minor B-movies anyway. By mid-decade, drive-ins had become family destinations. Amenities included

➧ **grease:** to pass a class.

➧ **hook a snake:** try to date a girl who is going steady with someone else, behavior mainly associated with *dormitory barbarians.*

➧ **hot sketch:** a lively companion, also known as a *hot ticket* or *hot spook.*

➧ **hub cap:** along with a *spoke,* one of the people who revolved around a big wheel on campus.

➧ **jelly tot:** a young teenager or preteen boy who tried to act older than his age.

➧ **krump out:** to get tired.

➧ **let's do what the wind does:** let's blow this joint.

➧ **lump lips:** to kiss.

➧ **maroon harpoon:** the shaft, such as a girl gave her guy when she dated a *dormitory barbarian.*

➧ **Motha Higby:** the fifties version of *hubba-hubba,* murmured meaningfully when a pretty girl walked by.

➧ **mullet:** a badly behaved person; a jerk.

➧ **My, how sanitary!:** I approve.

➧ **nosebleed:** a stupid person.

concession stands, playgrounds, outdoor dance floors, and drop-off laundries, as well as changing tables and bottle warmers for the little ones. Drive-ins now showed the latest films, competing with standard **hardtop,** or indoor, theaters.

An evening at the drive-in was an easy, low-cost way to enjoy a family night out. Children arrived dressed in pajamas, prepared to snooze through the second feature. Everyone indulged in tasty snacks of pizza, popcorn, hot dogs, or fried chicken. Meanwhile, laundry employees were washing and folding the clothes, which would be picked up on the way out. After the families left, night owls arrived for the *spook shows* that ran from midnight until sunrise.

As the fifties became the sixties , and property prices began to rise, many drive-in owners realized they could make more money by selling their theaters to developers than by keeping them open. By the 1970s very few ozoners were still operating, although occasionally a forlorn-looking movie screen can still be glimpsed from a secondary highway.

At the passion pit.

➤ **on the hook:** in love.

➤ **pink:** someone snooty, apparently unrelated to *pinko*, meaning 'communist'.

➤ **quirt counter:** a soda fountain.

➤ **rack:** to pass a class easily, also known as *to box one's grades*.

➤ **roach:** an unpopular girl.

➤ **scalp box:** a small box, to be filled with romantic souvenirs including letters and pictures. These little memento boxes were briefly the rage around the mid-fifties.

➤ **schnookle:** a loser.

➤ **scurve:** an unpopular person; a drip. These unfortunate types were also being called *nerds* for the first time, a word that has remained current.

➤ **shoe:** an adjective meaning 'loyal to the old alma mater; collegiate'.

➤ **Sophie:** a girlfriend.

➤ **squirrel:** a reckless driver.

➤ **tapper:** a boy who repeatedly pestered a girl for a date.

➤ **Vatican:** the school administration building.

➤ **warden:** a schoolteacher.

➤ **zorch:** terrific, the best. *Zorch* was among the words created by San

Francisco disk jockey Richard ("Red") Blanchard. His fans also enthu-
siastically adopted **nervous,** meaning 'wonderful', **threatened** for
'brand new', and **dimph,** which was even better than *zorch* or *nervous*.

SPEED SHOP

Another aspect of fifties car culture was the burgeoning devotion of
teenage boys to their souped-up *machines*. Hot rodding—driving or
racing cars modified for speed—was tremendously popular during this
decade. Serious hot rodders belonged to local timing associations,
groups organized to clock speeds over designated distances. These
local clubs were part of the National Hot Rod Association. For many
young men, however, tinkering with cars was just a casual hobby.
Cruises in their **street rod** and the occasional Saturday night **drag
race** were the highlights of their driving life.

Here are some of the less technical terms, selected from an abun-
dance of ever-changing regional and national hot rod jargon:

➤ **A-bomb:** a souped-up Model-A Ford.

➤ **abortion:** a poorly built car.

➤ **bear:** a car, also called a *beast*.

➤ **big rubber:** large rear tires, used to gain greater traction. **Small
rubber** was often used in front for a **dropped front end.**

➤ **bomb:** a very fast car.

DEEPIES

A short-lived but exciting movie craze was the three-dimensional movie,
usually referred to as a *3-D* or a **deepie.** 3-Ds were the film industry's
attempt to woo viewers away from the TV screen. In a process called
Natural Vision, two projectors threw polarized images onto the screen at
right angles to each other. When moviegoers wore special glasses provided
by the management, they saw a different image with each eye. Their brains
then melded the separate images into a single three-dimensional picture.
The effect was similar to that of an old-fashioned stereoscope.

The first full-length deepie was a clunker called *Bwana Devil,* the story of
rampaging lions attacking members of an African railroad-building crew. It
opened in November 1952, starring Robert Stack and Barbara Britton. Ads
promised the novel sensation of "A lion in your lap!" Viewers packed the
house for *Bwana Devil,* but after several more B-releases the novelty wore
thin. By the end of 1953 the 3-D fad was almost dead.

▶ **bucket of bolts:** a car that rattled a lot.

▶ **bull nose:** a hood from which the ornament was removed. Sometimes a smooth metal strip was added for a streamlined look.

▶ **channel:** to lower a car by cutting out the floor and dropping the body directly over the frame.

▶ **chatter:** vibrations caused by loose parts.

▶ **cherry:** a stock (standard) car, used, but in excellent condition.

▶ **choose off:** to challenge someone to a **drag race,** a quarter-mile race between two cars to determine which could accelerate faster. Drags could begin from a dead stop or a rolling start.

▶ **chop:** to cut a horizontal section out of the cab of a car, or take a horizontal strip off the windshield, still sometimes used. Chopping was often combined with **channeling** for a really, really low car. Short cars were in vogue even with adults—a 1953 Studebaker ad crows that its latest model is "Less than 5 feet high!"

▶ **draggin' wagon:** a car built for drag racing, also called a *dragster.*

▶ **dropped front end:** a front end that sat lower than an ordinary car, either through a dropped axle or a reworked frame. Also called a *raked* or *suicide front end,* or a *snow plow.*

▶ **five dollars a gear:** a race in which competitors determined who could go fastest in each gear. The winner in each gear collected five dollars. Big spenders could, of course, race for ten dollars a gear or more.

▶ **full-race:** a souped-up racing car that would stall at ordinary street speeds.

▶ **frenched:** having headlights or taillights molded into the fenders.

▶ **grind me off a hunk:** a complaint made when someone ground the gears while shifting.

▶ **herd:** to drive a car, as in *Herd that beast down the street!*

▶ **Johnson rod:** a nonexistent part that was blamed when anything mysterious went wrong with the car. A favorite joke of hot rodders was to yell out the car window, "Your Johnson rod's dragging!" to any driver who looked gullible enough to check it out.

▶ **lay a cool shift:** to shift without losing speed or grinding the gears.

▶ **Midnight Auto Supply:** a mythical shop where stolen car parts were supposedly purchased.

▶ **mill:** the car's motor.

▶ **necker's knob:** a steering wheel spinner knob, used to make one-armed driving easier, hence freeing the other arm for romantic purposes.

➤ **nerf:** to push another car around. The **nerf bar** was the bumper, sometimes made out of specially installed ornamental tubing.

➤ **purple death:** a volatile purple fuel, said to be a mixture of liquid explosives, although most rodders didn't actually know what was in it. Also called *purple stuff* or *purple goodies.*

➤ **rail job:** a hot rod without a body, used only for **drag racing.**

➤ **scat:** to go fast.

➤ **sex wagon:** the kind of car that teenage girls admired.

➤ **speed shop:** a place where engine parts and equipment were sold.

➤ **spook:** to drive around aimlessly, just for the pleasure of driving.

➤ **street rod:** a hot rod that could be driven in ordinary street traffic.

➤ **T-bone:** a Model T Ford.

➤ **Tromp it!:** Floor it!

JOY POPPERS

An exception to the conformism of the Silent Generation was the teenage delinquent. The 1950s saw a large jump in teenage crime, including gangs. Drugs were not necessarily a part of juvenile delinquency, but teenage *hopheads* were on the rise. Those other fifties nonconformists, beatniks, also indulged in all manner of illicit substances.

The jargon of an underground group like drug takers is ephemeral. By the time it filters into the mainstream, insiders have already adopted a new vocabulary. Some fifties drug words are still familiar today, but most of them didn't outlast the decade. Although the hophead crowd smoked some marijuana, also a favorite drug of the Beats, it stayed on the fringes of youth culture during this decade. Marijuana words are found in the sixties chapter, the era of its rise to recreational-drug stardom.

➤ **banging:** taking heroin intravenously, later used to mean 'drug taking' generally.

➤ **bindle:** a small packet of narcotics, folded in a special way. This word is borrowed from hobo slang for a rolled-up blanket or bedroll. (See the thirties chapter.)

➤ **black stuff:** opium.

➤ **buzzing:** trying to buy drugs.

➤ **Charlie:** cocaine.

➤ **coconuts:** cocaine.

➤ **deck:** drugs in a paper package.

➤ **go on the nod:** to start feeling depressed and lethargic rather than exhilarated after the initial impact of a drug dose wears off.

➤ **Have you got a thing?:** Do you have any drugs for sale?

▶ **ice cream man:** a drug dealer, especially an opium dealer. *Ice cream* can mean cocaine, morphine, or heroin in crystalline form.

▶ **joy popper:** an inexperienced drug user, probably analogous with *joy rider.*

▶ **let me hold something:** sell me some drugs.

▶ **live bait:** teenage addicts who sold drugs to other teenagers.

▶ **runners:** teenagers who recruited new drug users.

▶ **seeing Steve:** using cocaine.

▶ **set me straight:** sell me some drugs.

▶ **skin pumping:** injecting a drug below the skin rather than directly into a vein, indicating an inexperienced user. Also called a *skin pop* or *skin shot.*

▶ **toy:** a round tin salve container, emptied of salve and used to hold opium.

▶ **yellowjacket:** Nembutal, a barbiturate that came in a yellow capsule.

THE BEATS

Young people who weren't satisfied with being members of the Silent Generation opted to join the **Beat Generation** instead. The **Beats,** later called **beatniks,** originated as a small group of writers who rejected the bland conventionality of the mainstream 1950s. They included Jack Kerouac, who sounded the Beat manifesto in the cult classic *On the Road*; poet Allen Ginsberg, author of "Howl"; novelist William S. Burroughs; and Lawrence Ferlinghetti, poet and owner of the San Francisco bookshop City Lights. The Beats aimed for spontaneous, creative lives, inspired by Zen mysticism, jazz, casual sex, and the regular ingestion of mind-altering drugs. The Beats were, and wanted to be, as far away from bourgeois American values as they could get.

As always, having a separate identity depended partly on developing a group vernacular. Beatnik talk is largely a version of **hipster** slang, spoken by African-American musicians and bebop fans in 1950s New York. A variety of words expressed levels of hipness and squareness, from *gonesville* at one end of the scale to **cubistic** at the other. Beatniks were the first to abuse the innocent preposition *like,* using it constantly as a hedge: *It was like, something else, man.*

The larger Beat movement, sometimes called the **new Bohemians,** centered in New York's Greenwich Village and the North Beach area of San Francisco. Bearded young **cats** wore sandals and black berets, while their **chicks** dressed artistically in black leotards, flowing skirts, and inventive eye makeup. They *made the scene* at their favorite coffeehouses for evenings of poetry, jazz, and enlightenment. Or they *blew in*

to a friend's **pad** and dropped a **bennie** to get in the partying mood. It
was a real **gas,** man. That's **straight, no chaser.**

➤ **bennies:** Benzedrine, a popular stimulant drug.

➤ **bit:** what a person does, as in *"What's your bit?"*

➤ **beanery:** an inexpensive eating place; an old word, but popular
with beatniks.

➤ **blow one's jets:** get annoyed.

➤ **boss:** very good.

➤ **Breadsville:** the bank. *Bread* meant 'money'. This example is just
one of dozens of *-villes* coined during the 1950s. Using *-ville* to turn a
characteristic into a place was a verbal trick from as early as the 1890s,
but it really took off with the Beats. Other *-villes* included *chumpsville,
dullsville, nowheresville,* and *weirdsville,* as well the ones in this list.
Squaresville had been around since the 1940s.

BEAT, BEATNIK

The exact meaning of *Beat Generation* was disputed by the very person who
coined the term. In a *New York Times Magazine* article of November 16,
1952, author John Clellon Holmes quoted Jack Kerouac saying, "You know,
this is really a *beat* generation" [emphasis in the original]. Kerouac seemed
to be using the word *beat* in its sense of 'exhausted or beaten down', and
that's how Holmes interpreted it in his following discussion. Later, Kerouac
revised his definition. In a June 1959 *Playboy* article, he recalled sitting in
a church in his old hometown one afternoon, having "a vision of what I
must have really meant with 'beat' . . . ," which he now believed should
mean 'beatific'.

Part of Jack Kerouac's urge to refocus the word's meaning might have
been a response to the widespread adoption of *beatnik,* a term with much
less flattering connotations. *Beatnik* was invented by *San Francisco Chronicle*
columnist Herb Caen. In his April 2, 1958, column, he reported that *Look*
magazine had hosted a party for "50 beatniks," although more than 250
people had actually turned up for the food and drink. "They're only beat,
y'know," he quipped, "when it comes to work." With the *-nik* craze going
full blast, the word immediately gained currency. It soon became the general term for all bearded, bongo-playing, marginally employed members of
the younger generation. The new beatnik was a far cry from the original
Beats, and even farther away from any semblance of beatitude, except that
which might have been drug-induced.

➤ **butt me:** give me a cigarette.

➤ **cat:** a hipster; a man who appreciated jazz and all the cooler things of life

➤ **cube:** a major square, the opposite of a cat. **Cubistic** types displayed the attributes of a cube.

➤ **Daddy-O:** a form of address, originally from bebop. Also *Daddio*.

➤ **dexies:** Dexedrine, a stimulant.

➤ **dig:** to appreciate, enjoy, or simply understand.

➤ **eye heavy:** drunk.

➤ **Flipsville:** very exciting.

➤ **gas:** a very positive or funny situation—*What a gas!*

➤ **go rotary:** lose your temper.

➤ **gone:** the best and hippest. *Gonest* and *Gonesville* were even better.

➤ **heavy cream:** a chubby girlfriend.

➤ **hipster:** a man who is up to all the latest trends.

➤ **John Square:** a truly unhip, conformist type.

➤ **Kicksville:** a sister city to **Flipsville.**

➤ **Kitty:** a term of address for **hipsters.**

➤ **lay on:** to give someone something for free, including information or an opinion.

➤ **leapers:** stimulants like **bennies** and **dexies.**

➤ **mazuma:** money.

➤ **pad:** a beatnik's home.

➤ **popcorn:** someone with a real job.

➤ **rank on:** to disparage.

➤ **schmo from Kokomo:** a square.

➤ **scuffle:** to get by somehow without a regular job.

➤ **straight from the fridge:** absolutely cool; hip.

➤ **straight, no chaser:** the truth.

➤ **subterranean:** a **hipster** or cool dad, coined by Beat poet Allen Ginsberg.

➤ **Tapsville:** broke.

➤ **thumb:** a form of **hipster** handshake.

➤ **unhook your ears, Dad:** listen carefully.

➤ **wig out:** to go crazy.

➤ **word from the bird:** the truth.

ARRIVALS AND DEPARTURES

➤ **blow in on the scene, fall in, make the scene:** to arrive.

➤ **cut the scene, cut out, fall out, split no-tomorrow style:** to leave.

➤ **gimme some skin:** let's shake hands.
➤ **plant you now, dig you later; so long pal, stay pure:** good-bye.

A FEW MUSIC TERMS FOR COOL CATS

➤ **axe:** any musical instrument at all, not just 'a guitar' as it is now.
➤ **blow:** to play any musical instrument, including those featuring strings and keyboards.
➤ **finger popper:** a swinging **cat.**
➤ **loose wig:** a completely uninhibited musician.
➤ **monkey:** a music critic, who sees no music, hears no music, **digs** no music.
➤ **shucking:** faking the music when a **cat** doesn't know the tune.
➤ **terrible:** the best.
➤ **the ears are moving:** the audience is responding well.

FIFTIES BUZZWORDS

What got the **Affluent Society** buzzing was a mixture of politics and popular culture. As Americans watched the news on television for the first time, the **$64,000 Question** was, which scandal would grab the limelight next: quiz show, **payola,** or communist?

➤ **$64,000 Question:** the first of the major quiz shows, which shot to the top of the ratings soon after it came on the air in June 1955. The last and most valuable question was worth $64,000, so the term became a metaphor for a difficult, but significant, question. Earlier, *the $64 question* meant the same thing. The $64 question was part of an old radio quiz show, *Take It or Leave It.* President Franklin Roosevelt popularized **the $64 question** as an expression when he used it publicly to refer to a tricky issue. By the 1950s, inflation had set in and $64 no longer seemed very significant.

Players on *The $64,000 Question* won money by answering quiz questions, doubling their winnings with each correct answer. Contestants could quit at any time and keep what they won, but if they answered a question incorrectly they forfeited the money. The concept appealed to viewers. Other quiz shows soon appeared on the air. These shows eventually came to grief in the *quiz show scandals* of the late fifties. The scandals erupted when Charles Van Doren, a young Columbia professor who won $129,000 on the the show *Twenty-One,* admitted before a Congressional committee that he had received answers to some questions ahead of time. *Twenty-One* and other quiz shows routinely fed answers to popular contestants. They also paid unpopular ones to take a dive, all in the interest of higher ratings. Disillusioned viewers soon stopped watching, and quiz shows disappeared from television for many years. Humor columnist Art Buchwald struck a chord when he labeled the dishonest competitors **quizlings.**

⯈ **The Affluent Society:** the title of a 1958 book by economist John Kenneth Galbraith, later used to refer to the expanding middle class of the 1950s. Galbraith meant the title ironically. His book criticized a state of affairs in which many people were well off, but the country's schools, roads, and public places were crumbling. However, people often used the term positively to celebrate Americans' new postwar spending power.

⯈ ***Brown v. the Board of Education:*** one of the few Supreme Court cases known to Americans by name. (The complete title is actually *Brown v. the Board of Education of Topeka, Shawnee County, Kansas*). The result of this case was a unanimous 1954 ruling that school segregation was unconstitutional. Until this time, school districts were allowed to provide *separate but equal* school facilities for blacks and whites. Now the Supreme Court justices declared that separate was inherently unequal, and ordered segregated school districts to integrate as quickly as possible. *Brown v. the Board of Education* opened the way for the civil rights movement of the late 1950s and 1960s.

⯈ **The Kinsey Report:** a broad study of American female sexuality that caused people to run for their fallout shelters when it exploded onto the public consciousness in 1953. Dr. Alfred Kinsey interviewed 6,000 women for his report, titled *Sexual Behavior in the Human Female.* Among other bombshells he revealed that half the women questioned had indulged in sex before they were married, and one-quarter had committed adultery afterward. So much for the innocent fifties female. Dr. Kinsey had already published a report on males a few years earlier, but it generated much less excitement.

⯈ **Levittown:** a housing development built by William J. Levitt, or modeled after those designed by him. The name became a way of referring to suburbia generally. The original Levittown is in New York State, but similar housing developments were built in other places. The New York community was a low-cost housing project for World War II veterans, completed in 1951. Like later Levittowns, it was constructed to standard. Houses were all built to a uniform plan, and landscaping consisted mainly of trees planted systematically every 28 feet.

⯈ **McCarthyism:** behavior reminiscent of Senator Joseph McCarthy, who undermined political enemies by intensively investigating their backgrounds and implying that they might be communists. Political cartoonist Herblock (Herbert Block) invented the word in 1950.

Political writers still occasionally use it. The senator from Wisconsin first raised the issue of communists in the government during his 1950 reelection campaign. He announced to the startled members of the Wheeling, West Virginia Ladies' Republican Club that he had in his hand a list of government employees, "two hundred-five names known to the Secretary of State as being members of the Communist Party." A Senate committee convened to investigate this sensational claim, but concluded that McCarthy's list was a sham. Undaunted, he continued to fling accusations of treachery at members of the State Department and others in the government. Those who challenged him risked damaging their own careers at a time when anticommunist fever was high.

McCarthy overreached himself when he went after the U.S. Army. The army fought back during six weeks of televised hearings. Thousands of viewers heard the army's chief counsel, Joseph Welch, challenge McCarthy with the words, "At long last, sir, at long last, have you left no sense of decency?" Shortly afterward, the Senate voted to condemn McCarthy for contempt of the Senate, effectively destroying him as a political figure. He died of alcoholism a few years later at age 47.

➤ **payola:** paying radio disk jockeys to play a particular song. The **payola scandals** occurred in 1959, when a federal government subcommittee investigated the practice. Payola was so entrenched that some radio stations openly offered deals, such as one Detroit station's "Album of the Week" package. The station agreed to play a song or album 114 times a week for $350, with a six-week minimum. After the hearings, the FCC passed some regulations meant to stop payola, but scandals broke out again in the 1980s. Television and radio people also committed **plugola,** praising specific brand names without mentioning that they were being paid for the service.

Shortly after the payola hearings, the New York *Daily News* published the headline (typically truncated), "Arraign Cop in Laundrola." The article described a policeman who had taken protection money from neighborhood laundromats. Soon, people were adding *-ola* to almost anything to suggest shady dealings. *Baloneyola, fixola, freeola,* **ghostola** (uncredited speech writers), **royola** (unearned royalty payments), and **gayola** (payments to police for gay bar protection) were among the new terms. The suffix was already familiar from brand names like Victrola and Pianola. To fifties users, it may have had a similar ring to *-eroo* and other popular slang endings.

Power to the people!

The Sixties

Getting with It

In the sixties, **Camelot** went haywire. The decade started promisingly with President John F. Kennedy's **New Frontier,** but soon the conflict in Southeast Asia was heating up, **civil rightists** at home were **sitting in,** hippies were dropping out, and it looked like **Amerika** was in for some trouble.

At this time, the United States became involved in a new kind of war, one fought in the **boonies** against an enemy known as **Charlie,** *Chuck,* or *Mr. Charles.* While **Betty Crockers** were ensconced back at headquarters, **grunts** plodded through the Vietnamese back country trying not to get **dinged. Steve Canyons** provided air cover, taking off from **bird farms** stationed on the South China Sea. They all tried to avoid going to the **Hanoi Hilton** as POWs. After a year or so in Nam, short-timers could start counting the days to their **wake-up,** after which they'd be back in **the world.** President Nixon's 1969 **Vietnamization** policy gave Americans hope that all the troops would come home before too long.

Meanwhile, the situation stateside was far from quiet. **Yippies** and other **peaceniks** exhorted the government to **make love, not war. Trashing,** or strewing garbage around, was a popular protest activity on college campuses. A more rational option was a **teach-in,** where professors and others lectured on the war. Teach-ins were only one of the many *-ins* happening throughout the decade. The first, and most serious, was the **sit-in,** staged at Southern lunch counters to protest the continuing segregation of African Americans. Later, **join-ins, lie-ins, play-ins,** and **stand-ins** furthered the cause. Then hippies started organizing **be-ins,** and disgruntled **pot** users held **smoke-ins** to press for legalization of marijuana. **Power to the people!**

Besides being-in, hippies were **tuning in, turning on, and dropping out.** The **counterculture** believed in **flower power** and freedom from **hang-ups.** Denizens of **Hashbury** spent their time spreading

119

peace and love, especially **free love. If it feels good, do it.** They had **bad vibes** about **Clark Kent hippies,** though. In spite of the **love beads** and **Nehru jackets,** those **weekend hippies** just seemed so **uptight.** Maybe they needed to get **psychedelic** with a few drops of **instant zen.** Or how about a puff of **Acapulco gold?**

Not all young people were **flower children.** Plenty of mainstream teens were more excited by the **Fab Four** and the **British Invasion** than **love-ins.** Like teens of earlier eras, they still worried about **bagging z's** before a test so they wouldn't **flag** a course. They still tried to avoid **wimps, dimps,** and **squids,** and liked to play **huggy-bear** with their dates. If **long hitters crashed and burned** after drinking parties, they just wanted to put their heads down on **the great white biscuit.** The movie *Endless Summer* turned on teens in the rest of the country to a California **bag**—surfing. **Kooks** and **gremlins went over the falls,** while **hotdoggers** rode **heavies** with their **toes over.**

The youth culture seriously influenced sixties fashions. The style of the early 1960s was demure, featuring knee-length dresses and the little **pillbox hats** favored by first lady Jacqueline Kennedy. Then the **youthquake** swept in with a fashion revolution. **Go-go girls** looked cute in **microminis. Hippie chicks** loved to wear their **granny dresses,** while the guys decked themselves out in the **funk** look, with old-fashioned ruffles, leather-fringed jackets, and long, flowing hair. African Americans grew their hair into **'fros** and donned **dashikis** made of fabric patterned after African kente cloth. Coats could be **mini** or **maxi.** People just **did their own thing.** It was pretty **groovy.**

All through the 1960s, **jet jockeys** raced for space. **Spacefaring Apollonauts** traveled closer and closer to the moon while Kremlinologists kept an eye on how many **cosmodogs** the Russians were sending into orbit. Soon, **spacescapes** were as familiar to television-watching Americans as stereoscope pictures of Europe had been to their grandparents.

By 1969, the changes had come so fast and thick that most Americans, from the **jet set** to the **now generation,** were feeling exhausted. They had crossed the harsh frontier of the 1960s and were ready for something a little more frivolous. Fortunately, the seventies were on their way.

IN NAM

At the beginning of the decade, Vietnam (spelled Viet Nam until the mid-1960s) was an obscure, faraway place to most Americans. Yet by 1969 U.S. involvement there had become a defining feature of the era.

Before World War II, Vietnam was part of the French colony known as *Indochina.* After the war, the French struggled against Vietnamese communists for control of the country. The Geneva accords of 1954 temporarily split Vietnam at the 17th parallel, with the communist-led Democratic Republic of Viet Minh to the north and the American-backed Republic of Viet Nam to the south.

South Vietnamese leaders resisted reunification, believing it would put the North in power. The United States supported the South, first with money and advice, then with military aid. By the mid-sixties, nearly 400,000 American troops were engaged in the Southeast Asian conflict. The ground war gradually tapered off after 1969 as peace negotiations moved forward and **Vietnamization** took hold. The last American troops left in 1972. A few hundred advisors and other non-combatants remained until Saigon, the South Vietnamese capital, fell to the communists in 1975.

As in all wars, words from Vietnam reflect the soldiers' everyday experiences. American troops were in close contact with the civilian population as well as with South Vietnamese soldiers, so they adopted a number of Vietnamese words. A few words from Korea were still in vogue—*Chicom* for 'Chinese communist', *hooch* for a living place, **friendlies** for 'the South Vietnamese army', and of course the *DMZ,* or demilitarized zone, on either side of the 17th parallel. A lingering French influence provided *beaucoup,* 'a lot' (also popular during World War I), and *fini,* 'finished'. The abbreviations *POW* and *MIA* for *prisoner of war* and *missing in action* came into wide use now, although the terms were not new.

One noticeable difference between the conflict in Vietnam and previous American wars was the appearance of vocabulary that spoke of disillusionment with the American cause. Terms like **fragging, friendly fire, sorry about that,** and **winning hearts and minds** display a cynicism not found in earlier war slang. Drug-related terms were also part of the soldiers' language in Vietnam. Some of these are found in "Grass," the section on marijuana.

➤ **ARVN:** acronym for the Army of the Republic of Viet Nam (the South Vietnamese army). Americans pronounced it *Arvin* and called South Vietnamese soldiers **Arvins. Marvin-the-Arvin** was another nickname, as well as the contemptuous **As Really Very Nervous,** a reference to the Vietnamese soldiers' reputed unwillingness to engage in combat. The North Vietnamese army was known as **DRVN,** for the Democratic Republic of Viet Nam, or **PAVN,** for the People's Army of Viet Nam.

➤ **bird farm:** an aircraft carrier.

➤ **bombing pause:** a temporary halt in the bombing, meant to coax the North Vietnamese into negotiating.

➤ **boonies:** the Vietnamese back country, short for *boondocks,* a Tagalog (Philippine) word adopted by the Marines during the Spanish-American War. A **boonie rat** was someone who had spent a long time in the jungle.

➤ **Charlie:** a nickname for the Viet Cong, guerrillas who fought in South Vietnam for the communist cause. They were commonly known by the abbreviation *VC.* The name *Charlie* comes from "Victor-Charlie," the military code words for the letters *V* and *C.* Charlie also went by the more formal designations of *Mr. Charlie, Charles,* or *Mr. Charles,* or the more casual one of *Chuck.*

➤ **chicken plate:** a wraparound bulletproof vest sometimes worn by helicopter gunners.

➤ **choi oi:** mispronunciation of *troi oi,* a Vietnamese expression meaning something like 'Oh my God!'

➤ **counterinsurgency:** the U.S. government's tactics for fighting the Viet Cong guerrillas, whom the government considered *insurgents,* or revolutionaries.

➤ **cracker box:** a field ambulance.

➤ **dai uy:** the Vietnamese rank of army captain, a label generally assigned to anyone with authority.

➤ **dep chi:** a corruption of *dep trai,* meaning 'a handsome boy', a designation that Vietnamese bar girls awarded to all G.I.s.

➤ **di dai:** okay.

➤ **di di:** go away.

➤ **dinged:** wounded.

➤ **Dodge City:** Hanoi, the capital of North Vietnam.

➤ **dustoff:** a medical evacuation from the field, often by a **Huey** helicopter. The ability to rescue wounded soldiers and transport them to field hospitals within minutes was a life-saving advance over previous wars.

➤ **fini flight:** a pilot's last mission before going home.

➤ **flak jacket:** an armored vest worn by U.S. infantrymen to protect against shrapnel.

➤ **FNG:** foolish new guy, although in most soldierly dialects the *F* stood for a much ruder word. A more courteous version was **BNG,** brand new guy.

➤ **fragging:** the killing of an officer by his own men. At first fragging referred specifically to rolling a fragmentation grenade into the victim's tent, but later it meant killing an officer by any means, including shooting him while out on patrol. Officers who were overzealous in seeking out engagements with enemy soldiers were good candidates for fragging. Hundreds of cases were documented over the course of the war. It became more common toward the end, when soldiers were unwilling to risk themselves unnecessarily, knowing they would soon be going home. It was also a way of protesting the war itself.

➤ **freedom bird:** a plane that took a soldier home after his tour of duty was up.

➤ **friendlies:** usually members of ARVN, but also used to indicate civilians friendly to the South Vietnamese government or cooperative toward American soldiers.

➤ **friendly fire:** fire from American forces, mistakenly aimed at American positions.

➤ **grunt:** a slang term for an infantryman, which later entered the civilian lexicon as a word for anyone in a low-level job. Infantrymen were also called *snuffs* (because they snuffed out the enemy), *bluelegs, ground pounders, beetle stompers,* and *crunchies.*

➤ **Hanoi Hilton:** a prisoner-of-war camp in Hanoi, actually a former French colonial jail called Hoa Lo.

➤ **Ho Chi Minh trail:** a trail through the jungle, named after the leader of North Vietnam. The Ho Chi Minh trail led from North Vietnam, through neighboring Laos and Cambodia, and into South Vietnam. It was the main supply line from the North Vietnamese government to the Viet Cong.

➤ **Huey:** a popular name for the UH-1 Iroquois helicopter, which could carry up to 12 people and was frequently used for medical evacuations. Hueys lacking built-in weapons were called **slicks.**

➤ **immersion foot:** the Vietnam version of trench foot, caused by slogging through marshy fields and jungles.

➤ **in country:** in South Vietnam, especially as part of the ground war.

➤ **Indian country:** a hostile area where the population supported the Viet Cong and American troops could expect to be fired on.

➤ **jink:** a zigzag movement performed by a pilot to avoid anti-aircraft fire.

➤ **Kit Carson scout:** a former North Vietnamese soldier who defected to the South and served as a scout for the U.S. military, a reference to the legendary nineteenth-century U.S. Army scout.

➤ **LRRP rations:** freeze-dried meals sent with Long-Range Reconnaissance Patrols. They were lighter than C-rations, consisting mainly of a dish that would be hot if hot water was added—something like chicken stew or spaghetti with meat sauce—and a candy bar, nicknamed a **John Wayne bar.** They were also called *Lurp rations* or *long rats.*

➧ **number one, number ten:** expressions of approval and disapproval, with one being the best possibility and ten the worst. **Number ten thou'** was later added to mean something immeasurably worse than ten. For example, the Ia Drang Valley, site of the first large-scale North Vietnamese offensive in October 1965, was *boonies ten thou'.*

➧ **oil spot:** the first village in a hostile region to be converted to the South Vietnamese cause. Government troops would then use this village as a base, hoping their authority would spill over into the surrounding area like a widening pool of oil.

➧ **one-digit midget:** someone due to leave Vietnam in less than ten days.

➧ **outstanding:** a popular slang way of expressing approval of anything not absolutely terrible.

➧ **red dollars:** scrip issued to soldiers instead of real money.

➧ **Remington raider:** a clerk-typist, who may have worked on a Remington typewriter. Clerks were also called *desk jockeys, combat clerks, clerks and jerks,* and *rearies.*

WINNING HEARTS AND MINDS

A curious feature of the war in Vietnam was that many South Vietnamese civilians were more sympathetic to the Viet Cong than to the cause of their own government. The United States began a program of humanitarian aid and civic improvements in an attempt to gain support from South Vietnamese villagers. The government called it **winning hearts and minds.** Critics of the war began to use the phrase sarcastically to refer to less positive events, like the burning down of villages suspected of harboring Viet Cong.

Another expression adopted as an ironic catch phrase was **it became necessary to destroy the town in order to save it,** first heard during the **Tet offensive.** During the 1968 holiday of Tet, or the lunar new year, the Viet Cong overran numerous towns and villages. American forces nearly flattened some of the places before they could wrest them from the VC. The above statement was an army captain's way of explaining what happened to the town of Ben Tre, which Americans virtually demolished before they succeeded in dislodging the enemy.

➤ **rog:** short for *roger,* traditionally the army's way of acknowledging the reception of a radio message. It was used simply to mean 'yes' or 'understood'. **Affirmative** and **negative** were also favorite ways of saying *yes* and *no.*

➤ **saddle up:** to put on one's gear and get ready to leave.

➤ **shake 'n' bake:** an officer straight out of Officer Candidate School. New, noncommissioned officers were known as *shake 'n' bake sergeants* or *instant NCOs.* Shake 'n' Bake is a brand name for a product used in a quick method of cooking chicken, and the reference was to the quickness with which officers and NCOs were promoted and turned loose in the field.

➤ **Steve Canyon:** a pilot, a reference to Milton Caniff's tough comic-strip character, an Air Force pilot who appeared in newspapers from 1947 until 1988.

➤ **sao:** a jerk or creep, another bar girl contribution.

➤ **sorry about that:** an all-purpose expression of regret that first became popular in Vietnam and later spread to the folks back home. It was an understated way of indicating the soldier's realization that he could not solve any large or small problems connected with the war.

➤ **titi:** very little, from the Vietnamese.

➤ **tu dai:** a sign sometimes posted by the Viet Cong, warning the locals that an area was booby trapped.

➤ **Vietnamization:** President Nixon's name for a plan to turn the war over to South Vietnamese troops, while the Americans gradually withdrew. The term appeared during President Johnson's administration, but Nixon popularized it.

➤ **Vietvet:** a veteran of the Vietnam war.

➤ **wake-up:** a soldier's last day in Vietnam before he headed back home to the **world.**

➤ **waxed:** killed; also *zapped, greased, popped, capped,* or *wasted.*

➤ **world:** the United States, or, more generally, any place that wasn't Vietnam.

➤ **zero dark thirty:** before dawn.

➤ **zoomie:** a pilot.

MAKING THE GREAT SOCIETY

During the sixties, the home front was no more peaceful than the boonies. Besides protesting against the war in Vietnam, many students and other young people (and some older people) were involved in struggles to guarantee equal rights to all Americans. **Freedom riders**

Stokely Carmichael speaking at the University of California, Berkeley, during a Black Power rally.

rode buses around the segregated South. **Peaceniks** marched across campus. **Yippies** rioted through the Chicago streets. **Free speech** was important to those creating the **Great Society,** and the clamor could be heard throughout the decade.

➤ **Amerika:** the *Yippie* way of spelling America. The Germanic-looking *k* was meant to evoke echoes of fascism, an indirect accusation against the government. Radical newspapers sometimes spelled it *Amerikkka* to suggest the Ku Klux Klan. The **Yippies** were an unusual antiwar group, more lighthearted than most. For example, they threatened to disrupt the 1968 Democratic convention by dropping LSD into Chicago's water supply. They also paraded the streets with their proposed presidential candidate, a pig named Pigasus, until the police confiscated the animal. *Yippie* was originally meant to be a play on *hippie,* but later the group claimed it stood for Youth International Party.

➤ **black power:** a slogan that made its appearance during a 1966 civil rights march through Mississippi. It meant different things to different people. Generally, it expressed a rejection of the nonviolent integrationist principles of the early civil rights movement in favor of separatism and *black pride.* The **Black Panthers,** a militant group fighting for African-American rights, adopted black power as an ideal.

➤ **civil rightist:** someone committed to the fight for African-American civil rights.

➤ **credibility gap:** the difference between what politicians were telling people about the Vietnam conflict and what was actually happening. Many skeptics questioned casualty figures and other official information, especially toward the end of the war.

➤ **free speech:** the right to speak publicly on any topic. Students led by Mario Savio founded the **Free Speech Movement** in 1964 at the University of California at Berkeley. The movement was a response to the administration's ban against on-campus political activity. Protests included student strikes and a student takeover of the administration building. Eventually, the faculty voted to lift all restrictions on student speech. Unrest continued to trouble the Berkeley campus, leading some observers to call it *Berserkley.*

➤ **freedom riders:** civil rights activists, both black and white, who rode through the South on buses in 1961. They were pushing for enforcement of a recent Supreme Court decision making segregated buses and terminals unconstitutional. Riders were often beaten, jailed, or otherwise harassed, but they were effective. Soon after the freedom rides, the Interstate Commerce Commission ordered bus companies to desegregate their facilities.

➤ **Freedom Summer:** the summer of 1964, when young people, mostly college students, traveled to Mississippi to register African-American voters. Like the freedom rides, this activity was dangerous. Angry residents attacked and harassed participants, and several people were killed.

➤ **Great Society:** President Johnson's domestic policy. Johnson used the same name for his plan as Herbert Hoover had in the 1930s, and it encompassed some of the same ideas. Part of President Johnson's program was the **War on Poverty,** which included the Office of Economic Opportunity, Head Start for disadvantaged preschoolers, and VISTA, a domestic version of the Peace Corps. Important legislation included the Civil Rights Act of 1964 and the Voting Rights Act of 1965.

➤ **peace sign:** a gesture made by forming a "V" with the first two fingers, the same as Churchill's famous "V for victory" sign during World War II. President Nixon was also partial to the "V for victory" sign, made with both hands.

➤ **peacenik:** another *-nik* word, a hostile term for an antiwar demonstrator. A similar derogatory name was *Vietnik.*

➤ **red power:** a Native American political movement of the 1960s, modeled after **black power.** It was mainly based among the young. An early red power group was the National Indian Youth Council. Red power advocates orchestrated the **fish-ins** (see below). Also, Indians of All Nations occupied the former prison island of Alcatraz, claiming it was Native American property under treaty rights. The best known red power activists were members of **AIM,** the American Indian Movement. AIM was formed in 1968, but was most active during the 1970s.

➤ **trashing:** the practice of strewing garbage around college campuses as a way of protesting the Vietnam War.

➤ **women's lib:** a disparaging term for the feminist movement of the late 1960s, usually known as the *Women's Liberation Movement.* Members were known to the disapproving as *women's libbers* or *bra burners,* a reference to their reputed practice of burning their bras as a protest.

SIT-INS AND OTHER -INS

Sit-ins were a way of fighting segregation by sitting down in "whites only" sections of Southern restaurants. Four courageous young African-American men, college students in Greensboro, North Carolina, staged the first sit-in at the lunch counter of the local Woolworth's. Although they weren't served that day, they returned, and others gradually joined them. Sit-ins became a popular form of protest, generating variations such as **swim-ins** and **play-ins.**

With their usual love of a convenient suffix, Americans started tacking *-in* onto all sorts of gatherings, even when protest was not an issue. By the time the television variety show *Laugh-In* premiered in 1968, *-in*

BE-IN

The ultimate *-in* was one organized for the purpose of merely existing. These gatherings were also called *love-ins* or *happenings*. Hippies and other young people came together to get in touch with their spiritual selves through poetry reading, music, drug taking, and just plain hanging out. Probably the earliest be-in occurred in San Francisco's Golden Gate Park on January 14, 1967, the day LSD became illegal in California. The most impressive be-in was near Woodstock, New York, in the summer of 1969. More than 400,000 young people congregated in the pouring rain to sit naked in the mud, smoke pot, drink, make love, and groove to the music of Jimi Hendrix, The Who, Janis Joplin, Joan Baez, Arlo Guthrie, and others. But happenings happened everywhere in the late 1960s. It was a good time to be in.

had lost most of its original political meaning. Here are some notable *-ins,* mostly serious, a few less so:

➠ **fish-in:** events staged by Native Americans to assert their traditional fishing rights. The first fish-in took place in Washington State in 1964. Hundreds of people participated. Several other fish-ins followed.

➠ **hand-in:** an unjudged art show in which all artists were free to display their work.

➠ **join-in:** a plan of the Congress of Racial Equality to send pairs of African-American worshippers to various white churches in Baton Rouge on "race relations Sunday," February 11, 1962. CORE members also staged a **chain-in,** chaining themselves to seats in the observers' gallery of the Alabama legislature.

➠ **lie-in:** blocking subway trains or street traffic with one's body as a form of protest.

➠ **loot-in:** one reporter's way of describing a riot.

➠ **play-in:** taking children to play at segregated playgrounds.

➠ **shop-in:** a boycott against white shop owners, followed by a **buy-in,** staged by those who sympathized with the owners.

➠ **shrink-in:** a way of describing a psychiatrists' convention.

➠ **slop-in:** a student protest against bad cafeteria food.

➠ **smoke-in:** a demonstration supporting the legalization of marijuana.

➠ **stand-in:** instead of sitting down, standing; for example, at segregated movie theaters.

➠ **swim-in:** visiting segregated public swimming pools.

➠ **teach-in:** lectures offered by college professors outside of class time to educate students about the war, and also protest it. The first was held at the University of Michigan in 1965. Since then, teach-ins have sometimes been held as protests against other government actions, for example the Gulf War of 1991.

➠ **wade-in:** swimming at segregated beaches.

➠ **wed-in:** a hippie marriage that took place in Prospect Park, Brooklyn.

FLOWER POWER

The natural descendants of the Beat generation were the **hippies.** Although different in many ways—beatniks listened to jazz and wore black, hippies listened to rock and wore paisley—they were united in rejecting the conventions of mainstream society. Even the word *hippie* evolved from the earlier jazz term, *hipster.* In the 1940s, *hippie* meant someone who tried to be hip. By the 1950s, it meant someone who was hip. In the 1960s, whether *hippie* was a good or bad label just depended on your point of view.

Hippies borrowed other Beat lingo too, for example, *bread, chick, pad,* and *dig. Cool,* part of the hipster's dialect for a couple of decades, now entered the linguistic mainstream. In the 1940s, *cool* meant relaxed and low-key, effortlessly hip. In the 1960s, any good person or positive situation could be cool.

Hippies rejected materialistic goals in favor of a more meaningful existence. Many organized communes where they shared possessions and chores. They pursued spiritual enlightenment with the help of drugs. Although the movement faded after only a few years, it had a lasting cultural impact. Much of the *love generation's* language has a distinctly dated sound, but other words and expressions are now standard: *bummer,* **cop out,** *rip off, ego trip, check it out, that bugs me, right on,* and *get it together,* to name a few. And *cool* is still with us. Hippies also had a long-term effect on the slang of the drug world.

The words collected below are seldom heard now, even on the lips of fiftysomethings:

➤ **acid rock:** rock music associated with taking *acid,* or LSD. It tried to mimic the way people heard sounds when actually on the drug. The music was highly improvisational, featuring open-ended solos and electronic distortions. Some practitioners were Jefferson Airplane, the Grateful Dead, and Pink Floyd. It was also called *psychedelic rock.*

➤ **bag:** an interest or hobby; the thing you do, similar to the beatnik *bit.*

➤ **cop out:** to abandon one's principles, especially to become more conventional.

➤ **cosmic:** tremendously significant in some unexplainable but beautiful way, also spelled *kozmik.*

➤ **counterculture:** people against the dominant culture; hippies, war protesters, and the like. Journalist Theodore Roszak coined the term in 1968. It is still heard.

➤ **cracked house:** a vacant house that was "cracked open" so hippies could squat there. The behavior and the term were both more common in England than in the United States.

➤ **Edge City:** a place where people lived dangerously, reminiscent of the *-villes* of the 1950s.

➤ **Establishment:** anybody outside the **counterculture;** the people in charge.

➤ **far out:** extraordinary or bizarre. This expression was sometimes used as a rote response to any remark.

➤ **flower power:** the supposed power of pacifism and love to transcend the violence of the larger society. The idea was appealing to hippies, who were often called **flower children.** Antiwar protesters also adopted the flower motif. A famous picture of the time shows a line of National Guardsmen facing a crowd of peace marchers, one of whom, a young man, is inserting daisies into their rifle barrels.

free love: casual sex. Free love was mostly associated with communes, but others practiced it too, partly encouraged by the new availability of birth control pills.

hang-up: a problem, inhibition, or obsession. People got *hung up* on all sorts of issues.

Hashbury: a nickname for the Haight-Ashbury section of San Francisco, a central gathering place for the **counterculture** of the late sixties, no doubt named for the amount of hashish ingested there.

-head: a frequent user of drugs, as in *pothead.*

head shop: a place to buy drug paraphernalia.

heavy: very serious or substantive.

instant zen: the drug LSD.

magic mushrooms: psilocybin mushrooms, eaten to induce hallucinations.

mind-blowing: a property of consciousness-altering drugs. Later, it was used to describe any idea, incident, song, sexual encounter, or other stimulus that helped a person see life from a new angle. This term is one of several, like *psychedelic* and *trip,* that started out referring to drugs and eventually were applied to life in general.

now generation: young people of the 1960s, implying that they were up-to-the-minute, unlike their old-fashioned parents.

out of sight: amazingly good; very far out.

psychedelic: an adjective describing drugs that induced a state of perceptual distortion. The word was also applied to anything that startled the senses, including bright clashing colors, dizzying geometric patterns, strobe lights, and acid rock. One of the doctors who conducted experiments with LSD in the 1950s invented the word.

put on: a joke or hoax; a deliberately misleading statement.

rap session: a discussion or a conversation. It could also have the sense of a critique. *Rap* had a short shelf life. By the end of the decade, it was the sole property of would-be trendy adults who stupefied teenagers with the invitation "Let's rap!" The word reappeared in the 1980s as a term for a musical style that consisted of rhythmically spoken words over background music.

splitters: those who quit the **counterculture** and rejoined the **Establishment.** In other words, they *split the scene* (as both beatniks and hippies would have said).

➤ **Summer of Love:** the summer of 1967, when residents of Hashbury invited young people everywhere to travel to San Francisco for an alternative living experience. Thousands converged on Haight-Ashbury, creating chaos, boosting the crime rate, and inadvertently hastening the end of the hippie **counterculture** in that neighborhood.

➤ **teeny bopper:** a very young hippie wannabe.

➤ **trip:** to take drugs, also **trip out.** Later, it could mean to daydream or muse about some topic. A trip could also be any strange experience, not necessarily drug-induced. By the 1970s, a trip could be an eccentric person, and by the 1980s an entertaining event.

➤ **turn on:** to take drugs. Like **trip,** the meaning broadened to include other kinds of experiences. A **turn on** was anything that caused people to feel enthusiasm or excitement, including sex.

➤ **uptight:** tense and inhibited. Earlier it had an almost opposite meaning of 'very good'.

➤ **vibes:** an intuitive feeling about a person, place, or situation, short for *vibrations.* Vibes could be good or bad.

FREAK

Freaks came into their own during this decade. The word *freak* has had the double meaning of 'a weird person' or 'an enthusiast' since the early twentieth century. Some specialized meanings also appeared in midcentury. It could be slang for a sexual deviant or for a sexy young woman, a usage that was still around in the 1990s. Among forties jazz musicians, the word was a complimentary term for a player with an unorthodox musical style.

By the 1960s, *freak* meant 'a drug taker', or simply 'a hippie', a label the *longhaired freaks* of the counterculture embraced with pride. *To freak* or *freak out* was to have a bad experience with a hallucinogen. Later, it meant to lose your temper or to go wild with excitement, fear, outrage, or astonishment. The noun *freak-out* could also replace *happening* to mean 'a hippie gathering'.

At the same time, the word retained its meaning of 'an enthusiast', and *freak*-words proliferated among the young. Some of the freaks that one linguist heard mentioned on his own campus included *academic freak, airplane freak, Boone's-juice freak, clothes freak, diet freak, frat freak, health freak, ice-cream freak, Jesus freak* (a popular usage), *people freak* (also popular), *radio freak, shower freak, summer freak, TV freak, wine freak.* Freaks are still with us, although people now might be more apt to use the word *nut.*

➤ **weekend hippie:** an ordinary resident of suburbia who donned love beads and a leather fringe jacket for a weekend stroll through Haight-Ashbury or Greenwich Village. Also known as a *plastic hippie* or a *Clark Kent hippie.*

➤ **wrecked:** under the influence of drugs. Other popular terms were *spaced out, strung out, high, wasted, stoned.*

TELLING IT LIKE IT IS

The 1960s was a great decade for slogans. Buttons and posters were everywhere, giving voice to opinions from left to right. Here are a few of the more memorable, in no particular political order:

➤ **America—love it or leave it:** a slogan of the anti-antiwar protestors, often appearing as a bumper sticker.

➤ **Black is beautiful:** an expression of pride in African-American looks and style, including African print fabrics and natural, unstraightened hair.

➤ **Do your own thing:** a hippie motto encouraging people to be individualistic. Another version was *If it feels good, do it.*

➤ **Give a damn:** a button slogan expressing a theme of the times.

➤ **Keep America beautiful:** the slogan of Lady Bird Johnson's anti-litter campaign.

➤ **Make love not war:** an antiwar slogan frequently seen on buttons and posters.

➤ **Power to the people:** a demand for direct democracy, a goal of many sixties activists.

➤ **Sisterhood is powerful:** a slogan of the Women's Liberation Movement of the late 1960s.

➤ **Suppose they gave a war and nobody came:** a philosophical question found on antiwar posters.

➤ **Tell it like it is:** an exhortation to tell the truth, especially about controversial topics.

➤ **Tune in, turn on, drop out:** advice of former Harvard psychology lecturer Timothy Leary, encouraging youth to get in touch with their inner selves through hallucinogenic drug use.

➤ **War is not healthy for children and other living things:** a popular poster statement, usually illustrated with a flower drawing.

➤ **You can't trust anyone over thirty:** a piece of advice current among members of the youth movement, apparently first uttered by Jack Weinberg, a Berkeley graduate student.

GRASS

Marijuana use wasn't new—Americans started smoking it in the 1920s and it was declared illegal in 1937—but it remained on the fringes of the drug world until the sixties. Hippies, college students, radicals, and the troops in Vietnam all adopted it as their mind-altering substance of choice. By the late sixties, middle-class people were indulging in **pot parties. Blasting** joints became a new leisure activity for thousands of Americans.

Marijuana is derived from the Indian hemp plant (*Cannabis sativa*). A possible etymology is from the Spanish word for an intoxicant, *mariguana*. Occasionally, the word is spelled *marihuana*. The most popular name for marijuana in the sixties was *grass*, a word that had been in use since the forties. In the seventies, *dope* was the most heavily used term. The following words were part of the basic vocabulary for sixties marijuana smokers. Several have remained familiar.

➤ **A-bomb:** a cigarette made from marijuana combined with another drug, for example, heroin.

➤ **bad ounce:** three-quarters of an ounce of cheap Mexican grass.

➤ **baggie:** about an ounce of marijuana, sold in a small plastic bag.

➤ **bale of hay:** a bulky amount of marijuana, difficult to hide or dispose of.

➤ **balloon room:** place where dope was smoked.

➤ **blast:** to smoke marijuana, a word in use since the 1930s. *Blasted* meant high on the drug. Another word for smoking was *blow*.

➤ **bogart a joint:** to hang onto a marijuana cigarette longer than was polite before passing it on to the next smoker, from the image of Humphrey Bogart dangling a cigarette off his lip.

➤ **bong:** a pipe with an oversized bowl. As the marijuana burned, the bowl filled with smoke, providing a stready stream through the pipe. This piece of paraphernalia was introduced by returning G.I.s.

➤ **boxed:** under the influence of marijuana.

➤ **Buddha grass:** another word from the troops, meaning marijuana or hashish mixed with tobacco.

➤ **can:** one or two ounces of weed in a can, named for the Prince Albert tobacco cans in which it was sold during the 1930s and 1940s. **Can action** meant 'buying marijuana'.

➤ **cancelled stick:** an ordinary cigarette in which the tobacco had been replaced by marijuana, obviously a play on the slang term for a cigarette, *cancer stick*.

➤ **cocktail:** the butt of a joint twisted onto the end of an ordinary cigarette.

dime bag: $10 worth of marijuana. A **nickel bag** was $5 worth.

dinky dow: American spelling of a Vietnamese term for marijuana, literally meaning 'crazy'.

Jefferson Airplane: a paper match, split so that it would hold the butt end of a marijuana cigarette, named after the acid rock group. The butt end of a joint was called a **roach.** Various kinds of **roach clips** were employed to hold it. Joints were too expensive to throw away, so they were smoked to the very end. People who weren't handy with matches could buy roach clips at their local head shop.

koon sa: another Vietnamese word for marijuana

lid: a small plastic bag of un-cleaned marijuana. Later, a lid could be any bag of grass, cleaned or uncleaned.

manicure: to clean marijuana by removing the seeds and stems.

munchies: the feeling of acute hunger that marijuana users get after smoking a joint.

nod: a drug-induced stupor, simi-lar to the fifties expression *go on the nod.*

O.J.: an opium joint, a marijuana cigarette dipped in liquid opium, popular with the boys in Nam.

party pack: a package of ten joints, wrapped in plastic and sold by industrious Vietnamese vendors. **Kools** were ten-packs of regular ciga-rettes partly stuffed with marijuana.

pin: a very thin joint.

pot party: a party thrown for the purpose of *blowing* dope.

rainy day woman: a marijuana cigarette, after the Bob Dylan song

---

SIXTIES WORDS FOR MARIJUANA

Aunt Mary, boo, broccoli, bush, fennel, gangster, gates, gauge (from **ganja,** the word used in India and Jamaica), **hay, J** (for **joint,** meaning 'marijuana cigarette'), **jive stick, smoke, sweet Mary, tea** (becoming obso-lete by the 1960s), **weed, yerba** (from Spanish *hierba,* 'herb').

Some words that continued to be used after the 1960s are **dope, grass, joint, loco weed, Mary Jane, pot, reefer, spliff.**

TYPES OF MARIJUANA

Like real tea, marijuana came in black and green, and a few other colors as well. The most desirable, high-grade type of the drug was **Acapulco gold** or **Acapulco red.** Some other popular smokes were **African black, Bethesda gold, black hash, black Russian, cherry Leb** (Lebanese), **Columbus black, Congo brown, gold leaf, green Moroccan, Jersey green, Manhattan silver, Manhattan white, Mexican brown, Mexican green, Mexican red, Panama gold, Panama red, red Leb, Santa Maria gold, Santa Maria red, Zacatecas purple.**

of that name, possibly indicating that smoking was a good rainy-day activity.

➤ **square joint:** a joint smoked by squares, or, in other words, an ordinary cigarette.

➤ **thumb:** a fat joint.

YOUTHQUAKE

The majority of teens during the 1960s were not hippies, but conventional students intent on dating, drinking, and occasionally **acing a course.** Although slang frequently spilled over from the Haight to the dorm room, mainstream types also had a language of their own.

➤ **ace a course:** to get an A.

➤ **animal:** an athlete or other muscle-bound type.

➤ **bag z's:** to sleep.

➤ **Beatlemania:** hysterical excitment about the Beatles, whose first hit single, "From Me to You," burst on an unsuspecting teen world in 1963. Beatlemania reached a peak in the United States in 1964, when the *Fab Four* appeared on Ed Sullivan's variety show. The Beatles were also labeled the *Mop Tops* because of their longish, pudding-bowl haircuts. For teenage boys who couldn't grow their own mop tops, Beatle wigs were on sale.

➤ **bird-dog:** to move in on a friend's date; also to **cut in** during a dance, meaning 'to take a dancing woman away from her partner and start dancing with her yourself'.

➤ **bitchin':** said of anything good, from a classy car to an excellent grade; a word that resurfaces periodically, for example, in 1980s Valley Girl slang.

➤ **boonies:** secluded areas suitable for necking with a date. As with the Vietnam slang, the more general meaning is 'the middle of nowhere'.

➤ **British Invasion:** the swarm of British rock groups that followed the Beatles into the United States, including the Rolling Stones, the Dave Clark Five, Gerry and the Pacemakers, the Who, Herman's Hermits, and the Kinks. The British Invasion triggered a brief flare of interest in the *Mod* movement, centered in the neighborhood of London's Carnaby Street. Besides a look—Beatles-type haircuts, sleek suits, and square-toed *Carnaby* boots—the Mods imported a handful of words. The most successful were **luv** to address any female, **bird** to refer to a girl, and **gear, tuff,** or **fab** to voice approval.

➤ **crash and burn:** to suffer through a hangover.

➤ **dimp:** a loser; the same as a *wimp*, which came in about the same time.

➤ **dorf:** a clod or unattractive person.

➤ **flag a course:** to get an F.

➤ **flash:** to vomit.

➤ **flunkenstein:** an IBM computer that graded multiple-choice tests automatically.

➤ **funsies:** an ironic exclamation applied to an activity expected to be unpleasant, like exam-taking.

➤ **goose:** a socially unacceptable person.

➤ **grunge:** a dull date.

➤ **live in a tree:** to be unaware of what's going on around you.

➤ **long hitter:** a student who could hold his or her liquor.

➤ **mince:** a socially pathetic person.

➤ **mouse:** to kiss, also known as *playing huggy-bear* or *smash-mouth*.

➤ **seek the great white biscuit:** to seek one's pillow for the purpose of **bagging z's.**

GROOVY

Groovy is the slang word that just won't die. In the thirties jazz world, a musician who was **in the groove** was playing exceptionally smoothly. Later the expression extended to jazz fans who were carried away by the music. *Groovey* showed up in the early 1940s, still related to jazz. Gradually, it started to mean anything good, hip, or cool, but only to a small group of jive talkers. (See "Voutian Vocabulary" in the forties chapter.) By the fifties, *groovy* had been relegated to the margins of would-be hip, mostly appearing in television commercials.

Groovy wasn't finished yet, though. It had a second career in the 1960s as a full-blown part of the youth culture. Hippies used it, at least for a while, ordinary teenagers used it, and even preteens picked it up. To **groove on** something was to enjoy it, as in *I really groove on Pink Floyd.* **Groovin'** (never pronounced with the final *g*) meant having a good time. If some activity was **a groove,** it was fun.

Soon the word became a marker of the 1960s. Then, as the 1960s gave way to the 1970s, it became a marker of the hopelessly uncool. To nineties college students, **groovers** were pathetic people stuck in the past. But the story still isn't over. *Groovy* is being uttered again on twenty-first-century college campuses, and not as a joke.

- **smash:** to kiss.
- **squid:** a drippy person.
- **stay loose:** to relax.
- **straight skinny:** the absolute truth.
- **ugly stick:** what someone unattractive had supposedly been beaten with.
- **wig:** great.
- **woodsies:** romantic activities that took place in the **boonies**.
- **youthquake:** a term signifying the youth-oriented revolution in fashion and popular culture. The cult of youth worship was at its strongest in the 1960s when the largest bulge of the population was in its teens and twenties.
- **zot:** zero; nothing.

TOES OVER

During the sixties, a California craze called **surfing** swept the country. Even youngsters in land-locked states knew about **ho-daddies** and **hotdoggers,** thanks to movies like *Gidget* and *Beach Blanket Bingo*. The classic surfing documentary *The Endless Summer* also popularized the sport, while the California band the Beach Boys immortalized it in song. Surfers' slang eventually seeped into the teen lexicon, especially that of skateboarders (see the seventies chapter) and Valley Girls (see the eighties chapter). Here are a few colorful sixties surfing terms:

- **Cowabunga!:** a shout of happiness and exultation that could be loosely translated as "Surf's up!" Originally introduced by Chief Thunderthud on the 1950s children's television program *The Howdy Doody Show, Cowabunga* has remained in style as a general exclamation of surprise. It is a favorite expression of Bart Simpson on the animated television program *The Simpsons*.
- **curl:** the breaking part of a wave that curls over the rest of it, forming a tunnel.
- **freeboarding:** riding a surfboard while being pulled by a boat.
- **go over the falls:** to get caught in a breaking wave.
- **gremlin:** an apprentice surfer.
- **heavies:** big, surfable waves.
- **ho-daddy:** an intruder on the scene; a wiseguy; a nonsurfer. Also *hodaddy, hodad,* or *hoedad*.
- **hotdogger:** an accomplished surfer.
- **jams:** loose, knee-length swim trunks worn by surfers, usually in bright Hawaiian prints.
- **kook:** a rank beginner, also called an *egg*.

➤ **mushing wave:** a wave that broke quickly, resulting in a short ride,

➤ **pearl:** to have the surfboard take a nosedive into the waves.

➤ **surfwagon:** a remodeled vintage truck or station wagon, usually wood-paneled, perfect for carrying several surfers and their boards.

➤ **toes over:** surfing by balancing on the front of the board with your toes hanging over the edge. This position gave greater speed, but was tricky to do without falling. It was also called *ten over* or *hang ten.*

➤ **wipe out:** to fall off the board; to crash.

GO-GO GIRLS AND GRANNIES

When the decade opened, demure knee-length shifts and bouffant skirts were in fashion, along with little **pillbox hats** and white gloves for formal occasions. By the mid-1960s, the youthquake had shaken up the fashion world. Beatles haircuts morphed into long, flowing locks on male hippies. Women could wear their hair very short, like the supermodel Twiggy, or very long. Either way, it had to be straight. Boxy, sharply cut silhouettes were in vogue, along with space-age materials like plastic and metal. Most amazing of all were skirt lengths, which ranged from floor-length to mid-thigh.

➤ **Afro:** 'fro for short. An African-American hairstyle that expressed **black pride** by leaving in the hair's natural curl. The cut could be short and sleek or very long and full. Afros were kept in shape with careful trimming and an **Afro rake,** a wide-toothed, picklike comb. The Afro eventually became a look for anyone with very curly hair, black or white.

➤ **baby doll dress:** a loose-fitting minidress, sometimes with puffed sleeves, meant to project an innocent, girlish image. It was worn with **baby doll shoes,** round-toed low-heeled shoes with an ankle strap.

➤ **beehive:** a very bouffant hairstyle for women, most popular at the beginning of the decade. A beehive was achieved by teasing the hair into a cotton candy–like tower and hairspraying it heavily. A whole generation of young women learned to sleep with their heads hanging off the edge of the bed to preserve the geometric perfection of their beehives.

➤ **Chelsea boots:** men's ankle boots, featuring square toes and slightly raised square heels, introduced to the United States by the Beatles.

➤ **dashiki:** a loose-fitting, over-the-hips shirt, worn mostly by men, with patterns modeled after African kente cloth, a traditional woven fabric with colorful geometric designs. Most people simply wore cotton printed with kente-type patterns, which was cheaper and more accessible. Dashikis were part of the move toward ethnic dress. African

Americans adopted them first, but later, anyone who wanted to create an appearance of multicultural trendiness might wear one. Native American wear, such as feather necklaces, silver and turquoise jewelry, and moccasins, was also popular during this time.

➤ **fringe:** a haircut introduced by the Beatles, which looked as though it had been cut along the edge of a pudding bowl.

➤ **funk:** a look that combined offbeat, usually loud clothing in unexpected ways; for example, striped bell-bottom trousers with an Edwardian velvet smoking jacket. Later, the word *funky* was applied to anything offbeat or a little weird. It had been a jazz term for decades, meaning 'old-time, authentic jazz'.

➤ **go-go boots:** calf-length or hip-length boots, usually in white leather, with a square toe and a low square heel. These were also called *disco boots*. **Go-go girls,** the first to adopt this footwear, were young women who danced at *discothèques,* usually on a raised platform or in a cage raised over the dance floor. The word *discothèque,* meaning 'a place where disk jockeys spin records', was formed from the French word for 'library', *bibliothèque.*

➤ **go-go ring:** a chunky, brightly colored plastic ring.

➤ **granny dress:** a long-skirted, long-sleeved, high-necked dress, usually in a print pattern and romantically decorated with ruffles and lace. Hippie chicks favored this style.

➤ **granny glasses:** glasses worn by men and women with thin wire frames and small, circular lenses, sometimes tinted pink or blue.

➤ **love beads:** long necklaces strung with cheap plastic or glass beads, worn by men and women.

➤ **maxi:** floor-length skirt or coat, first worn by hippies in the late 1960s. Maxicoats were especially popular. Many women wore them over miniskirts.

➤ **midiskirt:** a calf-length skirt, really more popular in the 1970s.

➤ **miniskirt:** a short, tight skirt falling about eight inches above the knee. British fashion designer Mary Quant introduced the look, which usually included boots. **Microminis** were even shorter and had to be worn with tights if the wearer was to maintain any semblance of decency.

➤ **Nehru jacket:** a slim-fitting, hip-length jacket with a banded collar, named for Jawaharlal Nehru, the Indian prime minister. Nehru jackets were very popular among men of all ages and political persuasions.

➤ **pillbox hat:** a round, flat-topped hat that look best perched atop a bouffant hairdo, a look of the early 1960s. First lady Jacqueline

Kennedy frequently wore pillbox hats, adding greatly to their fashion-ableness.

➤ **unisex:** a look that could be worn by both men and women, consisting mainly of long hair, flowing shirts, and bell-bottoms.

ONE GIANT LEAP FOR MANKIND

Throughout the decade, the National Aeronautics and Space Administration (NASA) concentrated on reaching the moon. The *Apollo 8* space capsule entered the moon's orbit on December 24, 1968. Less than a year later, on July 20, 1969, *Apollo 11* astronaut Neil Armstrong became the first human being to set foot on the surface of the moon. Thousands of thrilled viewers in the United States and around the world watched the landing on television. As Armstrong stepped out of the lunar module he remarked, "That's one small step for a man, one giant leap for mankind." As the newscasters described it, the moon landing was a real **space spectacular.**

These are some of the new words that Americans learned from newspaper and magazine accounts of the space program.

➤ **Apollonaut:** an astronaut who flew on the Apollo space missions, which took place throughout the 1960s and early 1970s.

➤ **Apollo suit:** a space suit worn by **Apollonauts.**

➤ **astrodog:** one of the dogs used in the Soviet space program.

➤ **astromonk:** one of the monkeys used in space experiments.

➤ **cosmodog:** an **astrodog** that had actually traveled through outer space.

➤ **Geminaut:** an astronaut who flew on the Gemini space missions between 1964 and 1967.

➤ **jet jockey:** a pilot who was exceptionally skilled at flying the spacecraft after it reentered the earth's atmosphere.

➤ **moon car:** a vehicle for zipping around the moon's surface. A jazzier term was **moon jitney.**

➤ **moonmobile:** a fanciful vehicle designed to carry several people over the moon's surface.

➤ **moonship:** a spaceship designed for travel to the moon.

➤ **moonsuit:** a space suit to be worn on the moon.

➤ **spacefaring:** exploring outer space, a term invented by space capsule builder James McDowell, analogous to *seafaring.*

➤ **space highway:** a safety zone below the Van Allen radiation belts where astronauts could circle the earth without fear of being affected by radiation from solar flares.

➤ **spacenik:** an airman who lived experimentally inside an oxygen mixture that was being considered for use in spaceships.

➤ **spacescape:** a view of outer space.

SIXTIES BUZZWORDS

Most of these buzzwords refer to dramatic cultural change, in keeping with the mood of the 1960s. Everyone from hippies to **swinging singles** certainly would have recognized them.

➤ **Camelot:** the name given to President John F. Kennedy's administration. It expressed the hopeful belief of the early 1960s that Americans could achieve anything if they tried. The allusion to King Arthur's fabled court also seemed to fit the youthful president and his group of young, idealistic advisors. Kennedy himself labeled his policies the **New Frontier.** In an early speech, he told Americans that "we stand today on the edge of a new frontier—the frontier of the 1960s. . . . "

➤ **Chicago Seven:** originally the *Chicago Eight,* eight men who were arrested in the aftermath of the 1968 Chicago riots. The riots started when thousands of protesters jammed the streets outside the Democratic Party's convention site. Several of the Chicago Eight were well-known to the sixties public. They included Black Panther Bobby Seale, Yippies Abbie Hoffman and Jerry Rubin, and Tom Hayden and Rennie Davis, founders of Students for a Democratic Society (SDS). The trial was noisy, crowded, and sensational.

Eight became seven when the presiding judge declared a mistrial for Bobby Seale and jailed him on contempt charges. He was the only member of the group to serve jail time. All were acquitted of the charges, or had their convictions overturned.

➤ **Cuban Missile Crisis:** one of the most dangerous Cold War incidents, occuring in October 1962. When the administration got wind of Soviet missile installations in Cuba, President Kennedy demanded that the weapons be removed. For several days, the two countries balanced on the edge of a nuclear war. The turning point came when the U.S. Navy prepared to intercept Soviet merchant ships headed toward Cuba with more weaponry. The ships turned back before they reached the blockade. Finally, the Russians agreed to remove their missiles in exchange for an American promise not to invade Cuba and an understanding, not expressly stated, that American long-range missiles would be removed from Turkey (which they were). Kennedy's popularity reached a height after the Cuban Missile Crisis, but it cost Soviet Premier Khrushchev his career.

➤ **jet set:** wealthy people who spent their time jetting from one hot spot to the next. Commercial jet travel first became commonplace around the early 1960s. *Jet setters* were also known as *the Beautiful People.*

➤ **Nader's raiders:** young people working for lawyer Ralph Nader to expose unsafe or unhealthy business practices. Nader's raiders compiled studies on such disparate industries as agribusiness, the oil pipeline, the manufacture of TV sets, and meat processing. Nader was a pioneer of the consumer movement. His book *Unsafe at Any Speed* exposed the shoddy practices of the auto industry and led to the Highway and Traffic Safety Acts of 1966.

➤ **Stonewall:** the Stonewall Inn, a Greenwich Village gay bar that saw the beginnings of the gay liberation movement. On June 28, 1969, the police raided Stonewall. Police raids on gay bars were common because the bar owners were seldom granted liquor licenses. Usually, patrons went quietly, but this time they decided to fight back. Rioters filled the streets that night and the next. Newly radicalized gay men and lesbians formed the **Gay Liberation Front.** A broad spectrum of Americans were introduced to the homosexual meaning of *gay* for the first time, although people in the know had been using it since the nineteenth century.

➤ **swinging singles:** trendy, young, unmarried people. The sexual revolution made the single state a desirable way of life for the first time. Singles-only apartment buildings, resorts, cruises, bars, and other locales sprang up to accommodate the freewheeling lifestyle of the post–birth control pill crowd.

Not closet Trekkies.

Pet Rocks and Plumbers

American life took a turn for the frivolous in the seventies. During the **Me Decade,** people concentrated on encountering themselves rather than confronting the outside world. *Primal screams* echoed through the land, as the newly **self-realized** shed any inhibitions left over from the sixties. Those in search of quieter pursuits could stay at home and listen to their **eight-tracks** on the tape player. Or if they wanted a challenge, they could always spend time trying to solve their **Rubik's cubes.** **Trekfans** (or **trekfen**) were settled in front of the tube, catching syndicated reruns of their favorite show. If you weren't afraid of **future shock,** *Star Trek* could beam you up to a whole new universe.

How about getting up off the couch for a spot of **hustle**? **Disco** devotees were **psyched** for **body dancing,** back in fashion after a decade of free-form hopping. John Travolta dress-alikes in cream-colored **leisure suits** led their **foxy** ladies onto the floor while "Dancing Queen" boomed out a 4/4 beat over the sound system. Dresses swirled and gold chains glittered under the **disco ball. Mood rings** were a happy dark blue. It was **gravy!**

The seventies had something for everyone. For the antidisco crowd, there was **punk.** Male *punkers* used as much hair cream as male Bee Gees fans, but instead of slick modern pompadours they wore **liberty spikes. Skins** went even farther, with no hair at all. Girls wore **feather** haircuts. Although their clothes were often ripped, these early body piercers wore safety pins only on their faces.

Sidewalk surfing was another way to get off the couch. No longer a little-kid pastime, skateboarding attracted thousands of teenagers in the 1970s, including water surfers who switched to the sidewalk. When a hotdogger couldn't ride the waves, he (or occasionally she) could do **ollies, airs,** and **nose wheelies** on a hard surface. **Plank riders** had to be careful, though. If they **slammed** while getting **vertical,** they could pick up a bad case of **road rash.**

Speaking of road rash, a rash of CB operators hit the road during this decade. **Good buddies** with **handles** like *Gravy Train, Redneck Cowboy, Baby Cakes,* and *Bullfrog* tuned in for the **Smokey report. "Breaker, breaker good buddy**–any *plain wrappers* in sight or can I **put the hammer down?"**

"No **county mounties** on the road this morning."
"Ten-four Red Baron, **we gone.***"

College students in the mid- and late-seventies followed their elders in turning from society's improvement to self-improvement. After America pulled out of Vietnam, students could focus on their studies (although a few politically conscious teens took the time to **streak for impeachment** in 1974). To avoid turning into **pencil geeks,** students registered for **gut courses.** Only **gomes** felt like studying all the time. Nearly everyone occasionally pulled an all-nighter for some **heavy booking** before exams. Pretty **intense!** People were likely to **flake** after all that exertion, unless they were too **jacked** to fall asleep. The seventies did see one new cause—Mother Earth. Students all over the country observed the first **Earth Day** on April 22, 1970.

The decade's big political news, aside from our game of **ping-pong diplomacy** with China, came from a building in Washington, D.C., called the Watergate. At **that point in time,** Americans discovered **a cancer on the presidency.** With many **expletives deleted,** all the president's men revealed a remarkable cover-up of a **dirty tricks campaign** against the Democrats. Soon, the whole country was asking, *"What did the president know and when did he know it?"* The flood gates then opened for *-gate* words. Everything from **Altergate** to **Tailgate** came pouring out.

The first inklings of the new computer age sounded with the tap, tap, tapping of **keypunch operators.** Many of us dreamed of the time when we could purchase our first **computer kit.** Meanwhile, we were careful not to *fold, spindle, or mutilate* our **punch cards.** After all, **garbage in, garbage out.** We learned not to worry too much about the new technology though. We just figured it would all work out, and we'd **keep on truckin'** toward the future.

FRIVOLOUS FADS

In the seventies, people did lots of things just for fun. They dressed up for disco or got **structurally integrated** with **rolfing.** They bought **pet rocks** and **lava lamps** and **Rubik's cubes.** When the mood hit, they took off their clothes and **streaked** across campus. These are a few of the frivolous fads that occupied the seventies crowd:

➣ **body dancing:** a dance in which you used your whole body, swaying and moving your hips and flailing your arms. Couples danced either in parallel with, or touching, their partners. **Couple dancing** or **touch dancing,** with partners coordinating their steps, came back into favor in the seventies. The hottest touch dance was the *hustle,* made famous when Van McCoy recorded a song of that name in 1975. **Line dancing,** where dancers performed a series of steps in unison while standing side by side, was also popular.

The new dances were performed to **disco** music, a shortening of *discothèque.* Disco provided a continuous stream of music with a lively 4/4 beat, perfect for dancing. Song lyrics were light. Several songs, for example, Abba's "Dancing Queen," were about the dancing itself. Although musical sophisticates ridiculed disco in later decades, it was a powerful trend at the time. The 1977 movie *Saturday Night Fever,* starring John Travolta, helped popularize the disco lifestyle. Thousands of young people dreamed of spending their evenings gorgeously dressed, twirling to the music under the strobe lights and the mirrored, multifaceted **disco ball.**

➣ **eight-track (8-track):** a musical recording format that was very popular in the early 1970s, but has now virtually disappeared. An eight-track tape is an endless recording loop, similar to early film loops. The tape is divided into eight tracks, two of which play at a time. An eight-track tape deck was a must-have for early seventies teens, but, by 1975, the format was being replaced by technically superior cassette tapes. Nearly all recording labels stopped making eight-tracks by the early eighties. They're now available only as collector's items for diehard fans.

➣ **lava lamp:** a lamp with a base that appears to contain molten lava. The original lava lamp was invented in the 1960s by an Englishman named Edward Craven Walker. Two American businessmen saw the lamp at a German trade show and bought the U.S. distribution rights. They called it the Lava Lite. The lamp base contained Lava, a secret, patented substance

A lava lamp.

colored red or white, and a blue or yellow liquid. When a light bulb at the bottom of the lamp base was turned on, it heated up the lava, which moved up and down in the liquid.

Lava lamps fit right into the psychedelic lifestyle of the late sixties and early seventies. Once called "sexy things" by their inventor, they were an essential part of living room decor for swinging singles. These lamps are still being manufactured, although they are not as wildly trendy as they were in the 1970s.

➤ **mood ring:** a ring containing heat-sensitive liquid crystals that supposedly changed color with the wearer's mood. Invented by a New Yorker named Joshua Reynolds, the rings actually responded to body heat. Mood rings came with an instruction sheet that explained what the colors meant: dark blue—happy; green—relaxed and normal; amber—slightly nervous; gray—very nervous; black—highly stressed.

PUNK

An antidote to disco was the late seventies **punk** movement. The movement started among young working-class Londoners, and arrived in the United States around 1978. Punk rock was experimental music that prided itself on being raw and unsophisticated. It was characterized by the **wall of sound,** created with repeated guitar strumming, and lyrics that were meant to shock. The best known early punk band was the Sex Pistols. Others included the Clash, the Ramones, Television, and Siouxsie and the Banshees.

Punks were angst-ridden and nihilistic. They wore secondhand clothing in a jumble of styles and patterns. They ripped the knees of their jeans and poked safety pins through their cheeks. Men wore their hair in stiff spikes called **liberty spikes** or in a **Mohawk,** shaved on the sides and standing in a brush down the center of their heads. Women, sometimes known as **punkettes,** wore short, wispy **feather** haircuts. They highlighted their scanty locks with orange or puce streaks. **Skinheads,** also called *skulls, peanuts, boiled eggs,* or *cropheads,* dispensed with haircuts entirely in favor of shaved heads. If slightly grown out, they were **suedeheads.** *Skins* wore short, tight pants and Doc Marten work boots. Favorite *punker* activities while listening to music were *thrashing,* dancing the *pogo,* and **slam dancing—body dancing** with a real impact. By the 1980s, punk had morphed into **new wave,** a more conventional rock music style exemplified by such bands as the Talking Heads and Blondie.

➤ **pet rock:** the ultimate in easy-care pets, ideal for the self-absorbed seventies. The pet rock inspiration came to Gary Dahl, a California ad man, in 1975. He packaged a smooth, gray pebble from Rosarita Beach, Mexico, in a box shaped like a pet carrying case. He threw in a *Pet Rock Training Manual,* offering advice on such topics as how to housebreak your new pet (set it on a newspaper). Within a few months, Dahl had sold more than one million pet rocks for $3.95 apiece. Fickle Americans soon progressed to the next fad, but not before dozens of copycats rolled onto the market, along with support services like pet rock obedience lessons.

➤ **Rubik's cube:** a mathematical toy invented by Hungarian architecture professor Ernö Rubik. The cube was divided into three rows, with each row divided into three small cubes called **cubies,** for a total of nine cubies on each side of the main cube. The rows could be rotated

The word *punk* has been around since the seventeenth century. It has had many meanings, mostly negative. Its earliest usage was as a nickname for 'a young female prostitute'. At the turn of the twentieth century, the word meant 'something worthless, rotten, or inferior'. *Feeling punk* meant 'feeling low and miserable'. (See the first chapter, "Oh You Kid.") This meaning probably derived from the earlier use of *punk* as slang for 'touchwood'. Touchwood is rotting wood that burns easily. A *punk knot* in a tree indicates that the wood inside is rotten. From the nineteenth century, soldiers and hoboes used the jargon term *punk and plaster* to mean 'bread and margarine'.

Punk has also indicated 'a weak or unsatisfactory male' since the beginning of the twentieth century. The word sometimes had homosexual overtones, as when it referred to a hobo's young male companion. By the 1930s, *punk* was also a common label for hooligans or small-time criminals. In the 1950s, it usually referred to a juvenile delinquent. To *punk out* was 'to back out of a plan'. More recently, it has meant 'a young male prison inmate who is sexually victimized by older prisoners'.

Punks were no doubt pleased to embrace the antisocial connotations that came with their label. Ironically, they gave the word some respectability as the name of a genuine cultural trend.

both horizontally and vertically. Each face of an untouched Rubik's cube was a single bright color. As the player twisted the cube's rows, the colors got mixed up. The trick was to twist the rows back to their original positions, a feat that struck most people as nearly impossible. Potential color combinations ran into the billions.

One teenage *cubemeister* solved the puzzle in 28 seconds, but thousands spent every spare moment twiddling with no good result. Some cube owners finally admitted defeat and purchased one of several books that provided the solution. Others eventually buried the fiendish cube in the back of the closet or even in the bottom of the trash. Although Rubik designed his cube in 1974, cubist madness reached a peak in the U.S. around 1981. The colorful cube is seldom seen in public these days.

➤ **rolfing:** a system of deep tissue massage invented by physiotherapist Ida P. Rolf. Technically called a **structural integration,** rolfing (sometimes capitalized) was meant to realign the body with gravity. Rolf believed that people's experiences and lifestyles were connected with bodily asymmetries. By changing from stooped to straight, from crooked to balanced, people could change their personalities and outlook. Rolfing was one of the many ways that those in search of self-actualization enhanced their chances of finding it.

➤ **streaking:** running through a public place naked. Streaking was the most anti-Establishment activity on the mid-1970s campus. Reportedly, it started at Florida State University in Tallahassee. By 1974, large numbers of college students across the country were dropping their drawers. Five **parastreakers** jumped naked out of a Cessna airplane over the University of Georgia campus. Shortly before Nixon resigned, University of Pennsylvania students held a *streak for impeachment.* Colleges vied for group streak or *streak-in* records, sometimes rallying more than 1,000 *nude-niks* (as *Newsweek* put it). At Florida State, where it all began, students organized the **Streakers Party** to run candidates in that year's student government election.

Streaking was not confined to college campuses. People streaked down streets, across basketball courts and baseball diamonds, and through public gatherings. A Pan American airlines passenger streaked through a jumbo jet during a flight from London to New York. Nudist colonies staged fully clothed *streaks.* One Los Angeles radio station announced **streaker alerts** whenever listeners called in with sightings. Streaking broke through to the big time when a man named Robert Opel dashed naked across the stage before a stunned audience at the 1974 Academy Awards. Like most seventies versions of **ballyhoo,** the streaking fad was as short-lived as it was popular. By 1975, the party was over.

WHEELIES

Plank riding, otherwise known as skateboarding, was a kid's activity until the seventies. Early skateboards were not very sophisticated. Anyone attempting a complicated maneuver was asking for **road rash,** bad damage to the skin. In 1973, skateboards acquired urethane wheels. These allowed serious **sidewalk surfers** to move at high speed and to control the board to a much greater degree. The first skate park, complete with a U-shaped ramp called a **half pipe,** was built in Florida in 1976, taking skateboarding off the street and propelling it toward major sport status. As the sport developed, skaters borrowed or invented words to describe what they were doing. Many of these have stayed more or less current as a seminal core of jargon for later generations of plank riders. Moves being performed in the seventies included:

➤ **airs:** bringing the skateboard completely off the ground, usually with the aid of a transitional ramp. *Air* is short for *aerial.*

➤ **bailing:** falling deliberately in order to avoid **slamming,** or crashing.

➤ **berts:** a move named after surfer Larry Bertleman, in which the skater leans backward with one hand on the ground and moves the board in a circle or part-circle.

➤ **coffins:** riding while lying face-up on the board, a variation of a surfing move.

➤ **getting vertical:** what most people would call "getting horizontal," riding up the side of the ramp so that the skater was vertical to the side (and horizontal to the ground). Various tricks are performed while vertical.

➤ **goofy foot:** an old surfer expression that means riding with the right foot forward. Goofy footed skateboarders use the left foot to push. **Regular foot** or **natural foot** means using the right foot to push, the natural way for most right-handed people to skate.

➤ **inverts:** one-handed handstands, with the skater holding the board in the free hand, then landing on the board and continuing to skate.

➤ **nose wheelies:** riding on the board's two front wheels. A **heelie** means riding on the two back wheels.

➤ **ollies:** lifting the board off the ground by shifting your weight and tapping the board's tail on the ground.

➤ **pearling:** falling off the board, another surfing term.

BEAM ME UP, SCOTTY

In 1966 the starship USS *Enterprise* sailed out of the twenty-third century onto American television screens, and the future was at hand. Not just the future of the universe, but the future of science fiction programs. *Star Trek*, created by Gene Roddenberry, followed the adventures of the *Enterprise* crew, a mixed bag of Earthlings with one or two aliens. While exploring the galaxy, they encountered civilizations from around the known universe and helped solve their problems. Shows often alluded to events and issues important to 1960s Americans, such as racism.

Canceled after only three seasons, *Star Trek*'s real life began in 1970 with syndicated reruns. It gained a large following of devoted fans who published **trekzines** and organized **cons. Trufen** milled around in front of TV news cameras, wearing the traditional uniforms of the *Star Fleet*. Several decades later, television airwaves and movie theaters are still offering versions of *Star Trek* through nearly a dozen movies and four spinoff series.

Star Trek acquainted audiences with some new science-fictional technical terms. For example, starships were powered with *dilithium crystals. Warp drive* propelled the ships at *warp speed,* faster than the speed of light. The ship's *transporter beamed* people from one place to another by converting their matter into energy, then rematerializing them at their destination.

Viewers were enthralled with the transporter, operated by Mr. Scott, the ship's engineer. Before long, bumper stickers appeared with the request *"Beam me up, Scotty. There's no intelligent life on this planet."* Sadly, according to *The Oxford Dictionary of 20th Century Quotations,* no character ever said "Beam me up, Scotty." The closest anyone came was ship's captain James T. Kirk, who once said "Beam us up, Mr. Scott."

Even more interesting than the language of *Star Trek* was the language of *Star Trek* fans. Besides gathering for conferences, **Trekkers** wrote and read fan magazines. Many fans kept up lively correspondences through **LoC,** or letters of comment to their favorite **fanzines.** Most of their slang took the form of shortened and blended words. This abbreviated style is typical of the jargon of science fiction fans. Here is a sample:

➤ **BNF:** big-name fan, someone who is well-known in the world of *Star Trek* fandom.

➤ **closet Trekkie:** someone who watched the program secretly and was not involved in fan activities.

➤ **con:** a convention, also used in combinations such as **fancon** (a convention produced by fans), **trekcon** (a convention only for *Star Trek* fans as opposed to other sf, or science fiction, fans), and **concom** (conference committee).

➤ **fanac:** fan activities.

➤ **fanfic:** fiction written by fans, also called *trekfic.* A large amount of fiction was (and is) produced based on the series' characters.

➤ **fifth generation fan:** a recent fan who was not on the scene when fan clubs and magazines were originally being organized.

➤ **ish:** an issue of a magazine.

➤ **LoC:** a letter of comment, a letter to a fan magazine's editor.

➤ **neofan:** a serious new fan, learning the ropes of fandom.

➤ **STrekdom:** *Star Trek* fandom.

➤ **trekfan:** a *Star Trek* fan, with the plural **trekfen,** based on the alteration *man/men.* Totally committed fans were known as **trufen.** A variation was **STrekfan. Fen** was also used on its own.

➤ **Trekkie:** a *Star Trek* fan. Although nonfans used the term *Trekkie* innocently, fans considered it disrespectful. It derives from *trekkie bopper,* analogous with the sixties term *teeny bopper.* Trufen preferred the designation **Trekker.**

➤ **Welcommittee:** a welcoming, or service, committee for new fans. The largest one was the Star Trek Welcommittee, usually shortened to **STW.**

➤ **zine:** a fan magazine. Other compounds were **crudzine** (a badly written zine), **fanzine** (a magazine produced by a fan), **letterzine** (a magazine that published only fan letters), and **Trekzine** (a *Star Trek* **fanzine**). *Zine* was not exclusively a Trekker usage—other science fiction fans were already using it as early as the 1930s. It now has the more general meaning of a special interest magazine, typically produced by amateurs out of devotion to their topic.

CHIC IN THE SEVENTIES

Style in the seventies was very individual, following the general mood of the times. Even more so than in the sixties, people expressed themselves through their choice of outfits. Women could opt for the romantic gypsy look or a polished pantsuit. Batiking and tie-dyeing were popular, and ethnic wear was still in vogue. Long sideburns were popular for men. They wore their hair any length. So did women. By the end of the decade, everyone owned a pair of blue jeans, although Grandpa's might be made out of polyester.

➤ **army surplus:** an antifashion first adopted by a handful of teenagers, later embraced by **skinheads.** Skins favored nylon flight jackets and army boots. Other popular items were leather bomber jackets, navy pea coats, and army fatigues. Eventually, army surplus reached the mainstream. Those who wanted to wear olive drab and camouflage clothing didn't have to shop for it at actual army surplus stores anymore, it was available everywhere.

➣ **bell-bottoms:** denim jeans with legs that belled out at the bottom, a style that first became popular in the late sixties. Bell-bottoms were originally sailors' clothing, designed to be easily shed if their wearer fell into the water. Bells were for hippies in the sixties, but by the seventies everyone had a personalized pair. People decorated their jeans with embroidery, patches, or metal studs, or they widened the bottoms of the legs by sewing in colorful fabric triangles. Many jeans had waistlines that hugged the hips. A style with enormous legs was known as **elephant bells.** Near the end of the decade, the look was toned down to mildly belled pants called **flares.** By this time, flares were being sold in department stores everywhere, and could no longer be considered a radical look. Flared pants went away for a while, but returned in the nineties as high fashion.

➣ **body suit:** a one-piece outfit made of a stretchy fabric like spandex. Also called *body stockings,* these were usually worn underneath a skirt. Their popularity partly reflected the new fad for exercise. They were practical garments for disco dancing, skating, skateboarding, and aerobics classes. Television heroines and villains like Catwoman and Emma Peel of *The Avengers* popularized leather versions called **catsuits.**

➣ **bondage trousers:** a punk style designed by Malcolm McLaren and Vivienne Westwood, in which the trousers were tied together behind the knees.

➣ **Dr. Scholl's:** wooden-bottomed, nearly flat women's sandals with a broad leather strap across the top. The strap was red, white, or blue. The sandal, designed by orthopedic specialist Dr. William Scholl, was meant to tone the leg and foot as a woman walked. These shoes were invented in 1961, but reached their greatest popularity in the seventies.

➣ **earth shoes:** a leather lace-up shoe, designed so the heel was lower than the toe. Like **Dr. Scholl's,** these shoes were meant to be healthy for the foot and leg. They were created by a Danish yoga instructor named Anne Kals. Their introduction into the United States coincided with the first **Earth Day** (see "Seventies Buzzwords").

➣ **funky chic:** the fashion of not being in fashion, exemplified by socialites wearing ratty jeans and work shirts. No matter how astoundingly expensive such an outfit was, the wearer could still pretend that she was dressing for comfort and practicality rather than style. Funky chic evolved into **radical chic,** which required the further step of rubbing stylishly clad elbows with the proletariat. The best-known example of this style was the trend of inviting a few Black Panthers to one's

East Side apartment for drinks. Radically chic dressers aimed for a **countercultural** look, donning army surplus and faded denim to show their identification with the people. Both *funky chic* and *radical chic* were coined by the writer Tom Wolfe.

➧ **glam rock:** a rock music style that featured musicians in flashy, sexy clothes. The look was androgynous—both sexes wore tight, seductive clothes in slinky or shiny fabrics, glittery makeup, and gorgeous hair, sometimes dyed strange colors like orange. Glam rockers included David Bowie, Elton John, and Suzie Quattro.

➧ **hot pants:** extremely short, tight shorts, often worn with boots and stitched out of plush fabrics like satin, crushed velvet, and suede. Hot pants were just the outfit for an evening of disco.

➧ **leisure suit:** men's double-knit polyester suit, designed to be both comfortable and stylish. Leisure suits sometimes came with shirt-jackets rather than blazers. They were tailored in an assortment of colors, including pastels and plaids, and were worn with color-coordinated belts. Neckties were never part of the ensemble. After thirty years, leisure suits are the definitive icon of the seventies.

➧ **moon boots:** boots with thick rubber soles and nylon uppers, designed to look like an astronaut's boots (except that they came in more colors).

➧ **palazzo pants:** very wide, flowing trousers—at-home wear for women.

➧ **peasant skirt:** a long or midi-length skirt, usually made of soft cotton and printed with traditional Eastern European or Indian designs. Peasant skirts were part of the **gypsy look,** which meant softly draped skirts, romantically ruffled or embroidered blouses with wide flowing sleeves, shawls, bangle bracelets, and headscarves.

➧ **platform shoes:** women's shoes, usually sandals, with a very thick sole and a correspondingly high, wide heel. Soles were commonly made of stacked layers of wood or cork. Platforms had been stylish in the thirties, but came back in the seventies much higher off the ground. A two- or three-inch sole was typical.

➧ **shag:** a haircut that was short on top with long, wispy pieces over the neck and ears. Both men and women wore shags. They were a favorite cut of rock stars, from teen pop idol David Cassidy to glam rocker David Bowie. Jane Fonda popularized the cut for women. A short version, such as that worn by singer Rod Stewart, was called a **rooster.**

➧ **wedge:** a short, all-one-length woman's haircut, made famous by the 1976 figure skating gold medalist Dorothy Hamill. Wedges were for straight hair only. They were reminiscent of the traditional Victorian schoolboy's pudding bowl cut.

I HEAR THAT

Seventies teens were not much like sixties teens, but they did share a certain amount of vocabulary. Words like *cool* and *far out* were still used. Even *groovy* hung around for a while. The Me Generation also invented some slang of its own, although skimpier and more ephemeral than that of the previous era.

ME DECADE

Young people who spent the sixties grappling with the world's problems found a more interesting source of unresolved conflicts in the seventies—themselves. It was the dawn of the **Me Decade.** Sharp social observer Tom Wolfe nailed the era's chief feature, self-absorption, in an essay titled "The Me Decade and the Third Great Awakening." Wolfe compared the 1970s discovery of the inner self with the two Great Awakenings, American religious revivals of the eighteenth and nineteenth centuries. These evangelical movements were characterized by public revival meetings, where the preacher accused the congregation of sinning and they repented loudly and emotionally.

Seventies seekers of inner clarity did not visit revival tents—they attended **encounter groups.** Encounter groups were a form of group therapy that started in the late 1960s. Sessions were supposed to help individuals uncover their true selves by stripping away the culturally imposed layers of personality. Group members "helped" each other through criticism and haranguing, often leaving the victims in tears but promising to repent of their old, repressed ways. These harrowing sessions were worth it because they were a chance for each participant to command other group members' undivided attention for long stretches. People spent whole weekends focusing on the Real Me.

Self-realization and **consciousness-raising** were two important aspects of seventies self-help. The term *self-realization* was from the late nineteenth century, but gained its widest usage during the Me Decade. It meant 'realizing one's full potential as a person'. Consciousness-raising was used to raise someone's awareness of his or her particular needs. It also described the process of politicizing people. Feminist groups organized consciousness-raising sessions to sensitize women to their own and other women's social problems.

Popular places to encounter yourself and others were at Primal Scream Therapy, Lifespring, est (Erhard Seminars Training), and the Esalen Institute in Big Sur, California.

➤ **A.F.A.:** a signature that stood for *A Friend Always.*

➤ **all right!:** I agree or approve.

➤ **check you later:** good-bye.

➤ **dy-no-mite!:** terrific, really great; an exclamation popularized by the *Good Times* television show character J.J.

➤ **flake:** a disappointment or a failure; a strange, crazy person. To **flake** people **out** was the same as **freaking** them **out,** that is, shocking or scaring them. To **flake out** could also mean 'to pass out from exhaustion'. To **flake off** was 'to go away'. *Flake* to mean 'someone weird' was slang as early as the 1950s, but the word had much more flexible usage in the 1970s.

➤ **flip out:** to go crazy or lose control, another version of **freaking out.**

➤ **foxy:** attractive and sexy, usually applied to a young woman.

➤ **gravy:** excellent, cool, really fun. The word could be from an expression popular around 1910, *That's the gravy* or *That's some gravy.* Alternatively, it could be a play on *groovy.*

➤ **gut course:** an easy class that could be passed without studying. In some parts of the country, it was called a *cake course* or a *mick course* (short for Mickey Mouse).

➤ **I hear that:** I understand and agree with what you're saying.

➤ **intense!:** an all-purpose response that could mean anything from "that's terrific news" to "I heard what you just said."

➤ **jacked:** anxious or nervous.

➤ **jive turkey:** an insincere or phony person, originally African-American slang. Later, it just meant 'any kind of a jerk'. Hipsters used the expression as early as the fifties, but it didn't become widely popular until the seventies.

➤ **let it slide:** let's just forget it.

➤ **let's book:** let's leave.

➤ **lose it:** to lose your temper or your sanity.

➤ **mellow out:** to relax or calm down. Mellowing out could be achieved naturally or through taking drugs.

➤ **pencil geek:** someone who studied a lot. At different schools, this unpopular type was also known as a *cereb, spider, grub, weenie, wonk,* or *gome* (short for Gomer Pyle, the earnest, well-meaning, if not over-bright star of the late 1960s sitcom, *Gomer Pyle, U.S.M.C.*). At M.I.T., overstudiers were called **tools. Augers** were boring tools.

➤ **psyched:** excited.

➤ **psych out:** to astonish or scare someone; to play with a person's mind. *Psych!* meant 'Fooled you!'

➤ **scab:** an unappealing person, apparently unrelated to the union meaning of *scab* as a strike breaker.

➤ **scope out:** to look over or stare at. Scoping out was usually directed toward an object of romantic attraction.

➤ **see you on the flipside:** I'll see you later. *Flipside* was trucker and bus driver slang for 'the return trip'. More generally, the flipside meant 'the opposite of something'.

➤ **shed:** to study hard for a test, short for *woodshed*. This activity was also known as *heavy booking, megabooking,* or *speeding.*

➤ **solid:** a response to a suggestion, meaning 'okay, let's definitely do it'.

➤ **swift:** smart, clever. Sometimes used sarcastically.

➤ **throat:** a student who aimed for an A at any cost, even that of *megabooking.* Short for *cutthroat.*

➤ **wuss:** a feeble, indecisive person; a weakling.

BREAKER, BREAKER, GOOD BUDDY

During the mid-1970s, the long-haul trucker emerged as an American folk hero. C.W. McCall's country-music song "Convoy," about the exploits of a 1,000-truck convoy, was a nationwide hit. Part of the **four-wheeler's** new awareness of eighteen-wheelers came from the popularity of Citizens' Band radio, usually known by its abbreviation, *CB*.

CB radios were already standard equipment for truckers. Other drivers began to see their advantages after the national speed limit dropped from 65 mph to 55 mph in 1974. A large part of the conversation among CBers concerned where **Smokey** was holed up with the radar gun, and whether the driver could expect to get **green stamps** if he or she **put the hammer down.** By 1976, more than two million people held CB radio licenses. Thousands of others operated illegally while the FCC processed the huge backlog of applications. Even drivers without **ears** were familiar with the basics of CBers' jargon, which is highly allusive and sometimes made up on the spur of the moment.

SMOKEY REPORT

Any kind of police or highway patrols were known as **bears,** or **Smokies,** possibly because state troopers' headgear looks similar to that of the Forest Service's Smokey Bear. A number of terms took off from these two words:

➤ **bear bait:** a speeding car not equipped with a CB. These foolish drivers were bound to be pulled over, distracting the bears from speeding trucks coming up behind. They were also called *bear food.*

- **bear bite:** a speeding ticket.
- **bear in the air:** a police helicopter, also called *sky bear.*
- **bear story:** a report over the CB radio on police locations.
- **bear trap:** a police radar setup.
- **little bears:** local police.
- **polar bear:** a state trooper.
- **Smokey report:** a report on police whereabouts, same as *bear story.*
- **Smokey on rubber:** a moving patrol car.
- **Smokey on the ground:** police who were out of the patrol car.
- **Smokey with ears:** a police car equipped with a CB radio. Any driver equipped with a CB radio was described as having **ears.**

HELLO AND GOODBYE

A transmission was initiated with some form of **break** or **breaker–** *break-10, break-21, break, break,* or *break* followed by the channel number. Speakers then identified themselves by FCC call number and **handle,** their on-air nickname. Handles were colorful and self-descriptive. Some examples are *Country Bumpkin, Red Baron, Happy Hour, Gravy Train, Hot Lips, Double Trouble, Banana Man, Baby Cakes,* and *Goody Two Shoes.* Speakers asking for a response would say *back, back at you, bring it on, come back, come on, give me a shout,* or *go breaker.*

Good-byes were more varied than hellos. They included *clear, clear and rolling, down and gone, I'm through, out, we up, we down, we clear, we gone.* (Truckers had a habit of dropping the verb *to be* or using it uninflected, as in *we be rollin'.*) Some signoffs were more elaborate: *keep 'em between the ditches; keep the rolling side down and the shiny side up; nothing but a green light and a white line.* Many signoffs sent good wishes, often expressed through combinations of threes and eights, considered "good numbers": *threes and eights; stack them eights; eights and other good numbers; happy numbers.*

Here are some other useful terms for CB novices:

- **advertising:** a police car with its lights on.
- **backslide:** the return trip.
- **backyard:** the road behind the driver.
- **bob-tailing:** said of a car without a CB following a car or truck that does have one.
- **brown paper bag:** unmarked police car, also called a *plain wrapper.*
- **Charlie:** yes; also *Charlie Brown.*
- **collect call:** a radio call for a specific CB user.
- **convoy:** a procession of vehicles with CBs, driving together and keeping in touch via radio.

➤ **copy:** to understand the message, as in *do you copy?*

➤ **coupon:** a speeding ticket.

➤ **double buffalo:** the 55 mph speed limit, a reference to the buffalo-head nickel; also *double nickel.*

➤ **four-wheeler:** a car or small truck.

➤ **flip flop:** a return trip (see **see you on the flipside,** in the "I Hear That" section).

➤ **front door:** the first vehicle in a convoy. The last vehicle was the **back door.**

➤ **good buddy:** a trucker salutation that became enormously popular among other CBers and even non-CBers.

➤ **green stamp:** a speeding ticket.

➤ **left shoulder:** the opposite direction.

➤ **let the hammer down:** to go full speed ahead.

➤ **mercy:** one of the few exclamations that was legal over the air.

➤ **negatory:** no.

➤ **put the pedal to the metal:** to accelerate.

➤ **rocking chair:** the middle rigs in a convoy.

KEEP ON TRUCKIN'

Keep on truckin', meaning something like 'hang in there' or 'keep persevering', was a popular phrase of encouragement in the 1970s. Underground comic artist Robert Crumb created a "Keep on truckin'" poster showing a man with exaggeratedly long legs and large feet, strolling toward the edge of the poster. The phrase eventually turned up on greeting cards, T-shirts, and graffiti-laden walls. The young, the hip, and the casual adopted it as a way of saying "good-bye."

The term *trucking* did not come from truckers. It originated with railroad porters and baggage carriers as a way of saying 'move along', a reference to the baggage trucks used in railroad stations. An off-duty porter might say to his friends, "I think I'll truck on home." Dancer Bilo Russell invented a jazz step in the 1930s that became a common way of exiting from the stage. This move was also called *trucking. Trucking* was a popular dance in the thirties, based on a slow, ambling movement.

Since truckers were trendy during the seventies, the public naturally connected them with *keep on truckin'.* Bumper stickers began appearing on trucks of the four-wheel variety, and even on cars. It's more than likely that some of those trucks carried CB operators.

➤ **shake the leaves:** to check the road ahead for police or obstructions so other CB users could be warned.

➤ **smile and comb your hair:** there's radar up ahead.

➤ **ten-code:** an on-air numerical code, originally used by the police to save time, later adopted by CBers. The most widely known code number was *10-4,* 'message received'.

WATERGATE AND OTHER -GATES

The Watergate affair, one of the biggest political scandals in American history, was a buzzword bonanza. As the fascinated public read yet another shocking revelation, or watched former White House aides self-destruct on television, they acquired a whole new vocabulary. If the expletives had not been deleted, they might have learned even more.

It all began quietly enough. Five men, including a member of the Committee to Reelect the President (CREP), were caught breaking into the Democratic Party's national campaign headquarters on June 17, 1972. The headquarters was located in the Watergate, a large office and apartment complex in Washington, D.C. President Nixon denied that he or any of his staff were involved. This facade held until the burglars' trial early in 1973, when one of the convicted men, James McCord, implicated CREP and others closely connected to the president.

The Senate organized a Select Committee on Presidential Campaign Activities, better known as the Watergate Committee. In April 1973, Nixon was forced to fire several staff members whose complicity in the burglary and cover-up was clear. They included the head of CREP, John Mitchell, White House Chief of Staff, H. R. Haldeman, and Special Assistant on Domestic Affairs, John Erlichman. The president also fired White House counsel John Dean for suggesting to the Watergate Committee that Nixon himself had been involved from the beginning. Under pressure, Nixon appointed a special prosecutor, Archibald Cox, to investigate the matter. He assured the American people, "*I am not a crook.*"

Disaster struck for the White House when aide Alexander Butterfield revealed in televised hearings that the president had secretly installed a tape system to record all Oval Office conversations. It appeared that Senator Howard Baker's question "*What did the president know and when did he know it?*" would be answered at last. At first, President Nixon stood firm, but finally the Supreme Court forced him to turn over his tapes to the the special prosecutor. After the tapes revealed that Nixon had been aware of his staff's criminal activities, the House Judiciary Committee drew up articles of impeachment.

Nixon resigned the presidency at noon on August 9, 1974. He left a lasting impact, not least on the American language.

➤ **at this point in time:** now. *At that point in time* meant 'then'. These expressions were favorites of White House counsel John Dean, who used them repeatedly when he appeared before the Watergate Committee in June 1973. Later, they were widely parodied.

➤ **big enchilada:** John Erlichman's characterization of John Mitchell, heard on a White House tape. Erlichman's point was that Mitchell should be the fall guy for the Senate committee because, as the head of CREP, he was the big enchilada. Having nabbed Mitchell, the committee would presumably look no further.

➤ **cancer on the presidency:** John Dean's description of the cover-up, also heard on tape. Dean thought the cover-up maneuvers were eating away at Nixon's presidency and would eventually destroy it.

➤ **"creep":** preferred pronunciation of CREP, the Committee to Reelect the President, coined not by a frothing liberal, but by Republican National Committee chair Robert Dole.

➤ **Deep Throat:** the anonymous source who passed information about Watergate to *Washington Post* reporters Carl Bernstein and Bob Woodward. Woodward named their deep-background source after a highly popular 1970s pornographic movie. Deep Throat's identity is still unknown. Woodward claimed that he was someone highly placed in the Executive branch. Others have suspected that Deep Throat is really a composite of several members of the government.

➤ **dirty tricks:** tactics that the Nixon administration used against Democratic opponents and other enemies. These included spying and circulating slanderous literature. A common way of using the expression was in *dirty tricks campaign*.

➤ **eighteen-minute gap:** actually an eighteen-and-a-half-minute gap in recorded White House conversations, due to several erasures on one of the subpoenaed tapes.

➤ **expletive deleted:** a parenthetical notation in the transcripts of the Oval Office tapes, indicating that an obscene word or phrase had been left out. There were many such notations. The extreme saltiness of the president's language was as shocking to some as anything else the tapes recorded.

➤ **plumbers:** nickname for the administration's Special Investigative Unit, which included E. Howard Hunt and G. Gordon Liddy. Nixon had appointed the plumbers to stop information leaks and to participate in dirty tricks. They were the chief planners of the Watergate break-in.

➤ **Saturday night massacre:** the events of October 20, 1973. When Watergate special prosecutor Archibald Cox subpoenaed a number of Oval Office tapes and other records, Nixon resisted strenuously, claiming the tapes were vital to national security. The court ordered the president to release the tapes. In a desperate move, Nixon decided to fire the special prosecutor. However, when Attorney General Elliott L. Richardson was asked to do so, he refused, then resigned. His deputy, William D. Ruckelshaus, did the same thing. Solicitor General Robert Bork finally agreed to conduct the firing. After the Saturday night massacre, Nixon's popularity plummeted. He eventually appointed a new special prosecutor, Leon Jaworski.

OTHER -GATES

Almost immediately after *Watergate* became synonymous with political scandal, news reporters became **gateniks.** Any piece of corruption worth noticing was awarded a *-gate*. And the practice is still alive. During the 2002 Winter Olympics figure skating competition, suspicions of rigged voting came to light—the press lost no time in dubbing the situation **skategate.**

The vigilant folks from the American Dialect Society recorded more than four dozen new words formed with *-gate* between the late seventies and early eighties. Some of the more interesting include:

➤ **Altergate:** the suspicious affair of some transcript changes made to remarks of two Republican state representatives at an environmental hearing.

➤ **Billygate:** the scandalous activities of Billy Carter, brother of President Jimmy Carter, alternatively labeled *Billy-goat,* for obvious reasons.

➤ **Debategate:** the discovery that Ronald Reagan's 1980 presidential campaign organization had somehow acquired the briefing book and other materials that Jimmy Carter used to prepare for his debates with Reagan.

➤ **Floodgate:** the inquiry into activities of Rep. Daniel J. Flood of Pennsylvania.

➤ **Gategate:** the excessive use of the suffix *-gate,* a linguistic scandal.

➤ **Goldingate:** the questionable dealings of New York City Comptroller Harrison Goldin.

➤ **H_2Ogate:** an abbreviation made up of the chemical formula for *water*, plus *-gate*.

➤ **Tailgate:** a U.S. Army colonel's order to cover up the prominent Datsun logo on the tailgate of government-owned pickup trucks.

> **Waste-watergate:** the failure of the Environmental Protection Agency to clean up hazardous waste sites, also called *Sewergate*.

And then we have the *water-* words: **waterbugger,** meaning someone who plants a hidden microphone; **waterbungler,** one of the people who bungled the break-in; **Watergaters,** the people involved in the Watergate break-in; **waterfallout,** the fallout from Watergate.

DO NOT FOLD, SPINDLE, OR MUTILATE

After World War II, the technology wizards started working on making computers practical for government and business use. Remington Rand produced the UNIVAC (Universal Automatic Computer) in 1951. It ran on vacuum tubes and filled a small room. Eventually, transistors replaced vacuum tubes, and then integrated circuits replaced transistors. Seventies computers were much smaller and less expensive than the first-generation models. Even so, few people imagined owning their own computers. Computing still took place at work or school, and was the province of what were not yet called computer nerds. Some of the terms they used in those early days are seldom heard anymore.

> **chad box:** a metal box about the size of a trash can, used for collecting chads, the bits of paper that were punched out of punch cards. *Chad* was an unfamiliar word to most Americans, especially after punch cards became obsolete for business use. The term made a surprise comeback during the 2000 presidential election when it appeared that **hanging chads,** still dangling by a corner from the voter's punched card, caused the card-reading machines to miscount some votes.

> **computer kit:** a kit for building a microcomputer cheaply at home. *Home computers* or *personal computers* were also available, but were not cheap or easy to use.

> **data sheet:** a special form used to record information that would later be *keypunched* and entered into the computer.

> **"end-of-file":** a notation at the bottom of a computer-printed page, indicating the end of a set of data.

> **floppy disk:** an 8-inch-square flexible disk made of mylar, used to store information for microcomputers. The term is still around, but becoming less used, as today's floppies are actually 3.5-inch disks encased in hard plastic. Also called a *diskette*.

> **GIGO:** garbage in, garbage out. *Garbage* was 'useless, mixed up output from the computer', usually due to a machine malfunction or

an incorrectly written program. *GIGO* was a sad reminder that computers are only as good as the people running them.

➤ **keypunching:** recording coded data on cards by punching small rectangular holes in them with a **keypunch machine.** This work was the business of **keypunch operators.** The computer's **card reader** transferred information from the punched cards to the computer's memory bank, then spit the cards into a **card stacker.** *Keypunch cards,* also called *punch cards* or *punched cards,* measured roughly 3 inches by 8 inches and were divided into eighty columns. One character of code was punched into each column. By the 1980s, punch cards were becoming obsolete. Eighties computer operators who were hopelessly out-of-date were described as having **eighty-column minds.**

DO NOT FOLD, SPINDLE, OR MUTILATE

Punch cards predated computers by more than a century. They were first invented in 1801 as a way of programming Jacquard looms to weave specific designs. American Herman Hollerith created a version of these cards for the 1890 census. They were both punched and read using manually operated machines. Business and government soon adopted the punch cards for record keeping and data analysis. In the 1950s, IBM developed a system for using the cards with computers. Then companies took the next logical step. They started sending punch cards directly to their customers, as bills to be returned with payment. The cards were also used for college student registration.

The public couldn't be trusted to treat their cards right, so punch cards were printed with instructions such as "Do not fold or bend this card." The prototype warning was **"Do not fold, spindle, or mutilate."** (This expression has outlasted its individual words. Modern readers know what folding and mutilating are, but spindling is much less common. It refers to the nearly obsolete business practice of impaling paid bills on an upright spike, or spindle.)

Punch cards were a familiar symbol of a computerized society in the sixties, especially to students, who were handed thick stacks of them on registration day. The cards seemed to represent a bureaucratic, regimented world where human beings were just so many numbers. Naturally, sixties people protested this state of affairs. By the 1970s, the antipunch card slogan was well-established: *Human being—do not fold, spindle, or mutilate.*

➤ **line printer:** a printer that printed out computer data, one full line at a time.

➤ **mainframe:** the part of the computer system that actually processed data, also called the *central processing unit (CPU)*. These days, *mainframe* generally refers to a large, complex computer system.

➤ **multiprogramming:** running two or more programs on one computer at the same time—now called **multitasking.**

➤ **reproducing punch:** a machine that duplicated stacks of punched cards.

➤ **wheel printer:** a printer where the printing element consisted of a large wheel of metal spokes, with a type character attached to the end of each spoke. Wheel printers were widely used until the early eighties. They were also called *daisy wheel printers* because the spokes of the print element looked like daisy petals.

SEVENTIES BUZZWORDS

Not all the seventies news was faddish and frivolous, as these buzzwords show.

➤ **Earth Day:** a day of environmental education events, first suggested in 1969 by Senator Gaylord A. Nelson and planned by lawyer and environmentalist Denis Hayes. The first Earth Day was held on April 22, 1970. Students around the country gathered to have their consciousness raised about the disastrous state of the environment. More than 20 million people participated. That same year, Congress created the Environmental Protection Agency and passed the Clean Air Act. Millions still get together every year to raise awareness, protest ecological destruction, and pick up litter.

➤ **future shock:** the physical and mental distress caused by too many rapid technological advances and the social changes that go with them. *Future Shock* was the name of a 1970 book by futurologist Alvin Toffler, in which he compared the stress of dealing with unfamiliar technology with culture shock. He also offered some strategies for coping with it.

➤ **hostage crisis:** the takeover of the U.S. Embassy in Tehran, Iran, and the holding of 53 Americans hostage by Iranian militants. The crisis lasted 444 days, from November 4, 1979, to January 21, 1981, when Iran released the hostages in return for the unfreezing of Iranian assets. Iran had been ruled since 1953 by the Shah Reza Pahlavi, who was friendly to the United States. His government was overthrown in January 1979. He was replaced by the radically anti-

Western Ayatollah Ruholla Khomeini. Khomeini was deeply anti-American, calling the United States "the Great Satan." The immediate cause of the embassy takeover was the exiled shah's entry into the United States for medical treatment.

The hostage crisis was a terrible blow to the Carter presidency. The president's inability to get the captives released for more than a year, together with a failed rescue attempt, were heavy factors in his loss of the 1980 election. The Republicans were afraid that Carter would pull off an **October surprise,** using his presidential powers to get the hostages released at a politically advantageous moment, but the surprise never materialized.

➤ **misery index:** the combined rates of inflation and unemployment. Jimmy Carter coined the term when campaigning against incumbent Gerald Ford during the 1976 presidential election. It came back to haunt him later, as the misery index shot up during his term of office. Another word associated with Carter's time in office is **stagflation,** the combination of a stagnant economy with inflation.

➤ **Pentagon Papers:** a top-secret report on America's involvement in the Vietnam War, commissioned by the Secretary of Defense, Robert McNamara. Dr. Daniel Ellsberg, one of the report writers who became disillusioned with the war, decided to take the papers public. *The New York Times* and the *Washington Post* began publishing excerpts in June, 1971. Americans were shocked to learn that their government had hidden or distorted many facts about the war. The embattled administration tried to get the papers suppressed, but the Supreme Court ruled that the government had not shown a compelling reason for their suppression. The Pentagon Papers added greatly to the already high level of antiwar feeling. They also contributed indirectly to Nixon's downfall. They were the spur for organizing the **plumbers,** whose first job was to try to discredit Dr. Ellsberg.

➤ **ping-pong diplomacy:** the first step in friendlier relations between the United States and the People's Republic of China, taken in 1971, when China invited the U.S. table-tennis (ping-pong) team to a competition. The invitation to the *ping-pong diplomats* was a historic event. The United States and China had not shared diplomatic relations since the rise of Mao Zedong and the communists in 1949. China followed their *ping-pong gambit* with an invitation to President Nixon, who visited the country in February 1972. Excited Americans started talking about *the spirit of ping-pong* and speculating about what would happen in the world *post-ping-pong.*

The alpha geek himself, Bill Gates.

Tubular Times

The eighties almost looked like the twenties, at least if you were look-ing down Wall Street. The market was bullish, and everyone rushed to get **in the money. Fronters** in **boiler rooms** were busy **dialing and smiling,** hoping to land a **mullet.** These **bucketeers** were real experts. They **plucked** more **chickens** than a poultry farmer. **Lobby lizards** fol-lowed the ticker tape closely before buying, while **Aunt Jane** clung to her blue-chip stock.

The real securities action was in the world of corporate raiding. Tender offers, inviting shareholders to sell, were anything but tender. They could be **blitzkrieg,** hitting the company with lightning speed, or **creeping,** a slower method. Companies who felt the **teddy bear pat** could fend off raiders with a **crown jewel defense** or a **lollipop.** If they were lucky, a **white knight** would gallop to the rescue. Otherwise, the pat turned into a **strong bear hug.**

And what did Wall Street **yuppies** and **buppies** spend their profits on? At least some of it went to **power dressing.** Both women and men donned **power suits** for long days at the investment firm, although daring female **yups** might change into a **mini-crinoline** or **balloon skirt** for big evenings out. If headed for the latest trendy Ethiopian place, they could go casual in **alligator shirts** and **duck shoes.** The **preppie look** was **majorly** hot with **fast trackers.**

Not everyone worked on Wall Street. **Hackers** came into their own during the eighties, as microcomputers appeared on every office desk-top. While ordinary folks were trying to figure out the difference between RAM and ROM, **turbo nerds** were way ahead with a language all their own. They kept their **bogometers** running to avoid spending time with those who lacked the proper **hackitude.**

Computer geeks weren't the only ones living on a different plane. A **New Age** was at hand—the Age of Aquarius, that is. Those seeking a **consciousness revolution** visited **power spots** to improve their **auras.** 169

Ascended masters didn't need to hop on a plane. They engaged in **astral travel** for an **out-of-body experience.** The less fully enlightened sat at the feet of mystics who **channeled spirit guides,** usually for a hefty fee. Ramtha, Mafu, and others guided **New Agers** through many life trials. If asked, they might even advise disciples about when to buy low and sell high. When spirit guidance wasn't readily available, believers could at least tune up their **chakras** with a crystal or two. These chunky quartzes were good for everything from boosting energy to healing emotional wounds. And a small designer crystal was only $100.

Dudespeak and **Valspeak** were **happenin'** in the eighties. **Poindexters** didn't get it, but if you were **vogue,** it was **killer.** All your typical dude wanted was a little **face time** with a **bodacious dudette,** a few **serious** albums, and a **most excellent homey** to hang with. **Pre-car Valley Girls** thought a dude was like, **totally awesome** if he owned a black VW Rabbit convertible. If he had the **billys** to spend on a **bitchen** babe, it was like, **tubular, way rad,** right? But like, okay, what if the guy turns out to be a **slimeball?** I am totally not going out with some **Aqua Velva geek. Gag me with a spoon!** It's like, **grody to the max!**

Meanwhile, on the opposite coast from the San Fernando Valley, **b-boys** in baggy pants and **kicks** with the laces untied were out on the street showing their **breakin' moves—applejacks** and **six-steps** to start with. **Toprock** and **downrock** were **chilly the most.** The new music and street culture from the Bronx was called **hip-hop,** and it was **def. Crews** danced and **rapped** clever rhyming lyrics, **scratching** records to keep the beat. Rappers like Afrika Bambaataa and Run DMC stacked up the **cheese** with their **fresh** sound. Hip-hop was **all that.**

Americans hardly noticed when the eighties segued into the nineties. The century was speeding to its close, but we were having too good a time to put on the brakes. **Boo-yah!**

IN THE MONEY

In 1980, Ronald and Nancy Reagan entered the White House. For the first time since the early sixties, luxury and elegance were once again fashionable. Eighties young people admitted freely that they were **fast trackers,** out to earn some big dollars. One way to do so was to make a killing on the stock market. All sorts of people who didn't know a junk bond (risky, but high-yield) from a penny stock (cheap at less than $1 a share) began playing the market. **Odd lotters** and other amateur traders talked about being **in the money** when exercising their stock options would result in a profit.

Late-eighties newspapers splashed **insider trading** scandals across the front page, revealing that some investors had gotten impressively rich by illegally trading on confidential information. This news barely dented the public's market enthusiasm. Neither did **Black Monday,** the spectacular crash of October 19, 1987, when the Dow Jones Industrial Average dropped a record 508 points.

TENDER AND NOT-SO-TENDER OFFERS

The late 1970s and early 1980s saw an increasing trend of corporate raiders staging hostile takeovers of desirable companies. Every step of the process involved some highly descriptive slang.

➤ **blitzkrieg tender:** tendering an offer (that is, presenting it for formal acceptance) with a lightning speed reminiscent of Hitler's *blitzkrieg* attacks, thereby taking the target company by surprise.

➤ **blue-chip raider:** formerly "gentlemanly" blue-chip company that decided to grab a piece of the hostile takeover action. Ordinary raiders were called **pirates, buccaneers,** and **black knights.**

➤ **creeping tender:** almost the opposite of a **blitzkrieg,** in which the raider gradually and secretly amassed a large block of the victim's stock.

➤ **greenmail:** blackmail for greenbacks, buying a company's stock and then offering to sell it back to the shareholders at an inflated price. A subtler, camouflaged version was called **camomail.**

➤ **marriage broker:** the financial go-between who collected a fee if a merger succeeded.

➤ **sex without marriage:** takeover negotiations that didn't lead to a merger. Two companies that successfully merged were **brought to the altar.**

➤ **showstoppers:** questions about a target company that would halt a takeover, such as possible antitrust issues.

➤ **sleeping beauty:** the target company, passively awaiting takeover by anyone powerful enough to cut through the briar hedge.

➤ **strong bear hug:** a tender offer that named a specific price, so had to be made public. This tactic backed the victim into a corner because a company's directors have a responsibility to the shareholders to accept any good offer. Bear hug offers were pitched to be marginally too attractive to reject.

➤ **suitor:** a bidder in a friendly takeover.

➤ **teddy bear pat:** a letter or telephone call indicating that a suitor was about to make a takeover offer. This gave the target company a chance for a friendly merger.

▶ **tidal wave purchase:** a raider's open-market purchase of an over-whelming block of a company's shares.

▶ **toehold purchase:** a raider's purchase of an amount of stock just below that which the Securities and Exchange Commission requires to be made public.

KILLER BEES AND SHARK REPELLENT

The targets of corporate raiders did not always allow themselves to be swept up unresisting onto the front of the black knight's saddle. A number of defensive strategies were available.

▶ **crown jewel defense:** responding to a takeover bid by selling the company's most valuable asset to a third party. To avoid stockholder complaints, the asset had to be sold for its fair market value.

▶ **killer bees:** a team of specialists hired to protect a company from hostile takeovers; for example, lawyers and public relations firms.

▶ **lobster trap:** a mechanism that prevented people who held 10 percent or more of voting stock from converting their stocks into common shares. The lobster trap let the financial little guys escape but kept in the big guys.

▶ **lollipop:** an arrangement by which certain shareholders had the right to offer their shares for sale at a high price if a hostile bidder acquired some predetermined number of outstanding shares.

▶ **nuclear war:** what you got when two or more corporations competed for ownership of another corporation—mutually assured destruction.

▶ **scorched earth:** selling off a company's assets to make a takeover less attractive.

▶ **shark repellent:** changes in a corporation's charter that made taking it over less appealing.

▶ **white knight:** someone sympathetic to the target company's goals and practices who could outbid the **black knight.** A **white squire** was not quite as good because he could only purchase a large block of stock, not the whole company.

LOITERERS ON WALL STREET

These were a few of the people you might meet on the Street:

▶ **Aunt Jane:** a small stockholder who attended stockholders' meetings, usually imagined as a little old lady in tennis shoes.

▶ **barefoot pilgrim:** someone who had lost everything on the stock market, but might still be persuaded to invest again.

▶ **James Bond:** a U.S. Treasury bond due to mature in 2007.

▶ **lamb:** an innocent investor waiting to be fleeced. A highbrow lamb was a **lily.**

➤ **lobby lizard:** a client or potential client who spent hours in a brokerage firm's lobby, watching the electronic ticker tape, also called a *lobby rat. Lobby lizard* is patterned after **lounge lizard,** 'an idle man who spends a lot of time in clubs'.

➤ **mooch man:** an underworld operator who sold worthless stocks. The *mooch* was the sucker who fell for his patter.

➤ **mullet:** a gullible potential investor with a lot of money.

➤ **odd lotter:** an amateur investor who bought fewer than 100 shares of stock at a time. One hundred shares is a **round lot.**

BUCKET SHOP

Bucket shops were active as early as the 1870s, but gained new visibility in the 1980s. Originally the phrase indicated a shop where people could speculate on amounts of grain too small to be handled by the Chicago Board of Trade. In the early twentieth century, bucket shops for investors were set up to look like legitimate brokerage houses. Many were more like gambling dens. **Bucketeers** took orders from clients, but instead of executing the orders, they bet against the client on the stock rising or falling. Odds were, the client would lose. Besides not having to pay out a profit, bucketeers could charge a commission for their nonexistent services. *To bucket* was slang for 'to swindle', which no doubt reinforced the image of bucket shops as shady places.

The term **boiler room** is sometimes used interchangably with *bucket shop,* but it has a more specific meaning. It's a place where salespeople call potential clients and pressure them to buy questionable stocks. (The term is sometimes used to refer to places where intensive telephone sales of any kind take place.) This practice is also called **telefraud.** Like bucket shops, boiler rooms were in existence well before the eighties. The first ones appeared around 1910, shortly after telephones became a common household appliance, but the term became much more familiar during the 1980s. During this decade, even people who didn't play the market talked about it.

Eighties **yackers** who worked the telephones kept a **sucker list** of people likely to buy worthless stocks if the **razz,** or sales pitch, was strong enough. Calling potential clients was known as **stoking the boiler.** Beginning yackers were called **fronters.** They spent most of their time **dialing and smiling,** or making cold calls to prospective customers. More experienced colleagues then made follow-up calls to **pluck the chickens,** or sell them some stock.

POWER DRESSING

People were less inclined to pursue their own look in the eighties, although a few groups had distinctive styles. Preppie dressing gained new prominence as upwardly mobile young men and women strove to dress for success. Brooks Brothers suits for the office and Lacoste shirts for the golf course were two favored brands. Women tried to be **designer shoppers,** purchasing everything from dinner dresses to handbags from the same designer for a **total look.** Around this time, department stores stopped displaying clothing by type—skirts, sweaters, and so on—and started displaying it by maker.

Following the lead of the White House, those with enough money returned to traditional formality in the evenings. Women wore elegant gowns, while men were quietly suave in tuxedoes—not the pastel tuxes of the frivolous seventies, but the sober black dinner jackets of the ambitious eighties. Casual clothes revealed well-exercised, fat-free bodies. Health clubs proliferated, and running shoes were a basic item of footwear for nearly everyone. Women tucked their high heels into their briefcases and wore running shoes from home to work. About the only people who bucked the slick new eighties look were teenage **Goths** and hip-hop artists.

➤ **acid washed:** a description of denim, usually jeans, that was bleached to create washed-out streaks. This treatment made the jeans look old and worn out even when new. Another term was *frosted jeans.*

➤ **alligator shirt:** a cotton knit polo shirt made by Izod. In spite of the nickname, the creature sewn onto the shoulder was a crocodile. The shirts had been around for decades. French tennis star René Lacoste, known as "the crocodile," designed the first one in 1934. Lacoste shirts came in a variety of bright and pastel colors. Because the shirt was an established preppie look, it became a yuppie status symbol. The eighties fad was to wear the shirt with the collar turned up and the tail hanging out to show its longer-in-back design. Preps lucky enough to own multiple alligator shirts wore two together in contrasting colors.

➤ **banana clip:** a large, curved hair clip for holding women's hair in a ponytail.

➤ **belly shirt:** a cropped T-shirt or tank top that showed off tight abdominal muscles. For the less tight, some belly shirts came equipped with strips of fabric dangling from the hem to obscure the belly region.

➤ **bubble skirt:** a poufy skirt gathered in at the hem to form a bubble.

➤ **bustier:** a strapless corset, often decorated with ruffles and lace, and worn as street clothing. Bustiers were for the painfully young and trendy. They were part of the underwear-on-top look introduced by pop singer Madonna.

➤ **duck shoes:** distinctively designed waterproof shoes made of rubber and leather, sold in the L. L. Bean catalog. They were meant to be worn in the rugged outdoors, but stylish Wall Streeters considered them a fine wet-weather replacement for running shoes.

➤ **fade:** new style of Afro, flat on the sides, squared off on top, and sloping back from the forehead to the crown. A tall one was a

---

YUPPIE

The **yuppie,** which translates as either 'young urban professional' or occasionally 'young upwardly mobile professional', was a new breed of young adult. Yuppies were conventional, ambitious, and frankly interested in money, three traits that had not been widely admired since the fifties. Both male and female *yups* were unashamedly committed to getting ahead in lucrative professions like stockbrokerage or the law. They were also interested in enjoying the fruits of their labors after work. Yuppies preferred offbeat but elegant surroundings and well-chosen food and drink.

Because these superpreppies were very brand-oriented, certain types of possessions and ways of living became associated with *yuppieism.* The ultimate yuppie couple consisted of two young corporate lawyers who lived in a remodeled loft in an old warehouse district of Manhattan. They owned modular furniture, dhurrie rugs, and an Akita dog named Wolfgang. They ate in trendy little Ethiopian or Thai restaurants in Greenwich Village.

Unlike preppies, yuppies could hail from any class or ethnic group. **Suppies** were Southern yuppies, **buppies** were black, **guppies** were gay, **Juppies** were Japanese, and **Huppies** were Hispanic. Upwardly mobile Cuban Americans called themselves **yucas.** One local newspaper in the Northwest Territory suggested that young couples who moved north and built environmentally coordinated houses be labeled **yappies**—young Arctic professionals. High-quality oversized paperback books, widely popular in the 1980s, were nicknamed **yuppiebacks.** Yuppies even had their own **yuppie disease,** Epstein-Barr syndrome. Epstein-Barr, a mysterious illness that causes chronic fatigue, began to be prevalent during the yuppie decade, primarily striking young upwardly mobile adults. Another version of yuppies that came along late in the 1980s was the **dink** couple—double income, no kids.

high-top fade. A cut that was angled to one side was a **gumby,** after the cartoon character.

➤ **Gothic:** an option for the disaffected teen, based on the styles seen in old horror movies. **Goths** dressed head to toe in black clothing. Black-rimmed eyes stared out of dead white faces. The overall look was similar to punk, but in black and white.

➤ **Jheri curls:** loose, wet-looking curls worn by African-American men, including pop star Michael Jackson. To achieve the right curl, men used a curl-relaxing process invented by Jheri Redding hair care manufacturers, plus liberal amounts of hair oil. The style lasted only briefly, to be replaced by fades.

➤ **mini-crinoline:** a short, bouffant crinoline, a Vivienne Westwood design. If a woman wore a mini-crinoline with a bustier, she could go out wearing nothing but underwear and shoes.

➤ **parachute pants:** pants made out of parachute nylon and trimmed with multiple zippers along the legs. These pants were fashionable among breakdancers because their slickness allowed for easy spinning on the ground.

➤ **power suit:** a type of suit worn by both sexes, in black, gray, or navy. The jacket featured wide, square, padded shoulders and a nipped-in waist. Women wore knee-length straight skirts and men wore narrow-legged pants. Men had the further option of spicing things up with a boldly colored tie, while women usually went for a white blouse. Power suits were part of **power dressing,** dressing conservatively but expensively to exude an aura of power and wealth. Power dressers favored designer labels, Italian shoes, and Rolex watches.

➤ **slouch socks:** long, bulky socks worn pushed down around the ankle. They were a casual look, meant to be worn with jeans, shorts, or exercise outfits.

➤ **stirrup pants:** another body-hugging style for the workout crowd, stretchy Lycra pants for women made with a stirrup attached to the hem. When the wearer slipped her foot into the stirrup, the pants pulled tight and wouldn't ride up. Stirrup pants were modeled on ski pants. They were often worn with baggy, oversize sweaters and shirts.

HACKERS

By the 1980s, computers were no longer an optional purchase for businesses or a novelty item for individuals. They had shrunk from room size to desk size, and were cheaper and easier to use. As computers became more commonplace, **hackers,** or computer programmers, moved to the forefront of American culture. In some ways the opposite of yuppies, *turbo nerds* only got rich by accident. They were devoted to the design and programming of computers, and happily spent many hours hunched over their machines. They dressed for comfort in scruffy jeans and running shoes and ate takeout Chinese or pizza.

Like all closed and closely knit groups, hackers developed a richly detailed jargon, most of it comprehensible only to other hackers. Here are a few terms that entered the linguistic mainstream, evolving in interesting ways as they did so:

➤ **bogus:** nonfunctional or useless. *Bogus* was a very popular piece of slang in the 1980s, but the hacker meaning of 'nonfunctional' was much narrower than its usage in the general population. **Bogus** had already been an African-American word for 'phony' for several decades. It became part of rapper slang, then part of general youth slang as a catch-all description of 'anything bad, stupid, or false'. To Valley Girls, *bogus* meant 'pretentious'.

Hackers spun several terms out of the original word. **Bogosity** was the degree to which people and things were nonfunctional. Both humans and computer programs could **bogue out** unexpectedly, instilling in some hackers an **autobogophobia,** or fear of becoming *bogofied.* **Bogons** were the elementary particles of bogosity (following the form of words like *proton* and *neutron*). The **bogometer** was a mythical instrument for measuring their presence.

➤ **computer geek:** someone who would rather sit in front of a computer than eat or sleep, also known as a *turbo nerd* or *turbo geek.* The original *geeks* were carnival performers whose act consisted of biting the heads off live snakes or chickens. In the seventies and eighties, it was considered an insult to call someone a computer geek unless you were one yourself. The venerable *Hacker's Dictionary* defines geeks as fulfilling "all the dreariest negative stereotypes about hackers." They were asocial monomaniacs, pale from spending all their time in the computer room. They were inclined to **geek out** at parties, rushing over to fool around with the host's desktop model. *Geek* by itself or with other adjectives was used freely in the 1980s to describe various types of social misfits. (See **Aqua Velva geek** in the "Totally Tubular" section.) **Geeking out** has been used more recently to describe the behavior of people high on cocaine. Nonetheless, beginning in the 1990s, computer geeks embraced the label as a positive indication of their special qualities. By the end of the nineties, a programmer's most knowledgeable colleague was known as the **alpha geek.**

➤ **hacker:** a computing enthusiast, someone who loves to program and is really good at it. Unfortunately, to eighties computer illiterates a hacker was a kind of evil computer genius who broke through other people's security systems. This definition has remained widespread. Hackers themselves prefer the word *cracker* for such people. Some attempt was made to introduce *worm* as a word for people who engaged in illegal systems break-ins, but it never caught on. Not only do computer types consider the term *hacker* an honorable one, they believe that it's a title best bestowed by others. Just as most people prefer not to label themselves brilliant in case they can't live up to it, hackers prefer to let others recognize their hacking merits. Some computer in-group uses of *hacker* are **hack attack** or **hacking run,** meaning a marathon computer session of at least twelve hours; **hackitude** or **hackishness,** the positive group of characteristics associated with being a hacker; and **true-hacker,** a loyal member of the hacking community, in much the same way as a **trufan** is loyal to the *Star Trek* community.

Hacker may have started out as a negative or self-deprecating label. In the forties, fifties, and sixties, a hacker was someone who played golf or tennis poorly or, more generally, a beginner at some activity who was in need of more practice.

➤ **shareware:** uncopyrighted software that anyone is free to use. Nonhacker citizens use this term interchangably with *freeware,* but to hackers **freeware** means 'software that really is free', while shareware is usually accompanied by the author's plea for payment. The **charity-ware** or **careware** version requests a donation to a selected charity. **Guiltware** simply points out that the author has worked very hard on this program and those users who don't see their way to reimbursement are being a little unappreciative. The term *freeware* is now being replaced by **open source** and **free software. Payware** is commercially marketed software.

CHANNELING THE NEW AGE

Combining elements of the occult, astrology, faith healing, and various Eastern religions, **New Age** was the 1980s version of self-realization. The actress Shirley Maclaine publicized the movement in books like *Don't Fall off the Mountain* and *Out on a Limb,* which detailed her spiritual journeys. Since this was the eighties, one purpose of spirit-guided self-discovery for many people was to get ahead in the material world. Dozens of companies sponsored human-potential seminars for their employees. Soon, 1980s incarnations of Madame Sarah the Fortune Teller were channeling advice from their ancient **spirit guides.** Quite a few channelers got rich by conveying these musings to eager audiences for a fee.

New Agers who couldn't afford access to a channeler created new realities for themselves through meditation, crystal use, and star charts. **New Age music,** soothing instrumental music performed by such artists as pianist George Winston, was also popular during this decade.

Here are some of the terms that New Agers contributed to the 1980s vocabulary. Most are not New Age inventions, but borrowings from the Hindu religion or from spiritualism.

➤ **akashic record:** a permanent record of everything that has happened in the world, including every thought and deed of every human. *Akasha* is 'ether', one of the five Hindu elements.

➤ **ascended masters:** those who have reached the highest plane of spiritual existence.

➤ **astral body:** a person's spiritual body, distinct from his or her physical body. People's astral bodies engaged in **astral travel** or **out-of-body experiences.** *Astral* generally means 'connected with the heavenly plane'.

➤ **aura:** an energy field surrounding every human being, a spiritualist notion. Auras are invisible to most people, but to New Agers sensitive enough to see them, auras were color-coded. Violet indicated a very highly evolved person. Greens were reasonably conscious. Black meant serious trouble.

➤ **chakra:** the energy centers of the body, from the Sanskrit word meaning 'wheel'. Hindu gods are sometimes pictured holding a circular chakra. According to New Age theory, people have seven chakras, located in strategic places between the feet and the crown of the head. Each chakra is associated with a different color.

➤ **channeling:** providing vocal cords for visitors from the spirit world, much as mediums did in earlier decades. (See the twenties chapter, "Messages from the Other Side.") Instead of holding a séance to talk to Great Uncle Fred, New Agers sat at the feet of eighties mediums to receive general comments from spirits who were strangers.

➤ **crystals:** pieces of rock that contained healing and energizing powers. Different colored crystals had different uses: rose quartz was for emotional healing; clear quartz provided energy; tiger's eye boosted personal power; amethyst calmed the nerves. Crystals could also be placed on a person's **chakras** to balance them.

➤ **power spot:** a place that generated extra spiritual energy, such as Stonehenge and the Great Pyramids.

➤ **psychic healer:** someone who cured ills by sending out waves of mental energy.

➤ **retrocognition:** paranormal knowledge of past events.

➤ **spirit guide:** a spirit entity who provided guidance and advice through a medium. Spirit guides frequently hailed from ancient Middle Eastern cultures.

➤ **third eye:** an imaginary eye in the middle of the forehead, the center of psychic vision.

HOSERS AND HAPPY CAMPERS

As usual, teenagers were busily evolving their own words of the moment. The language of students, Valley Girls, and hip-hoppers overlapped quite a bit. Many words that eventually entered the larger slang world originated among rappers. Mainstream teens and Valley Girls also borrowed extensively from surfers.

➤ **awesome:** amazingly good, from surfer slang.

➤ **Barney:** an unattractive male, a reference to Barney Rubble of the television cartoon *The Flintstones.*

➤ **beer goggles:** a loss of judgment due to having drunk too much.

➤ **bimbette:** an eighties version of *bimbo,* a word first popularized in the twenties, meaning 'a scatterbrained, giddy, or promiscuous young woman'. The word probably derives from the Italian word for 'child', *bambino/bambina.* Male bimbos in the eighties were **himbos** or **himbettes.**

➤ **bodacious:** outstanding; excellent. This word has long been part of Southeastern dialects, where it means 'impudent', 'audacious', 'thorough', or 'remarkable'.

➤ **bow-head:** a preppie female who wore her hair pulled back with a bow; a silly girl.

➤ **box tonsils:** to kiss.

➤ **buzz crusher:** a killjoy.

➤ **crispy:** hung over.

➤ **dweeb:** a dork, a nerd, etc.

➤ **excellent:** excellent; also very good, fine, or okay. Anything pleasing to a young person was excellent, *most* excellent, or *majorly* excellent.

➤ **face time:** time spent necking, also called **interfacing** or, unfortunately, **sucking face.**

➤ **generic:** dull and boring.

➤ **granola:** someone who believed in a natural, healthy lifestyle; a throwback to the sixties.

➤ **happenin':** stylish or important; trendy. **'Zhappenin'?** was a common greeting.

➤ **happy camper:** someone who was pleased or content with a situation, but almost always used in the negative context of being *not* a happy camper.

➤ **heinous:** very bad.

➤ **hoser:** a stupid or crude person. This word was popularized by the Canadian characters Bob and Doug McKenzie on the television program *Second City Television.*

➤ **lame:** bad, pathetic, or **bogus.**

➤ **major:** the favored way of saying that something was very important. **Majorly** also became highly popular during this decade to mean 'extremely', as in *he is majorly weird* and *that test was majorly hard.*

➤ **mint:** memorable or priceless, often said of an event.

➤ **poindexter:** a nerdish young person, *dexter* for short.

➤ **pond scum:** a low life.

➤ **poser:** a phony.

➤ **power nap:** the deep sleep of exhaustion.

➤ **radical:** especially good or cool, often shortened to *rad.* Surfers used this word to describe a difficult or impressive surfing move. Skateboarders then adopted it to describe a challenging skating situation. In the eighties, the general teen population picked it up and broadened its meaning to cover 'anything positive'.

➤ **'rents:** parents.

➤ **serious:** exceptionally good or interesting, as in *a serious album collection.*

➤ **vogue:** a well-dressed person or a stylish item of clothing—not *in vogue,* just *vogue.* **Voguing** was a type of dance in which the dancer struck and held poses as if he or she were a *Vogue* magazine model.

➤ **waldo:** a hopeless wimp, from the picture book series *Where's Waldo?*

➤ **way:** very, originally surfspeak. The word was also used as an affirmative. When someone expressed incredulity by saying, "*no way,*" the correct response was "*way!*"

➤ **wicked:** very, very good.

TOTALLY TUBULAR

The Valley Girl arose to brief, but **tubular,** fame in the early 1980s. The Valley in question was the San Fernando Valley, north of Los Angeles. The Girl in question was a certain type of well-dressed **airhead** who spent quality time at the shopping mall and free evenings watching soap operas like *Dynasty.* The rest of the country heard about Valley Girls when musician Frank Zappa joined with his daughter

Moon Unit to record a song titled "Valley Girl." The song is a monologue touching on the Val Gal's struggles with orthodonists, uncool mothers, and other tribulations.

Valley Girl slang relied heavily on surfer jargon. Valley Girls introduced well-established surfer words like *rad, way, awesome,* and *tubular* to a wider audience. Vals also indulged in the excruciating overuse of **like,** not only as a hedge word, but as a substitute for *say.* I'm like, "Wow! Now it's totally a widespread usage!"

➤ **airhead:** a dimwit, also **space cadet.**

➤ **all the way live:** exciting, animated; usually used to describe parties, concerts, and other lively events.

➤ **Aqua Velva geek:** a male of a certain age who wore tight, double-knit polyester pants and gold chains nestled in his chest hair. He considered himself a swinger and probably lived in a singles complex.

➤ **bag it:** get rid of it, often said of things that are not easy to get rid of, such as **bag your face.**

➤ **beasty:** repellent or dorky.

➤ **beige:** boring, bland.

➤ **billys:** money (dollar bills).

➤ **bitchen (bitchin'):** absolutely wonderful, said of a person or item.

DUDE

Dude! Yo, dude! This way cool eighties word has hung around for an amazingly long time, although it had to keep changing meanings to do it. Its probable origin is an eighth-century Northern English word, *duddes,* meaning 'male clothing'. By the fifteenth century the variation *dudes* was used specifically to indicate 'raggedy old clothes'. A **dudesman** was 'a scarecrow'. **Duds,** an old-fashioned slang word for 'clothes', is almost certainly related.

As late as the nineteenth century, *dude* still referred to clothing. *Duded up* was common slang for 'dressed up' until recent decades. In the American West, the dude first made his appearance as a well-dressed gentleman, who might also be called a *dandy.* Since most dudes were newly arrived Easterners the word soon acquired the connotation of an outsider or an inexperienced person. It could also suggest a sissy or, alternatively, a ladies' man. The meaning gradually narrowed to describe a slick, Eastern city boy, with the underlying notion that such a person was well-dressed.

➤ **crill:** utterly low and inferior, named for the creatures that float in the ocean and are sucked up by whales.

➤ **fer shurr:** what I am saying is definitely true, or, alternatively, I agree emphatically with what you just said.

➤ **gag me with a spoon:** literally, make me vomit, but really a suggestion that what the Val is talking about is enough to make anyone sick. A slightly less colorful version was **barf me out.**

➤ **gnarly:** excellent; awesome. This word was first used by surfers to describe scary waves, but Valley Girls made it popular as a general compliment.

➤ **grody:** disgusting, yucky, gross.

➤ **I am so sure:** I really don't think so. An alternative expression was **as if,** said with eyes rolling.

➤ **jel:** an idiot, short for Jell-O brain.

➤ **Joanie:** totally out-of-date and frumpy, possibly a reference to Joanie Cunningham from the television program Happy Days, which ran from 1974 to 1984.

➤ **kill:** an adjective meaning 'remarkably good'. **Kill** and **killer** usually mean something positive in youth slang. In earlier decades, to kill someone meant 'to fascinate or favorably impress' the person.

➤ **max:** the most, usually used in the phrase **to the max.**

In the mid-twentieth century, the meaning of *dude* shifted again. It meant 'a sharp dresser', but was used positively by zoot suiters to refer to themselves or their friends. (See the forties chapter for the sidebar "Zoot Suit.") Then, it gradually broadened to be a way of addressing or referring to a male. In the 1950s it was used mainly by hipsters, with a similar meaning to *cat*.

Dude was propelled to the highest level of slangdom by surfers, a route that many other recent slang words have taken. Any surfer or friend of a surfer was a dude. A female surfer was a **dudette.** Another variation was **dudester.** The word *dude* received national exposure in the 1982 movie *Fast Times at Ridgemont High.* By the mid-1980s, any male under the age of 40 was a dude. **Dudical** meant 'cool'. By the end of the eighties, dudesters were using the word *dude* as both a form of address and a general exclamation when anything surprising happened, either good or bad. *Dude! I lost my car keys. Dude! That babe is way happenin'. You found my car keys? Du-u-u-de!*

➤ **pre-car:** not old enough for a driver's license. It was also used metaphorically to mean 'not old enough to do anything fun', including have sex.

➤ **scarf out:** to overeat.

➤ **shine:** to ignore someone. Later, it could mean to disparage someone.

➤ **skanky:** disgusting, grody.

➤ **slimeball:** a jerk.

➤ **totally:** completely, the most popular Valspeak adverb **fer shurr.**

➤ **tubular:** so totally **bitchen** it's almost unbelieveable, borrowed from the surfing term for a well-formed wave.

➤ **tude:** an attitude, usually a bad one.

➤ **twitchen** (**twitchin'**): very positive, almost like **bitchen.**

➤ **zod:** something really bizarre.

-SPEAK

Valspeak, or the language of Valley Girls, was only one of various kinds of **-speak** that came into vogue in the 1980s. This combination form was based on George Orwell's *Newspeak,* the government double talk described in his 1949 novel *Nineteen Eighty-Four.* Virtually anything called *-speak* was negative. The form has stayed active over the past couple of decades. It is now used for the language of all sorts of groups. A few examples of *Eighties-speak -speaks* are listed below.

➤ **computerspeak:** the jargon of computer experts, also called *machinespeak.*

➤ **governmentspeak:** the jargon used by federal government workers.

➤ **Haigspeak:** pompous but vacuous verbosity, a trademark of Reagan's first secretary of state, Alexander Haig. Prime examples of Haigspeak include *careful caution, nuanceal differences,* and *this is not an experience I haven't been through before.*

➤ **libspeak:** the buzzwords of the women's liberation movement.

➤ **nounspeak:** the use of long strings of modifying nouns, for example *aircraft fuel systems equipment mechanics instructions booklet.* Literary critic Jacques Barzun referred to this syndrome as the **noun plague.**

➤ **sciencespeak:** scientific-sounding prose used for advertising purposes or to otherwise impress the unwary.

➤ **sportspeak:** the unique language of sports announcers.

➤ **whitespeak:** a euphemistic, falsely bright style of speech used by white liberals when speaking to or about blacks. Writer Meg Greenfield coined the term in an April 18, 1983, *Newsweek* essay.

RAPPER'S DELIGHT

Rap music arose out of **hip-hop,** the mid-1970s black street culture of the South Bronx. Besides music, hip-hop included graffiti art and **breakdancing.** In the early days of hip-hop, disk jockeys would sometimes perform out on the sidewalk. They powered their record players by plugging them into street lamps (called **lamping**). DJs like Kool Herc and DJ Hollywood would work with identical records on two turntables. By switching back and forth between the two, they could extend sound breaks in the songs indefinitely. Over the breaks they **toasted,** a Jamaican form of word play that includes jokes and boasting. Later DJs introduced the techniques of **quick mixing,** combining short sound bites from different records, and **scratching,** moving the needle forward and back in the record's groove to create background noise. These were the beginnings of the rap sound.

Hip-hop culture put a premium on personal style and verbal quickness. Rap was a version of *playing the dozens* or *shooting the dozens,* a stylized system of trading insults. These were usually about someone's appearance or, if really serious, about his family. (Most often, it's males who play the dozens.) Being able to manipulate hip slang was important, but spontaneous linguistic creation was even better. To dozens players, *rap* meant 'aggressive or persuasive talk', a way of displaying your personality vocally.

A rap song is a set of rhyming lines spoken rythmically over a background beat. Songs usually describe the rapper's life and opinions. Much of it is political; some is violent. The first rap record to get national exposure was the Sugarhill Gang's *Rapper's Delight,* released in 1979. Other early practitioners were Run-DMC, LL Cool J, Public Enemy, and Afrika Bambaataa. Since then, breakdancing and graffiti art have dwindled, but rap is stronger than ever. Although rappers' slang is constantly evolving, some words that were **fresh** and **chill** in the eighties are still around. They are preserved here as soon-to-be obsolete, but important, slang.

➤ **all that:** having some seriously good qualities; extraordinary.

➤ **amped:** wound up; ready to go.

➤ **b-boy:** a boy who breakdanced, short for *break boy.* Also *b-girl. B-boy* can also mean a pal or someone who's involved in hip-hop culture.

➤ **bag on:** to insult.

➤ **bank:** money. Other words for money were *cheese, dead presidents, scratch, scrilla,* and *snaps.*

➤ **big up:** to flatter someone, as in *Don't big me up!*

➤ **bite:** to copy other people's rap lyrics or graffiti style.

➤ **boo-yah!:** an exclamation meaning 'extremely good, very fine'.

➤ **bust a move:** to dance. **Busting a rhyme** is rapping.

➤ **Casper:** to be gone, from *Casper the Friendly Ghost.* A variation was *I'm ghost.*

➤ **chill:** stylish, cool. Very cool was **chilly the most.** Among mainstream teens *chill* could also mean 'relaxed', and *to chill* was 'to relax or calm down'. **Chill hard** was 'to survive'.

➤ **cramped:** ugly.

➤ **crew:** the group of people you breakdance or rap with, also called a **posse.**

➤ **dead up:** absolutely; I'm telling it straight.

➤ **def:** excellent, from *death,* which in this case is positive, by way of Jamaican English.

➤ **dip:** to leave.

➤ **dis:** to insult or show disrespect for someone. *Dis* can also be a noun.

➤ **dope:** very hip.

➤ **down with:** in agreement with or approving of, as in *I'm down with that.*

➤ **flavor:** style.

➤ **flowstress:** a female rapper.

➤ **fly:** very attractive and stylish; talented. Earlier, it was a jive word meaning 'a smooth type'. From the eighteenth to the early twentieth centuries, *fly* meant clever, on the ball, even sharp to the point of dishonesty. It might have been said of a pickpocket, for instance. By the late nineteenth century, it could also mean socially wild or sexually experienced.

➤ **fresh:** stylish, original, appealing. By the 1990s the word was becoming outdated among rappers, but was sometimes found in mainstream slang.

➤ **hard roller:** someone with an affluent lifestyle.

➤ **high five:** a form of greeting in which two people slap their right hands together around shoulder level. A **low five** takes place at the waist.

➤ **ho:** a whore. This pronunciation and spelling was later adopted by the broader youth culture.

➤ **homey:** a good friend, short for *homeboy.* Another way to say it was *home slice.*

➤ **hottie:** an attractive girl.

➤ **ill:** obnoxious, bad-tempered, or behaving irrationally. **Illin'** was the verb. *Ill* with the meaning 'bad-tempered' is a Southeastern dialect word used by both black and white speakers.

➤ **it's all good:** everything is fine, going well.

➤ **kick the ballistics:** to converse.

➤ **kicks:** sneakers.

➤ **level the vibes:** to create a relaxed atmosphere.

➤ **macadocious:** great; very stylish.

➤ **marinate:** to hang around.

➤ **mic:** a new way of spelling *mike,* short for *microphone.*

➤ **my bad:** sorry, my fault.

➤ **off the dome:** spontaneously; off the top of one's head.

➤ **phat:** well-off, rich. Also describing some stylish or upscale possession, as in a *phat car. Fat* has meant 'flush with money' since the seventeenth century. Using *ph* to spell *f* is a typical slangster joke (see
"Winchellese" in the thirties chapter).

➤ **piecing:** creating graffiti masterpieces.

➤ **riff:** to complain, argue, or boast. To **riff on** someone else is to
insult the person.

➤ **rolling with:** hanging around with.

➤ **sampling:** incorporating other people's recorded music into your
own.

➤ **shout out:** an acknowledgment or a credit during a rap performance.

➤ **shuck:** to deceive.

➤ **step to:** to confront or compete with.

➤ **styling:** looking good.

➤ **tag:** someone's graffiti signature. **Tagging up** was writing graffiti.

➤ **throw down:** to party.

➤ **treach:** very good, short for *treacherous.*

➤ **twisted:** drunk.

➤ **wack:** worthless; of poor quality.

➤ **wheels of steel:** turntables.

➤ **word!:** that's the truth; I agree with you. This exclamation was later
adopted by the *dude* crowd. A variation is **word up.**

➤ **yo!:** a greeting, also dudeish.

➤ **zoning:** cruising around in a car.

BREAKIN' MOVES

The breaks in rap music were filled with dance. Young men, and occasionally women, improvised athletic dance routines called **breaking** or
breakdancing. Sometimes, breakdancing was competitive, especially
as an alternative to fighting. Dancers introduced a unique clothing
style that made it easy to move freely and to roll on their backs and
heads. Outfits featured baggy shorts or jeans and sweatshirts with

Downrock.

hoods or hats. Women might wear spandex. Leather was also a good look. Untied running shoes or basketball shoes were a requirement.

Early breakdance was in the **electric boogie** style. Dancers usually stayed upright, concentrating on **popping,** or making sharp, jerky robotlike motions. They also **glided** and did the **moon walk,** a backward glide made famous by Michael Jackson. Upright dancing was called **toprock,** dancing on or near the floor was called **downrock.** Here are a few of the steps that amazed the crowd:

applejack: a basic move to challenge another b-boy to a competition, squatting down, falling back onto your hands, and kicking one leg high in the air, then springing back onto both legs.

body slam: falling on your back.

bronco: bouncing from a handstand to your feet in one move.

crab: spinning or walking on your hands with legs curled forward around your arms.

cricket: spinning while supporting yourself on one hand.

float: balancing on your hands with legs curled toward your body.

helicopter: spinning your straight right leg around under your bent left leg while balancing on your hands.

kip-up: rolling from a position flat on your back to an upright stance in one movement. Doing it repeatedly is called the **rubber band.**

➤ **one-hand glide:** spinning on one hand.

➤ **six-step:** spinning your legs around in a circle while supporting your body first on one hand, then the other, switching from hand to hand to keep from blocking your legs, a kind of moving handstand.

➤ **swipe:** spinning from your left side to your right side, starting from a back bend position.

➤ **windmill:** rolling from shoulder to shoulder, legs spinning in the air.

EIGHTIES BUZZWORDS

The biggest buzz of the eighties concerned **Reaganauts** and their policies, from **Star Wars** to **Reaganomics.** Yuppies tuned in to CNN (available from 1980) to hear all the latest.

➤ **go ballistic:** go out of control with anger. Ballistics refers to the motion of projectiles through space. In the 1980s, projectiles meant intercontinental ballistic missiles. The expression was first used literally to describe out-of-control guided missiles. Later, it extended to people. Someone who was only moderately angry was **semiballistic.** *Going ballistic* could also mean reaching a whole new level. For example, if a pop singer won a Grammy, her career was sure to go ballistic. In the early nineties, **ballistics** were forcibly delivered rap lyrics.

➤ **Reaganomics:** the economic policies of President Ronald Reagan. Reagan's program consisted of reducing federal taxes, reducing the size of the government, deregulating businesses, and tightening the money supply. These policies were also known as *supply-side* or *trickle-down* economics. Another word for Reaganomics was *Reaganism.*

The president loaned his name to a number of new terms in the eighties. **Reaganauts** were his loyal supporters, who were also called *Reaganites.* Editorial writers spoke of **Reaganesque** political trends. **Reagan Democrats** were those who traditionally voted Democrat, but nonetheless voted for Reagan for president, often on a split ticket. The president's wife, Nancy, also made a contribution: **Reagan red,** for the first lady's trademark bright-red dresses and suits.

➤ **Star Wars:** nickname for the Strategic Defense Initiative, after the popular science fiction film that appeared in 1977. The goal of Star Wars was to keep intercontinental ballistic missiles from hitting the United States by intercepting them after they left the earth's atmosphere. The program was never implemented, mainly because of the $1 trillion price tag and questions about the Initiative's viability. With the collapse of the Soviet Union in 1991, the defense system seemed less crucial. In 1993, President Clinton announced its abandonment.

Internet digerati exhorted the rest of us to get cyberized.

The Nineties

Dot-Comming into Y2K

As Americans entered the last decade of the twentieth century, the country was once again at war. Hardly had the nineties begun when the **mother of all battles** was joined between the United States and Iraq. Americans and their allies used their **aerial assets** to engage in **inconvenience bombing.** The Iraqis responded with **golden BBs. Line doggies** on the ground just wanted to **shoot and scoot.** Even when soldiers wore **bone domes,** the heat of **Big Red** out in the desert, or **the beach,** as it was also known, could be tough to take. **Ragged out** soldiers patronized the mobile **roach coach** to **get their guts right** with **grease** and **nuclear coffee.**

Operation Desert Storm was the first real **media war. Video canaries** from the major networks holed up in **Little Hollywood,** broadcasting news flashes at all hours. Some people thought television's **Boys of Baghdad** were practicing **gulf-ploitation.** Meanwhile, **Baghdad Betty** did her part for the other side by broadcasting propaganda messages.

The conflict in the Persian Gulf turned out to be a **McWar,** over by the spring of 1991. Americans then turned their attention to the domestic front, especially the part of California known as Silicon Valley. Computers were hotter than ever. The World Wide Web was the place to be, for everything from e-mail to **e-tail.** Internet **digerati** exhorted the rest of us to get **cyberized. Screenagers,** born during the Information Age, quickly became **Net vets.** Older folks, traveling along the **information superhighway** without a map, felt a bad case of **iconitis** coming on. How can **newbies** transform themselves into **knowbies** when their electronic messages keep fading into **ether mail?** Did someone push the **bozo button?**

Generation X was one group that definitely had a clue about the Web, as well as all other modern technology. **Gen Xers** were the **MTV generation.** No **dead tree editions** for them—bring on the **e-zines.**

Even **slackers** and **phase shifters** wouldn't **fan** a chance to be **cyber-capitalists.** Starting your own **dot-com** was a great way to **make bank. Telephone number salaries** were **mondo cool.** Just don't blow it, **brainiac,** or you'll end up as **cyber-roadkill.** Sadly, many **twenty-somethings** were stuck in **McJobs,** living with their parents and barely earning enough **mint** to **score** a few CDs and pay for a tongue piercing. Hey, it's an **alternative lifestyle,** right? **Whatever.**

The Internet changed the workaday world in the nineties. It ushered in the era of **cafeteria officing,** allowing more people to work at home. Even **legacy** businesses like banking had flexible work arrangements. Telecommuters had the chance to **sunlight** at home or catch a **webisode** during their **downtime. Home officing** was convenient for those on the **mommy track** or the **daughter track.** Every day was **casual Friday. Hoteling** worked well for the few who still showed up at the office. Actually, hotelers moved from office to office, depending on which day of the week it was.

Still, some aspects of computers were less than perfect. As the decade neared its end, **cyberjunkies** were suddenly scrambling to get **Y2K compliant.** Otherwise, their systems might crash at midnight on December 31, 1999. Most computer owners wanted to wipe out the **millennium bug** before the **event horizon** actually arrived. Waiting to **fix-on-failure** could lead to global breakdown, **the end of the world as we know it.** What would the world be like if people couldn't **instant message,** or **dialogue** with other **Netizens?** Let's **workshop** this problem so we can **transition** smoothly to the year 2000.

DESERT STORM

On August 2, 1990, Iraq took control of the tiny neighboring country of Kuwait, claiming that its historical status as part of the Ottoman Empire made Kuwait an Iraqi province. Both the United Nations and the Arab League immediately condemned the invasion. The United Nations also imposed an economic boycott on Iraq.

U.S. President George Bush organized a broad coalition that included Great Britain, France, Germany, and several other Western European countries, as well as Japan, Australia, and much of the Middle East. When Iraq ignored the United Nations' January 15 deadline for withdrawal from Kuwait, the coalition launched **Operation Desert Storm.** A massive bombing campaign began on January 16, 1991. Ground troops invaded southwestern Iraq on February 24. Although Saddam Hussein had predicted *"the mother of all battles,"* the ground war lasted only four days. Coalition troops quickly surrounded

Kuwait, and the Iraqis retreated. A cease-fire was declared on February 28.

Although the Persian Gulf War was short, it was long enough for soldiers in the field to accumulate a hoard of war-related slang. Much of it was current military slang, including many technical terms. Other words reflect particular features of the Gulf War, for example the heavy reliance on air power, the overwhelming presence of the desert, and the crowd of journalists on the scene. And, of course, a few food terms were knocking around.

➤ **aerial assets:** the coalition's air power.

➤ **air tasking order:** an Air Force battle plan. In the nineties, no one was assigned tasks—they were **tasked,** *task* being one of the many words that verbalized during this era (see "Verbing Nouns" below).

➤ **ashtray:** the desert, also referred to as *the beach.*

➤ **assertive disarmament:** war, an assertive way of convincing Iraq to disarm.

➤ **Baghdad Betty:** an Iraqi propagandist who waged psychological war against U.S. troops through radio broadcasts.

➤ **Baghdad Biltmore:** a building where prisoners of war were held.

➤ **Big Red:** the desert sun.

➤ **Big Ugly:** a B-52 bomber.

➤ **black clandestine:** a phony radio transmission, used to spread false information.

➤ **blue on blue:** friendly fire, an allusion to the blue uniforms that Union soldiers wore during the Civil War.

➤ **boloed:** destroyed. A Purple Heart was called a **bolo badge,** especially when awarded for a foolhardy action.

➤ **bomb-a-minute attack:** a massive air attack.

➤ **bomber's night:** a moonless night.

➤ **bone dome:** a helmet.

➤ **carpet bomb:** originally, to inflict saturation bombing, but used metaphorically to mean 'severely criticize'.

➤ **checkbook diplomacy:** the conduct of international affairs through economic relations rather than military power. During the Gulf War, Germany and Japan helped finance the coalition, but did not send troops. This approach was known as **checkbook participation.**

➤ **chocolate chips:** the brown-splotched desert camouflage uniforms.

➤ **clean bombing:** bombing with great accuracy.

➤ **collateral damage:** the incidental consequences of bombing military targets, frequently used as a euphemism for 'civilian deaths'. Another euphemism was **damage assessment** for 'body count'.

➧ **deconflict:** to separate airplanes during an attack so that they didn't inadvertently interfere with each other.

➧ **desert cherry:** a recently arrived, untried soldier.

➧ **Desert Shield:** the prewar military buildup in the Middle East, initially intended to protect Saudi Arabia from Iraqi aggression. The war itself was named **Desert Storm.**

➧ **discriminate deterrence:** bombing with pinpoint accuracy.

➧ **dog out:** to criticize.

➧ **echelons beyond reality:** command decisions.

➧ **finger of death:** a hotdog.

➧ **fragger:** someone who determined bombing targets. Compare this use with the sixties **fragging.**

➧ **furballs:** pilot's jargon for dogfights with other planes.

➧ **G-day:** the first day of the Gulf War's ground campaign.

➧ **generic mail:** mail from the United States addressed to "Any Soldier."

➧ **get your guts right:** to eat.

➧ **G.I. Jo:** a female soldier.

➧ **grease:** food.

➧ **gulfspeak:** euphemistic and emotionally loaded words used to discuss the war.

➧ **highway of death:** the road from Kuwait to Iraq, heavily bombed by U.S. warplanes.

➧ **human shield:** someone kept hostage at a likely bombing site, such as a military compound. Early in the conflict Saddam Hussein rounded up foreign nationals and placed them in sensitive areas to deter possible bomb attacks. He later released them as a diplomatic gesture.

➧ **inconvenience bombing:** bombing targets that will cause inconvenience if destroyed, such as power plants.

➧ **insult bombing:** bombing a country's statues and monuments.

➧ **Iraqispeak:** Iraq's version of **gulfspeak.**

➧ **Iraqnophobia:** loss of confidence among businesspeople as a result of the Gulf crisis.

➧ **K-day:** January 15, 1991, the deadline for Iraqi withdrawal from Kuwait. The day after the start of the war was **K-plus.**

➧ **kill sack:** an area in which all moving objects are to be destroyed.

➧ **leg:** paratrooper slang for 'nonparatroopers'.

➧ **line doggie:** a soldier on the front lines.

➧ **McWar:** a military conflict that is fast and cheap (see **McJob** in "Hangin' with the Yuffies" below).

➧ **mort out:** when allied planes shoot each other down accidentally.

From the Latin for 'death', probably by way of *mortal*. *Mort* is an archaic word for 'the note blown on a hunting horn when an animal is killed', but it's doubtful that many Gulf soldiers were familiar with that meaning.

➤ **MRE:** meal, ready-to-eat, the new vacuum-packed C-rations. This source of nourishment went by various pseudonyms, including *meals rarely edible, meals rejected by Ethiopians, might require emergency,* and disregarding the initials, *Airwing Alpo.*

➤ **nuclear coffee:** the mixture of powdered coffee, powdered cocoa, creamer, and sugar included in MREs.

➤ **over the shoulder toss:** low-altitude bombing.

➤ **pinprick raids:** a series of small-scale attacks in preparation for a major offensive.

➤ **ragged out:** exhausted.

➤ **roach coach:** the lunch wagon.

➤ **rototilling:** carpet bombing.

➤ **Sammy:** a nickname for Saddam Hussein.

➤ **Saudi champagne:** a nonalcoholic beverage made of apple juice and Perrier water.

➤ **Scud:** originally a nickname for a Soviet-made surface-to-surface missile used by Iraq, but later used metaphorically to mean something of no value. To **scud** was 'to bash or beat', and to **scud in with** was 'to criticize unfairly'. **Scudded** meant 'drunk', a reference to the missile's unpredictable flight path.

➤ **service the target:** to kill the enemy.

➤ **shoot and scoot:** to fire, then move before the enemy can return fire.

➤ **surface engagement:** a ground battle.

➤ **target-rich environment:** Iraq, from a bomber's perspective.

➤ **terrain alteration:** the effect of bombs on the landscape.

➤ **T ration:** a tray of food serving eighteen people.

➤ **wolfburger stand:** a mobile food wagon.

THE PRIME-TIME WAR

The Persian Gulf War was the first overseas conflict that Americans were able to watch as it actually unfolded. All the major networks were established in Baghdad before the outbreak of hostilities, but the star was the fledgling Cable News Network (CNN), a 24-hour news channel barely eleven years old. CNN rocketed to the big time when a bombing attack on Iraq's central communications tower knocked out the other networks' transmissions capabilities. CNN continued broadcasting over a dedicated telephone circuit to Jordan.

Americans stared for hours at CNN's minute-by-minute coverage. And they weren't the only viewers. Diplomats, even government heads, admitted keeping informed partly through television news. Soon, the involved parties were framing statements with a view to how they would play over the air. The media's high profile during the war also had an effect on both soldiers' and civilians' language use.

THE MOTHER OF ALL BATTLES

Saddam Hussein unintentionally introduced Americans to one of the most popular non-English terms since *Sputnik* when he predicted that a ground war in Iraq would be **the mother of all battles.** 'Mother of' is a loose translation of a common Arabic rhetorical device. It means 'the best or greatest of its kind'.

Soon after Americans first heard the expression, dozens of English variations popped up, most of them meant to be humorous. *Mother of* is still out there. A recent Internet search retrieved *the mother of all web pages* and *the mother of all search engines,* among others.

Several terms from the nineties referred to the war itself:

➧ **mother of all briefings:** General Norman Schwarzkopf's television briefing at the end of the war. Schwarzkopf was the commander of the coalition troops.

➧ **mother of all corners:** the position in which Saddam Hussein found himself, followed by the *mother of all routs* and the *mother of all defeats.*

➧ **mother of all journalistic changes:** novel reporting techniques used during the war.

➧ **mother of all homecomings:** Tampa's homecoming parade for General Schwarzkopf.

➧ **mother of all parades:** New York City's victory parade for the troops.

Other examples are *mother of all ACC tournament games; mother of all clichés* (the expression *mother of* itself, also named *mother of all metaphors*); *mother of all grudges; mother of all mailing lists; mother of all mothers; mother of all storms* (a 1991 windstorm in Detroit); *mother of all theories* (Einstein's Unified Field Theory); *mother of all Whistlers* (portrait known as "Whistler's Mother").

Inventing *mother-of* expressions became something of a sport. David Grimes, a columnist for the *Sarasota Herald-Tribune,* made up nineteen variants, which included *mother of all chopped, shaped, artificially flavored and colored food-substance products* (Spam); *mother of all lawn weeds* (crab grass); *mother of all impersonated rock stars* (Elvis Presley).

➤ **Boys of Baghdad:** reporters for CNN, also called *Baghdad Boys.*

➤ **gulf-ploitation:** the use of Gulf War themes in popular entertainment programs.

➤ **information anxiety:** an anxiety to be fully informed about the progress of the war, often expressed by obsessive viewing of CNN.

➤ **jib rat:** a journalist who depended for information on the Joint Information Bureau (JIB), also known as a *jiblet.*

➤ **Little Hollywood:** the back veranda of the Dhahran International Hotel, headquarters for the television networks.

➤ **media war:** the Persian Gulf War, also called the *made-for-TV war* and the *prime-time war* because of its saturation media coverage.

➤ **pack journalism:** controlled, generic reporting by **pool journalists,** reporters chosen to witness the conflict from the front lines and report back to nonpool journalists in the rear echelon.

➤ **Patriot baiter:** a TV correspondent. The reference is to Patriot missiles, and the reporters' tendency to stand on the veranda or roof of their hotel when such missiles were being fired. They were also called *Scud watchers* because of similar behavior during Scud missile attacks.

➤ **pencil:** a news correspondent, although few of them would have been so behind the times that they actually used pencils.

➤ **reporteress:** a female reporter.

➤ **Scud-a-vision:** CNN.

➤ **total immersion:** continuous coverage of the war.

➤ **video canary:** a TV correspondent.

ZOOMING DOWN THE ELECTRONIC HIGHWAY

Computers once again demonstrated their world-changing capacities when the Internet became accessible to ordinary home computer users. The Internet is a vast computer network connecting a very large number of small computer networks (called internets with a small *i*). The Internet existed during the seventies and eighties, but was difficult to use effectively. It was reserved mainly for academic researchers and the military. When the World Wide Web (WWW) was introduced in 1989, followed by software programs that allowed untrained users to browse for information, the Internet became much easier to navigate. A new world suddenly opened to nontechnocrats. Not only could individuals connect with each other through electronic mail, they could search for homework answers, the latest interest rates, tips on orchid growing, and all sorts of other information. They could also purchase anything from books to used cars online.

Here are some words that couldn't have been coined before the nineties:

➤ **bozo button:** a filter that eliminates e-mail messages from specified sources, for example, from places that frequently send ads.

➤ **cancelbot:** a software program that searches the Internet for commercial mass mailings or other targeted material, and deletes it.

➤ **chiphead:** someone who spends an inordinate amount of time on the computer.

➤ **digerati:** Internet insiders; those at the top of the computer technology heap. The word is formed from *digital* and *literati*.

➤ **ether mail:** e-mail that remains undelivered, therefore lost; the online version of the dead letter office.

➤ **ghost site:** a website so out of date that it is virtually defunct.

➤ **iconitis:** the condition of having too many icons on your computer screen to use them conveniently.

➤ **infofreak:** someone who likes to collect information over the Internet, also **infojunkie.**

➤ **infosize:** to access the Internet's information sources efficiently.

➤ **keyboard plaque:** the dirt, grime, and gunk that accumulates on computer keyboards.

➤ **knowbot:** a software robot that will search through large databases looking for pertinent information.

➤ **lapjack:** to steal a laptop computer from someone, also called **notebook nabbing.**

➤ **mail bomb:** a high volume of e-mail sent to an address in retaliation for the recipient's bad online behavior.

➤ **mouse potato:** a couch potato for the Internet, a *Webaholic* who likes to spend the day in front of the computer screen clicking the mouse. The bane of a mouse potato is a **back-seat mouser** who offers advice about where to point and click. (*Couch potato,* meaning 'someone who spends long hours in front of the television', was introduced in 1976 and trademarked by Robert Armstrong.)

➤ **nastygram:** a rude or unpleasant electronic message. The verb for sending such messages is **flame.**

➤ **newbie:** an Internet neophyte. The opposite is a **knowbie.**

➤ **Netiquette:** proper online behavior.

➤ **Netizen:** a person who uses the Internet, also called a **Net surfer.** Frequent and knowledgeable users are **Netheads** and longtime users are **Net vets.**

➤ **screenager:** someone who was between 13 and 29 during the 1990s, entirely comfortable with both computer technology and cable television.

➤ **spam:** unsolicited e-mail, usually a commercial, high-volume mailing or, in other words, electronic junk mail. **Spammers** send it and **spammees** receive it. The word derives from the Hormel canned meat product. **Meatloaf** is unsolicited noncommercial e-mail, for example anecdotes and jokes, sent out to a selected group of people. **Paraspam** is an e-mail discussion about spam. *Spam* is also used figuratively as a verb meaning 'to push pointless information on someone' or 'to chat aimlessly'.

➤ **techno-addict:** a person who uses computer technology excessively, for instance by conducting romances over the Internet rather than in person.

➤ **technoliterati:** those who are literate in new computer technology.

➤ **word of mouse:** computer-based communication.

CYBERWORDS

Cybernetics is the science of automatic communications and control systems in both living creatures and machines. In the nineties, *cybernetics* was shortened to *cyber-*, which stood for computers, especially the Internet. Author William Gibson started the trend in his 1984 novel *Neuromancer*. He introduced the word **cyberspace** to describe the virtual reality experienced by the humans in his book, whose brains were connected to a computer network. Other people started using *cyberspace* to mean 'the notional place where all Internet activities occur'. The prefix *cyber-* combines beautifully with practically every English vowel and consonant, so it wasn't long before cyberwords proliferated. Here are some of the more promising:

➤ **cybercafe:** a place that provides beverages, food, and computers, with patrons paying a set fee for time on the Internet.

➤ **cybercapitalism:** the global spread of consumerism by means of the World Wide Web.

➤ **cybercast:** a live broadcast over the Internet.

➤ **cybercrime:** cracking the codes that keep computer accounts, cellular telephones, and other electronic devices private.

➤ **cyberculture:** the culture of the post-Internet age.

➤ **cyberfare:** whatever can be accessed and read online.

➤ **cyberians:** librarians who use computers.

➤ **cyberize:** to cause someone to become interested in computers and the Net.

➤ **cyber-lifestyle:** the sort of lifestyle you can only acquire by using the Internet.

➤ **cyberpal:** someone you meet online.

➤ **cyberpicket:** a union protest displayed at a website.

➤ **cyberpork:** government money that can be earned by working on the Net.

➤ **cyberporn:** electronic pornography. A specific type of cyberporn is the **cyber mistress,** who strips over a live Internet feed.

➤ **cyberpunk:** a type of science fiction that centers on computer technology, such as William Gibson's *Neuromancer*. In the mid-nineties the meaning broadened to cover people who break into computer networks (called **crackers** or **hackers** in the 1980s), from the 'petty criminal' meaning of **punk.**

➤ **cyber-roadkill:** useless websites littering the information superhighway.

➤ **cybersquatter:** someone who registers an Internet address likely to be wanted by a company that can afford to pay well for it. Cybersquatters don't actually use the address, but hold it as an investment.

➤ **cybersurfer:** a person who surfs the Net, visiting numerous websites.

➤ **cyberwonk:** an Internet technology nerd.

INFORMATION SUPERHIGHWAY

The **information superhighway** is the Internet as imagined by politicians and the computer industry. It's an online road that all Americans can travel; a quick, cheap way to access the information we need. Vice-Presidential candidate Al Gore talked about it during the 1992 presidential campaign. He called for a network of "information superhighways" that would link businesses, schools, government agencies, private institutions, and homes. The concept was so widely discussed in the early nineties that the American Dialect Society chose *information superhighway* as its 1993 Word of the Year.

Competing terms were *data highway* or *superhighway* and *electronic highway* or *superhighway*. Another variant was *databahn*, based on the German word *autobahn*, meaning 'highway'. Then there is the **information snooper-highway,** describing users' vulnerability to having their privacy invaded online, and the **information superhypeway,** a reference to the massive amounts of advertising that eventually appeared there.

LIVING IN THE E-WORLD

Another word that became a word part in the 1990s was *electronic*, shortened to *e-* and combined at will. Most forms are self-explanatory. Besides **e-mail,** they include the less common **e-bouquet** (electronically transmitted picture of flowers), e-business, e-commerce, **e-democracy** (online town hall meeting), e-gossip, e-manners, e-paper, **e-postage** (proposed charge for sending e-mail messages), **e-surgery** (performed by one doctor on the scene and one connected via computer), **e-tail** (electronic retailing), e-ticket, e-vite, **e-zine** (online magazine).

HANGIN' WITH THE YUFFIES

The 1960s was the decade of the baby boomers; the nineties saw the **baby busters. Generation X,** named after a 1991 novel by Douglas Coupland, includes young people born sometime between the early sixties and the late seventies. Also called *twentysomethings, post-boomers, boomlets, slackers,* and *grunge kids,* their popular image was that of disenchanted underachievers, frustrated by what they perceived as fewer opportunities than previous generations had enjoyed. Their slang shows that they were ironic, clever, occasionally cynical, and tuned in to the consumer world.

➤ **alternative:** nonconformist, especially noncommercial, most often heard in the phrase *alternative lifestyle.*

➤ **bag:** to harass or criticize, a meaning change from the Valley Girl meaning of 'get rid of'

➤ **Baldwin:** an attractive young male, possibly a reference to the popular family of actors Alec, Daniel, Stephen, and William Baldwin.

➤ **Betty:** an attractive young female, probably from the cartoon character Betty Flintstone. The names of other characters from the animated sit-com *The Flintstones* were also used as labels: **Fred** for a nerd and **Wilma** for a female nitwit. **Barney** was eighties slang for an unattractive male.

➤ **bigtime:** totally. It appears at the end of the sentence, as in *You just blew it bigtime.*

➤ **biscuit head:** a lame, pathetic person.

➤ **brainiac:** very smart, often used sarcastically.

➤ **bump'n:** very high quality, as in *a bump'n CD collection.*

➤ **cheesedog:** the opposite of a topdog; a nerd or loser.

➤ **cool beans:** an expression of mild approval.

➤ **dead tree edition:** a paper version of a magazine, as opposed to an **e-zine.**

➧ **dode:** a fool.

➧ **doe:** stupid, probably from *D'oh,* a puzzled response heard frequently on the animated sit-com *The Simpsons.*

➧ **eat chain:** drop dead, short for *eat a chainsaw.*

➧ **fan:** to pass up an opportunity, possibly from baseball, where *fan* means 'to strike out'.

➧ **flex:** to depart.

➧ **get faced:** become intoxicated.

➧ **get your boogies on:** dance.

➧ **get off with your bad self:** gloat.

➧ **grind:** to eat.

➧ **grobbling:** complaining.

➧ **grumpies:** grownups.

➧ **hangin':** what used to be called *hanging out,* that is, spending time with your friends doing nothing.

➧ **insane:** fearless, especially while engaging in potentially dangerous sports like skateboarding and mountain biking. **Kodak courage** is what makes you fearless when you know that the cameras are pointed in your direction.

➧ **jonesing:** wanting something badly, from an earlier use of *jones* meaning 'a drug addiction' or 'drug withdrawal symptoms'. By the 1990s, *jones* meant 'any kind of strong craving', and was often used jokingly as in a *caffeine jones.*

➧ **lates:** I'll see you later.

➧ **madd:** crowded, as in *this place is madd with grumpies.*

➧ **make bank:** to earn good money. *Bank* to mean 'money' is borrowed from rap. **Bank geeks** were teens slightly younger than Xers, characterized by conservatism and nerdishness.

➧ **McJob:** low-paid, unchallenging work, frequently in the service sector. McJobs garnered a **McSalary.** The term appears in Douglas Coupland's novel *Generation X. Mc* was a popular prefix in the nineties to indicate a simplified or mass-market version of something. (See **McWar** above.) It apparently derives from the name of the fast-food chain, McDonald's.

➧ **microserf:** a low-paid computer worker.

➧ **mint:** money.

➧ **mondo:** extremely.

➧ **MTV Generation:** the group of young people that grew up in the 1980s, with the Music Television channel as their chief source of cultural knowledge.

➧ **nappy:** gross.

➤ **nectar:** beautiful.

➤ **phase shifter:** someone who sleeps all day and parties all night.

➤ **plug:** name for a temporary worker who's covering for a permanent employee on leave.

➤ **postal:** crazy and violent, especially used in the phrase **go postal.** The expression comes from an incident in which a fired postal worker went out of control and shot several former colleagues.

➤ **rager:** a wild party.

➤ **rave:** a huge, semipublic party, often thrown in an abandoned warehouse, a field, or some other illegal location, and featuring music, dancing, and drugs. Raves often end with the arrival of the police.

➤ **raw:** great, very good; nice-looking.

➤ **scenic:** an attention-grabbing event, such as a fistfight in a restaurant.

➤ **score:** to acquire. The word had meant 'buy drugs' from the 1930s. In the 1970s, the meaning shifted to cover the acquisition of sex. By the 1990s it could refer to any item.

➤ **stud muffin:** a sexy guy.

➤ **stupid fresh:** even better than fresh; really outstanding.

➤ **sunflower:** a cute girl.

➤ **telephone number salary:** a seven-digit yearly income.

➤ **whatever:** yeah, okay. I don't care about it enough to argue with you. This sense of the word was first heard in the eighties, but became

---

SLACKER

A special subgroup of the X Generation was that of **slackers.** A *slacker* has been a person who avoids work since the nineteenth century. A new twist in the nineties was that the term could have positive connotations, depending on your point of view. Slackers of this era were generally college-educated and middle- or upper-middle-class. They deliberately chose to be marginally employed (called **occupational slumming**), either because they rejected nineties consumerism or because they were reluctant to sign on for a conventional, work-oriented adulthood. During their free time, slackers often pursued quirky or specialized interests. Like the beatniks before them, they spent a lot of time in coffeehouses and cybercafes with like-minded companions. Slackers were often found living on the fringes of their old university. Richard Linklater's 1991 movie, *Slacker,* showcased the Austin, Texas, manifestation of this type.

much more prevalent in the underenergized nineties. Now it is virtually standard English.

➧ **yuffie:** young urban failure.

XERS ON WALL STREET

Not all of the younger generation were slackers in the 1990s. Some took advantage of their familiarity with computers to start online businesses. **Dot-coms** were a major part of the business boom of the late nineties. Owners and investors got rich—on paper, at least—when stock prices for online companies shot into the financial stratosphere. The crash came all too soon. Shortly into the next century, dot-coms began turning into **dot-compost,** but for a while Silicon Valley and Wall Street were happily joined.

➧ **bandwidth:** a computerized communication system's data transfer rate, used figuratively to describe someone's level of brain power, as in *He doesn't have the bandwidth for this project.*

➧ **cafeteria officing:** when an employer gives a worker the choice of coming to work at a central location or setting up a home office.

➧ **dot-com:** a shorthand way of referring to an Internet business. The main part of an Internet address is its domain name, which identifies the website's provider, followed by a period (*dot*), and, in the United States, a three-letter indicator of what type of entity it is. The addresses of commercial enterprises generally end in *.com* (for instance, *www.somebusiness.com*). Other common endings are *.edu* for educational institutions, *.org* for nonprofit organizations, and *.gov* for the federal government. **Dot-communists** are those who believe in a big future for the Internet, either people who work for a dot-com, or cybernerds who think the Internet should be widely available, but noncommercial. **Dot-compost** describes the reusable assets from a failed dot-com.

➧ **downtime:** the time when a computer is not running, but also used to mean occasions when humans take work breaks.

➧ **dumbsizing:** cutting back on the number of employees so drastically that it hurts the business. This word is a takeoff on **downsizing,** a gentle term for firing people. An even more delicate expression is **rightsizing,** or making the work force the right size by getting rid of excess people. A similar euphemism is **decruitment,** the opposite of recruitment. During the dot-com boom, **upsizing** also occasionally took place.

➧ **emailingering:** the Internet way to hang around the water cooler, reading and writing e-mail and fiddling around on the Internet to avoid doing work.

entreprenerd: a computer person who starts an Internet business.

firewall: a security system that prevents sensitive information from being accessed by outsiders.

high tech, high wreck: a prescient saying that indicates some concern about the dot-coms' ability to sustain their high nineties stock prices.

hoteling: moving office workers from one cubicle to another, depending on who happens to be around on a given day. Hoteling is a way to get along with less office space in a situation where many employees have flexible hours or work at home.

incubator: an established company that provides office space, managerial support, and financing to a start-up company.

legacy: the way companies did things before the Internet; for example, *legacy banking systems*.

price-to-fantasy: a way to measure a company's current stock price against its greatest potential price. The stock price of dot-coms was often more fantasy than reality.

starter castle: the first home of a newly rich dot-commer, also known as a *McMansion*.

sunlighting: accepting an outside project while working for your regular employer at home. This practice is the same as moonlighting, but telecommuters don't have to wait until the evening to take on a second job because they are not physically present at a central office.

webisode: a short television program, usually less than ten minutes, delivered over the Web.

DRESSING FOR THE NEW MILLENNIUM

During the nineties, fashion continued its trend of "anything goes." Here are a few distinctive looks of the decade:

casual Friday: the corporate innovation of wearing casual clothes to work on Friday, also called *dress-down Friday*. Casual Friday was not completely casual, as jeans were usually not allowed. A typical outfit would be khakis, a denim work shirt, and a blazer or sports jacket.

Club Kid style: the flamboyant wardrobe favored by youths who frequented **raves** and dance clubs, including glitter makeup, exaggerated platform shoes, and see-through vinyl clothing.

grunge chic: a style that emulated the clothing of grunge rock fans. *Grunge* is a Seattle-based heavy metal sound, an outgrowth of punk. Some 1990s grunge bands were Nirvana, Alice in Chains, Pearl Jam, and Soundgarden. **Grungers** dressed in loose, sloppy, mismatched layers, perhaps combining thermal underwear with cutoff jeans and a flannel shirt. Women sometimes wore droopy cotton dresses over long

Grunge chic.

underwear or tights. In a word, the look was grungy (although it should be noted that many of these clothes were highly practical in Seattle's climate). The best and cheapest way to collect grungewear was to go **thrifting** in secondhand shops.

➤ **Hammer pants:** an exaggerated harem pants look, introduced by the nineties rapper MC Hammer. These pants were a logical extension of the hip-hop artist's loose, comfortable clothing. They featured a pleated waist, legs that ballooned out to a tapered ankle, and a crotch that drooped about midway to the knee.

➤ **mullet:** a restyled shag haircut, shorter on top and with longer back strands that resemble a fish tail.

➤ **riot grrl:** the look of some very tough young females, exemplified by grunge rocker Courtney Love of the band Hole. Riot grrls emphasized both their freedom from conventional feminine restrictions and their pride in their sexuality. They might wear a baby doll dress with combat boots and fishnet stockings. They tattooed and practiced body piercing—inserting what were once known as earrings in their lips, eyebrows, tongues, navels, and other body parts. Makeup was obvious and messily applied. Young female **digerati** were sometimes known as *cybergrrls, webgrrls,* or *technogrrls.*

VERBING NOUNS

Nouns that turn into verbs are nothing new in English. That process has been taking place for centuries. However, the usual trickle of words from one category to the other became a flood in the 1990s. People were verbing all sorts of nouns that would have been unlikely candidates in earlier times, including compound nouns and nouns that have already been adapted once from another part of speech. Here are some innovative forms. A few (**transition, instant message, workshop**) have made it into the mainstream. Most have not found widespread use.

➤ **to agent:** to act as someone's agent.

➤ **to calendar:** to mark an event on one's calendar.

➤ **to college:** to attend college.

➤ **to dialogue:** to talk with another person, that is, to have a dialogue.

➤ **to effort:** to make an effort to accomplish something, a word from the Gulf War, used in sentences like "We are efforting television coverage of that event." Another noun/verb from the Gulf is **to bunker,** which means 'to search Iraqi bunkers for souvenirs'.

➤ **to error:** the same thing as *to err,* but with one additional syllable.

➤ **to fellowship:** to worship or share fellowship at a church.

➤ **to fetish:** to make a fetish of some idea or object.

➤ **to fountain:** to shoot up in a stream, as a fountain does.

➤ **to guilt:** to make someone feel guilty.

➤ **to household:** to send one mailing per household instead of sending to individuals within the household; for example, sending one annual report to two people who hold shares in the same company.

➤ **to instant message:** to converse with someone over the Internet by sending messages back and forth when you are both online. **Message** alone is also used as a verb.

➤ **to journal:** to keep a journal.

➤ **to keynote:** to present a keynote address.

➤ **to multitask:** to make a computer perform more than one function at a time. Later, it meant a human's performance of more than one task at a time.

➤ **to no-hit:** to pitch a baseball game in which no batter scores a hit, or, in other words, to pitch a no-hitter.

➤ **to pie:** to hit someone in the face with a pie as a political statement.

➤ **to pond:** to place hatchery fish in a pond, a turn of phrase favored by the U.S. Army Corps of Engineers.

➤ **to privilege:** to place some person, group, or idea in a privileged position. This verb has been used to the point of saturation by trendy literary scholars, although it is not often heard among the general population.

➤ **to PR:** to market to people through public relations. *PR* is an abbreviation of *public relations,* but the unabbreviated form doesn't seem to work as a verb (so far).

➤ **to office:** to supply the types of services usually found in a business office, such as photocopying and sending fax messages, or simply to have an office, used in expressions such as *she offices downtown.*

➤ **to rehome:** to place a stray animal in a new home, noted on a British website, "Cats Online."

➤ **to sewer:** to install sewers in a neighborhood.

➤ **to single-parent:** to raise a child as its only available parent.

➤ **to source:** to find a source for, usually used by businesspeople. A related word is **outsource,** meaning 'to hire temporary workers or independent consultants rather than using permanent employees'.

➤ **to taboo:** to forbid a subject's discussion; that is, to make the subject taboo.

➤ **to task:** to assign a task to someone. Note the difference in perspective between this word and *multitask.*

➤ **to timeline:** to give someone a timeline or assign a timeline for a project.

➤ **to transition:** to make a transition from one state of being to another state, such as transitioning from a noun to a verb. An earlier verb, *transit,* as in *to transit the desert,* is the basis for the noun *transition.*

➤ **to vision:** to have or develop a vision; to envision.

➤ **to wordsmith:** to talk loosely or chat about a topic.

➤ **to workshop:** to get together in a group to talk over ideas and solutions to problems.

THE END OF THE WORLD AS WE KNOW IT

As the year 2000 approached, people became aware of a potentially serious computer glitch. In earlier decades, computers were designed to store dates as two-digit numbers. For instance, the year 1979 was encoded as "79." This feature saved on computer memory, but was shortsighted. At the turn of the century, the date was set to roll over to "00," which the computer would interpret as 1900. This situation was known as the *Year 2000 problem* or, more commonly, **Y2K,** with *K* representing the number 1,000. Unless the problem was corrected, computer systems were predicted to malfunction, causing chaos.

In spite of assurances that the government and businesses were busy correcting the **millennium bug,** many Americans expected the end of the world as we know it and the emergence of a new, technology-free environment. A Y2K cottage industry sprang up, producing a flurry of print articles and websites describing the apocalyptic consequences of computer breakdown. These included failure of electrical and telephone systems and the possibility that nuclear weapons would fire by accident. The Y2K industry abruptly collapsed on the morning of January 1, 2000, when it became clear that the modern world's operating systems had reached **compliance** in time.

» **changeover:** the change from dates beginning with 19 to dates beginning with 20, also called **rollover** or *date rollover.*

» **digital doomsday:** one way of describing the Y2K problem.

» **event horizon:** the date when a system would start having problems because of not being able to correctly process 00 as 2000.

» **fix-on-failure:** a strategy of waiting until Y2K computer problems occurred before attempting to fix them.

» **millennial meltdown:** what would happen if computer date problems weren't fixed in time.

» **millennium bug:** the glitch that caused computers to be unable to interpret 00 correctly, sometimes called the *Y2K bug.*

» **Y2K compliance:** updating the computer's hardware and software so that it can correctly interpret the date 00 as 2000, also called *Y2K conformity* and *Y2K readiness.* The expected crisis was called **Y2Kaos,** while the ease with which computers actually rolled over was labeled **Y2Kake.**

NINETIES BUZZWORDS

These buzzwords show that human relations were still important in the computer age, even as digital doomsday neared. Lifestyles, alternative and otherwise, were in the news.

» **Contract with America:** a Republican proposal for federal government reform, especially budgetary reform. On September 27, 1994, three hundred Republican congressional candidates pledged themselves to a Contract with America if they were elected. Their proposals included a constitutional amendment requiring a balanced federal budget, term limits for legislators, revised welfare laws, tax cuts, a boost in the military budget, a reduction in the size of the federal government, and a presidential line-item veto to make it easier for the president to eliminate wasteful spending.

Those who considered the plan unworkable sometimes referred to it as the *Contract on America.* However, it appealed to voters. Many newly elected Republicans swept into Congress during the 1994 midterm elections. Once there, hampered by infighting and the threat of presidential vetoes, they were unable to enact some major components of the Contract. The plan had run out of steam by the 1996 elections, although Republicans retained their majorities in both the House and the Senate.

Ebonics: name for the speech style of some African Americans, more often known as African-American Vernacular English. The word is a blend of *ebony* and *phonics,* and has been in use among specialists since the 1970s. *Ebonics* burst into the popular consciousness in December 1996, when the school board in Oakland, California, passed a resolution describing it as "the predominantly primary language of African-American students." The Board proposed to start treating Ebonics as a separate language rather than a nonstandard dialect of English. They wanted to use the same teaching methods for Ebonics speakers that were used for other bilinguals. They also planned to earmark special funds to support the teaching program.

When the Board's resolution made the news, commentators of all colors and political leanings felt moved to weigh in with their opinions. Although responses varied, nearly all were sharply negative. Some people accused Oakland of making an ill-disguised grab for extra funding. At the heart of the controversy was the issue of whether Ebonics is a language or merely a corrupt form of English. School Board members based their conclusions on decades of research demonstrating that African-American speech patterns have their own structure and logic. The Linguistic Society of America supported Oakland, affirming that Ebonics is systematic and rule-governed, like all language. However, the Society's expert opinion made only a small splash in the ocean of general disapproval. The hard-pressed Board quickly wrote an amended resolution. This time, they referred to "language patterns" rather than "primary language" and emphasized the need to teach standard English.

sandwich generation: men and women who take care of their children and their parents at the same time, usually baby boomers in their forties or fifties. This term reflects some new social realities that were becoming apparent in the nineties, a longer-lived population and greater numbers of people who have children late in life. Two related terms are **daughter track** and **granny track** to refer to women who need flexible work schedules so they can care for their elderly parents. Both terms are based on **mommy track,** the less challenging, less economically rewarding career path that mothers of small children often follow. Occasionally, members of the sandwich generation practiced **granny dumping,** the abandonment of elderly relatives in hospital emergency rooms.

➤ **soccer mom:** an upper-middle-class white suburban woman who spends a lot of time running the kids to soccer practice and other after-school activities. Both political parties saw the soccer mom as an important force during the 1996 election campaigns. They pitched family-oriented proposals in hopes of acquiring her vote. Many women, however, considered the term derogatory. Less-used labels were *soccer dad* and *soccer parent.* Another important voting bloc was the **waitress mom,** or working-class woman, although that term was also less widely used.

Afterword

Good-Bye to a Great Century

It's been a wild, but fascinating, hundred-year ride. We started out driving **flivvers** and ended up traveling the **data highway.** Now it's time for **jazz babies, flower children,** and **grunge kids** to roll over to the new century. **Twenty-three skiddoo!** Or, in other words:

See you in the funny papers! (1900/1910s)

Don't take any wooden nickels (1900/1910s)

Toodle-pip (1920s)

Abyssinia! (1930s)

Got to take a fast powder (1940s)

Black time's here, termite (1950s)

It's been real (1960s)

See you on the flipside (1970s)

I'm outie (1980s)

Buh-bye (1990s)

Bibliography

GENERAL SOURCES

Auchter, Dorothy. *Dictionary of Historical Allusions and Eponyms*. Santa Barbara, Calif.: ABC-Clio, 1998.

Ayto, John. *The Oxford Dictionary of Slang*. Oxford; New York: Oxford University Press, 1998.

Barnhart, Robert K., ed. *The Barnhart Dictionary of Etymology*. New York: The H.W. Wilson Co., 1988.

Berry, Lester V., and Melvin Van den Bark. *The American Thesaurus of Slang: A Complete Reference Book of Colloquial Speech*. New York: Crowell, 1953.

Browne, Ray B., and Pat Browne, eds. *The Guide to United States Popular Culture*. Bowling Green, Ohio: Bowling Green State University Popular Press, 2001.

Chapman, Robert L., ed. *New Dictionary of American Slang*. New York: Harper & Row, 1986.

Cumming, Valeria, and Elane Feldman, series eds. *Fashions of a Decade*. New York: Facts on File, 1991– .

Dalzell, Tom. *Flappers 2 Rappers: American Youth Slang*. Springfield, Mass.: Merriam-Webster, 1996.

Flexner, Stuart Berg. *I Hear America Talking*. New York: Van Nostrand Reinhold, 1976.

Flexner, Stuart Berg. *Listening to America*. New York: Simon and Schuster, 1982.

Green, Jonathon. *The Cassell Dictionary of Slang*. London: Cassell, 1998.

Hendrickson, Robert. *The Facts on File Encyclopedia of Word and Phrase Origins*. New York: Facts on File, 1987.

Inge, M. Thomas, ed. *Handbook of American Popular Culture*. New York: Greenwood Press, 1989.

Lighter, Jonathan, ed. *The Random House Historical Dictionary of American Slang*. New York: Random House, 1994.

Mallery, Richard Davis. *Our American Language*. Garden City, N.Y.: Halcyon House, 1947.

Mencken, H. L. *The American Language*, 3rd ed. New York: Alfred A. Knopf, 1923.

Mencken, H. L. *The American Language*, 4th ed. New York: Alfred A. Knopf, 1938.

Morris, William, and Mary Morris. *Dictionary of Word and Phrase Origins*. New York: Harper & Row, 1962–1967.

Moss, George Donelson. *America in the Twentieth Century*, 2nd ed. Englewood Cliffs, N.J.: Prentice Hall, 1993.

Panati, Charles. *Panati's Parade of Fads, Follies and Manias: The Origins of Our Most Cherished Obsessions*. New York: Harper Perennial, 1991.

Partridge, Eric. *A Dictionary of Catch Phrases*, Revised and Updated Edition, edited by Paul Beale. New York: Stein and Day, 1986.

Partridge, Eric. *Slang Today and Yesterday*, 4th ed. London: Routledge & Kegan Paul, 1970.

Rollin, Lucy. *Twentieth-Century Teen Culture by the Decades*. Westport, Conn.: Greenwood Press, 1999.

Room, Adrian. *Brewer's Dictionary of Modern Phrase and Fable.* London: Cassell, 2000.

Simpson, J. A., and E. S. C. Weiner. *The Oxford English Dictionary,* 2nd ed. Oxford: Clarendon Press, 1989.

Spears, Richard A. *NTC's Dictionary of American Slang and Colloquial Expressions.* Chicago: NTC Publishing Group, 2000.

This Fabulous Century: Sixty Years of American Life. New York: Time-Life Books, 1969–1970.

Wentworth, Harold, and Stuart Berg Flexner. *Dictionary of American Slang.* New York: Crowell, 1975.

WEBSITES

"American Cultural History—The Twentieth Century." Kingwood College Library (Kingwood, Texas). *http://kclibrary.nhmccd.edu/decades.html*

"American Dialect Society E-mail List Archive." *www.americandialect.org/adsl.html*

1900–1919

A Dictionary of Catch Phrases and the *Dictionary of American Slang* provide detailed discussions of possible sources for *twenty-three skiddoo.* H. L. Mencken also speculates on the derivation of this term in the third edition of *The American Language.*

Cakewalks are described in *The International Encyclopedia of Dance,* Selma Jeanne Cohen, founding editor (New York: Oxford University Press, 1998).

Terms for early-twentieth-century inventions, including automobiles and moving pictures, are found in Frederick Lewis Allen, *The Big Change: America Transforms Itself 1900–1950* (New York: Harper and Bros., 1952); Lloyd Morris, *Not So Long Ago* (New York: Random House, 1949); and a second book by Morris, *Postscript to Yesterday: America: The Last Fifty Years* (New York: Random House, 1947).

Magazines of the time devoted many pages to motors and motoring. Two that are especially useful for terminology are *Illustrated World* and *Country Life in America.* Some auto words and lore are also from Bill Bryson, *Made in America: An Informal History of the English Language in the United States* (New York: William Morrow and Co., 1994). *Tin Lizzie* language is collected in B. A. Botkin, "The Lore of the Lizzie Label," *American Speech* 6 (Dec. 1930): 81–93.

Vaudeville terms are listed on the website "Vaudeville Memories," *http://members. rogers.com/vaudeville/vaudslang.htm.*

The Case Western slang is from Robert Bolwell, "College Slang Words and Phrases from Western Reserve University," *Dialect Notes* IV, part 3 (1915): 231–238.

The clothing terms in this chapter are from magazines, the 1900–1910 and 1910–1920 volumes of *This Fabulous Century: Sixty Years of American Life,* and Lloyd Morris's *Not So Long Ago.*

Nearly all the war words are from Mencken's *The American Language,* 3rd. ed., or from Jonathan Lighter, "The Slang of the American Expeditionary Forces, 1917–1919," *American Speech* 47 (Spring-Summer 1972): 5–142.

-Fest words are from Louise Pound, "Domestications of the Suffix *-fest,*" *Dialect Notes* IV, Part V (1916): 353–354.

Wobbly jargon is recorded in Stewart H. Holbrook, "Wobbly Talk," *The American Mercury* 7 (Jan. 1926): 62–65.

1920s

Lists of flapper slang abound. Most of the flapper words in this chapter are from Mencken, *The American Language,* 3rd ed.; the 1920–1930 volume of *This Fabulous Century*; "College Slang: A Language All Its Own," *The Literary Digest,* 14 March 1925, 64–65; M.C. McPhee, "College Slang," *American Speech* 3 (Dec. 1927): 131–133;

and F. Walter Pollock, "Courtship Slang," *American Speech* 2 (Jan. 1927): 202–203. Material about the *vampire baby* comes from the American Dialect Society E-mail List Archive.

Virtually all the clothing terms for this and subsequent chapters are from *Fashions of a Decade* and, starting in the 1940s, the website "Yesterdayland Fashion." A few for this chapter are from Kevin Rayburn's website "The 1920s" (offline at time of writing).

Many music dictionaries discuss the origins of the word *jazz*, including Peter Clayton and Peter Gammond, *Jazz A–Z* (Enfield, Middlesex: Guinness Superlatives, 1986) and Robert Gold, *A Jazz Lexicon* (New York: A.A. Knopf, 1964). A very complete account is Alan P. Merriam and Fradley H. Garner, "Jazz—The Word," *Ethnomusicology* 12 (Sep. 1968): 373–396. The American Dialect Society E-mail List Archive includes an extensive discussion of *jazz*, covering, among other issues, the question of its earliest usage and whether it originally connoted sexual activity. Some jazz terms are from Murray L. Pfeffer's "The Big Bands Database," *http://nfo.net/*.

Alcohol is another major twenties topic. The words in this chapter come from Achsah Hardin, "Volstead English," *American Speech* 7 (Dec. 1931): 81–88; "The Lexicon of Prohibition," *The New Republic*, 9 March 1927, 71–72; and Manuel Prenner, "Slang Synonyms for Drunk," *American Speech* 4 (Dec. 1928): 102–103, as well as some of the *flapper* word lists.

Sources of the gangster slang are James P. Burke, "The Argot of Racketeers," *The American Mercury*, Dec. 1930, 454–458 and the website "Twists, Slugs and Roscoes: A Glossary of Hardboiled Slang," compiled by William Denton, *www.miskatonic.org/slang.html*.

Charles Wolverton discusses possible etymologies for *ballyhoo* in "Ballyhoo," *American Speech* 10 (Dec. 1935): 289–291.

The spiritualism terms were collected from the many magazine articles on the subject that appeared during the 1920s.

Aviation slang comes from "Aviators Speak a Language All Their Own," *The Literary Digest*, 12 May 1928, 73–74; Paul Robert Beath, "Aviation Lingo," *American Speech* 6 (April 1930): 289–290; Capt. Scott Townsend, "Winged Words You Should Know," *Popular Mechanics*, August 1926, 291–293.

Two general sources of twenties terminology are Frederick Lewis Allen, *Only Yesterday: An Informal History of the 1920's* (New York: Harper & Row, 1931) and the website "The 1920s."

1930s

Words and abbreviations of the Depression and New Deal are mostly from Moss, *America in the Twentieth Century* and Flexner, *I Hear America Talking*. Some of the words, including Hoover words, are found in *Panati's Parade of Fads, Follies and Manias*. Other Hoover words are in the 1930s volume of *This Fabulous Century*. Dust Bowl words are scattered throughout 1930s *American Speech* Miscellanies. Donald Worster describes *suitcase farming* in *Dust Bowl: The Southern Plains in the 1930s* (New York: Oxford University Press, 1979).

My main sources of hobo slang were Dean Stiff (real name Nels Anderson), *The Milk and Honey Route: A Handbook for Hoboes* (New York: Vanguard Press, 1930) and Carl Jacobsen, "Jargon of the Road," *American Speech* 11 (April 1936): 278. Some discussion of the differences among hoboes, tramps, and bums is found on the American Dialect Society E-mail List Archive.

Swing words come from the 1930s volume of *This Fabulous Century*; Carl Cons, "The Slanguage of Swing," *Down Beat*, July 1994, 20 (a reprint of a 1935 list); and H. Brook Webb, "The Slang of Jazz," *American Speech* 12 (Oct. 1937): 179–184.

S. P. Lawton, *Radio Speech* (Boston: Expression Co., 1932) provided some of the radio slang. Other sources were "Some Radio Terms," *Fortune,* May 1938, 54 and *American Speech* Miscellanies. Walter Winchell's distinctive language is recorded in Paul Robert Beath, "Winchellese," *American Speech* 7 (Oct. 1931): 44–46 and in biographical articles about Winchell.

Harold W. Bentley, "Linguistic Concoctions of the Soda Jerker," *American Speech* 11 (Feb. 1936): 37–45 and John Lancaster Riordan, "Soda Fountain Lingo," *California Folklore Quarterly* 4 (1945): 50–57 provided the colorful soda fountain terms.

Levette Jay Davidson records thirties road words in "Auto-tourist Talk," *American Speech* 9 (April 1934):110–114. The latest terminology is also found in many magazine articles of the period. All the Burma-Shave jingles are listed in a delightful little book by Frank Rowsome, Jr., *The Verse by the Side of the Road: The Story of Burma-Shave Signs and Jingles* (Brattleboro, Vt.: Stephen Greene Press, 1965).

Information about Maury Paul and Café Society is from Eve Brown, *Champagne Cholly: The Life and Times of Maury Paul* (New York: E. P. Dutton, 1947). Frank M. Calabria wrote in detail about dance marathons in "The Dance Marathon Craze," *Journal of Popular Culture* 10 (Summer 1976): 54–69. The material on sit-down strikes is from George E. Peter, *American Speech* 12 (Feb. 1937): 31–33. Most of the information about the *War of the Worlds* broadcast is from the University of Virginia American Studies Program's 1930s Project, *http://xroads.virginia.edu/~1930s/front.html,* and the American Cultural History website. The quoted conversation is reported in "Radio Listeners in Panic, Taking War Drama as Fact," *The New York Times,* 31 Oct. 1938.

A good source of thirties terms and historical background is Frederick Lewis Allen's *Since Yesterday: The 1930s in America* (New York: Harper and Row, 1939).

1940s

Sources for World War II words and phrases are plentiful. I used Joseph W. Bishop Jr., "American Army Speech in the European Theater," *American Speech* 21 (Dec. 1946): 241–252; "Glossary of Army Slang" (from the Public Relations Division of the U.S. Army), *American Speech* 16 (Oct. 1941): 163–169; A. Marjorie Taylor, *The Language of World War II* (New York: The H. W. Wilson Co., 1948); as well as *I Hear America Talking* and the 1940s volume of *This Fabulous Century.* The POW terms are from Frederika D. Borchard, "From Behind Barbed Wire," *The New York Times Magazine,* 4 Nov. 1945, 12. Richard R. Lingeman's *Don't You Know There's a War On?* (New York: G. P. Putnam's Sons, 1970) provided some military and home front terms, as did *Slanguage Dictionary of Modern American Slang* (Newton, Iowa: The L. B. Robison Co., 1944).

Various versions of the Kilroy legend popped up in magazine articles after the war. Many are recounted at the website "Kilroy Was Here," Patrick A. Tillery, webmaster, *www.kilroywashere.org.* Discussion of the term *fifth column* is mainly from Dwight L. Bolinger, "Fifth Column Marches On," *American Speech* 19 (Feb. 1944): 47–49.

The teen slang can be found in "Is Your Sub-Deb Slang up-to-Date?" *Ladies Home Journal,* Dec. 1944, 152–153; Catherine Mackenzie, "Teen-Age Slang," *The New York Times Magazine,* 5 Dec. 1953, 32; Doris Willens, "It's Oogley, Also Bong," *The New York Times Magazine,* 6 March 1949, 33–35. Arthur K. Moore reviews early forms of *juke* in "Jouk," *American Speech* 16 (Dec. 1941): 319–320.

Forties jive talk comes from *Slanguage Dictionary of Modern Slang* and Babs Gonzales, *Be-Bop Dictionary* (New York: Arlain Publishing, 1949). A few words are from Richard O. Boyer, "Bop," *The New Yorker,* 3 July 1948, 28–37. "The Voutians," *Life,* 5 May 1947, 129–135 provided most of the Voutian vocabulary. A few words came from Tom Dalzell's *Flappers 2 Rappers.*

Harold Wentworth collected words with "The Neo-Pseudo-Suffix 'eroo'" in *American Speech* 17 (Feb. 1942): 10–15. A. D. Weinberg discusses *hubba-hubba* in "Some Data and Conjectures on the History of 'Hubba-hubba'," *American Speech* 22 (Feb. 1947): 34–39.

1950s

Most of the words relating to the bomb and communism come from Douglas T. Miller and Marion Nowak, *The Fifties: The Way We Really Were* (Garden City, N.Y.: Doubleday and Co., 1977) and *America in the Twentieth Century*. Different words for bomb shelters can be found in magazine articles and advertisements, especially in *Time* and *Newsweek*. The term *red market* appeared in "Steel Head Assails Vicious 'Red Market'," *The New York Times*, 13 Oct. 1950, 41. The information about the Doomsday Clock is from the website of the Bulletin of Atomic Scientists, *www.bullatomsci.org/clock/doomsdayclock.html.*

Sputnik-based words are collected in Louise M. Ackerman, "Facetious Variations of 'Sputnik'," *American Speech* 33 (May 1958, Part 1): 154–156; William White, "Sputnik and Its Satellites," *American Speech* 33 (May 1958, Part I): 153–154; and Philip C. Kolin, "*Successniks*," *American Speech* 57 (Winter 1982): 255.

Words from the Korean War are elusive. A few of those listed are found in *I Hear America Talking*. Most are from Paul Dickson, *War Slang: American Fighting Words and Phrases from the Civil War to the Gulf War* (New York: Pocket Books, 1994). War-related words also appear occasionally in 1950s volumes of *American Speech*.

Teenage slang is from "Gator Gab," *Time*, 24 Aug. 1959, 46; "It's Zorch," *Newsweek*, June 8, 1953, 60; "Jelly Tot, Square Bear-Man," *Newsweek*, 8 Oct. 1951, 28–29; Jan Landon, "When You Say That, Smile!" *Good Housekeeping*, Oct. 1954, 18; "Zorch Is Dimph," *Life*, 13 July 1953, 41–42. Teen drug words are collected in William C. De Lannoy and Elizabeth Masterson, "Teen-age Hophead Jargon," *American Speech* 28 (Feb. 1952): 23–31.

A number of articles on drive-ins and 3–D movies appeared in fifties magazines such as *Time* and *Life*. They are also covered in *This Fabulous Century*.

Hot rod vocabulary is from "Hod Rod Dictionary," *Popular Science Monthly*, Dec. 1952, 185–188; "Hot-Rod Terms for Teen-Age Girls," *Good Housekeeping*, Sep. 1958, 143; Don Mansell and Joseph S. Hall, "Hot Rod Terms in the Pasadena Area," *American Speech* 29 (May 1954): 89–104.

Most of the beat lingo is found in Max Décharné, *Straight from the Fridge, Dad* (New York: Broadway Books, 2001). Some is from Ashley Talbot's *Beat Speak* (Sudbury, Mass.: Water Row Press, 1996).

William Randle offers a detailed discussion of *payola* and its offshoots in "Payola," *American Speech* 36 (May 1961): 104–116. Material on the $64,000 question is from *TV Guide: The First 25 Years*, compiled and edited by Jay S. Harris (New York: Simon & Schuster, 1978) and *Museum of Broadcast Communications Encyclopedia of Television*, edited by Horace Newcomb (Chicago: Fitzroy Dearborn Publications, 1997).

1960s

Most of the Vietnam vocabulary comes from newspaper and magazine articles: R. W. Apple Jr., "G.I.'s Vocabulary in Vietnam is Beaucoup Exotic," *The New York Times*, 3 Nov. 1965, 2; "In the Boonies, It's Numbah Ten Thou'," *Time*, 10 Dec. 1965, 34; Jack Langguth, "A New G.I. Argot Can Be Heard in Vietnam Hooches (Barracks)," *The New York Times*, 20 Sep. 1964, 4; Joseph Treaster, "G-Eye View of Vietnam," *The New York Times Magazine*, 30 Oct. 1966, 100, 102, 104, 106, 109. The Vietnam Veterans Home Page, Bill McBride, webmaster, has a word list at *www.vietvet.org*. Another source is Gregory R. Clark, *Words of the Vietnam War*

(Jefferson, N.C.: McFarland & Co., 1990). Also, personal narratives of the Vietnam War often include glossaries.

Hippie talk is from John Bassett McLeary, *The Hippie Dictionary: A Cultural Encyclopedia (and Phraseicon) of the 1960s and 1970s* (Berkeley, Calif.: Ten Speed Press, 2002) and the glossaries of Robert J. Glessing, *The Underground Press in America* (Bloomington, Ind.: Indiana University Press, 1970) and Louis Yablonsky, *The Hippie Trip* (New York: Pegasus, 1968). Two magazine sources are "The Freaks Had a Word for It," *Newsweek,* 29 Dec. 1969, 18 and Mike Jahn, "If You Think It's Groovy to Rap, You're Shucking," *The New York Times Magazine,* 6 June 1971, 28–29, 93–95, 98. Marijuana slang is usually part of hippie or college student glossaries, but a more complete source is Ernest L. Abel, *A Marihuana Dictionary: Words, Terms, Events, and Persons Relating to Cannabis* (Westport, Conn.: Greenwood Press, 1982).

Kelsie B. Harder provides an impressive list of *-in* words in "Coinages of the Type of 'Sit-in'," *American Speech* 43 (Feb. 1968): 58–64. Freaks are listed in Paul A. Eschholz, "*Freak* Compounds for 'Argot Freaks'," *American Speech* 44 (Winter 1969): 306–307.

Mainstream teenage slang comes from Lynda Bird Johnson, "A Glossary of Campus Slang," *McCall's,* April 1967, 56; Lawrence Poston III and Francis J. Stillman, "Notes on Campus Vocabulary, 1964," *American Speech* 40 (Oct. 1965): 193–195; "The Slang Bag," *Time,* 1 Jan. 1965, 57–58; Angela Taylor, "For the Parent Who Is a 'Grunge': A Glossary of New College Slang," *The New York Times,* 27 Dec. 1965, 20. Most of the surfer words are listed in "The Mad Happy Surfers," *Life,* 1 Sep. 1961, 47–53. Other words plus background are from a most excellent surfing compendium by Trevor Cralle, *The Surfin'ary* (Berkeley, Calif.: Ten Speed Press, 1991).

Margaret M. Bryant collected words from the space program in "Space Exploration Terms," *American Speech* 43 (Oct. 1968): 163–181. More words are found in Berger Evans, "New World, New Words," *The New York Times Magazine,* 9 April 1961, 62, 64, 66.

A good background source for the sixties is William L. O'Neill, *Coming Apart* (Chicago: Quadrangle Books, 1971).

1970s

Details of seventies fads come from *The United States Guide to Popular Culture*; "Super70s.com," *www.super70s.com/Super70s/*; "8-Track Heaven," *www.8track-heaven.com*; Mary Bellis, "Lava Lite Lamp," *www.inventors.about.com/library/weekly/aa092297.htm.* Another source for pet rock information is Jane and Michael Stern, *Encyclopedia of POP Culture* (New York: Harper Perennial Press, 1992). Two useful magazine articles on Rubik's cubes are "Hot-Selling Hungarian Horror," *Time,* 23 March 1981 and "The Cube: Method in the Madness," *Newsweek,* 10 August 1981, 76. Streaking words are collected in the "Among the New Words" section of *American Speech* 48 (Spring–Summer 1973): 140–142. More words are found in "Streaking: One Way to Get a B.A.," *Newsweek,* 18 March 1974, 41–42.

Most of the punker words are from Facts on File's *Fashions of a Decade.* Good coverage of the different meanings of *punk* is found in *The Cassell Dictionary of Slang. The Oxford English Dictionary* also provides a detailed list of meanings.

"Star Trek Glossary of Terms," *www.uspnsanfrancisco.com/microsites/startrek/glossary_stng.asp,* provides a brief list of some words used on *Star Trek.* The Trekker slang is from Patricia Byrd, "Star Trek Lives: Trekker Slang," *American Speech* 53 (Spring 1978): 52–58.

Peter Hill and Stephen Hill, *Skate Hard* (Fitzroy, Victoria: The Five Mile Press, 1988) offers a brief history of skateboarding in the 1970s, as well as explanations of the moves performed at the time.

Teenage slang comes from Charles R. Grosvenor Jr., "In the 70s," *www.inthe70s.com/generated/terms.shtml*; William Safire, "Words for Nerds," *The New York Times Magazine*, 20 July 1980, 8, 10; *Flappers 2 Rappers*.

Lanie Dills provides a very complete listing of CB terms in *The CB Slanguage Language Dictionary* (Nashville, Tenn.: self-published, 1975). Other sources are Kenneth L. Woodward, "The Trucker Mystique," *Newsweek*, 26 January 1976, 45–46; Sherman Wantz, "How to Use CB Radio 'Buzz' Words," *Popular Electronics*, January 1976, 91–92; Ivan Berger, "How CB Can Make Your Vacation Better," *Popular Mechanics*, July 1976, 58–60; W. Clark Hendley, "'What's Your Handle, Good Buddy?' Names of Citizens Band Users," *American Speech* 54 (Winter 1979): 307–310. The history of *keep on truckin'* is from *A Dictionary of Catch Phrases* and H. Brook Webb, "The Slang of Jazz" (see 1930s citations).

Watergate terminology is included in most descriptions of the events. A good discussion of several terms is Hugh Rawson's "The Words of Watergate," *American Heritage*, October 1997, 24–27, 30, 32, 34, 36–38, 40, 42. *-Gate* words are recorded in the "Among the New Words" sections of various volumes of *American Speech* between 1978 and 1984.

Donald D. Spencer, *Computer Dictionary for Everyone* (New York: Charles Scribner's Sons, 1979) provides a compilation of computer words current in the 1970s. Information about the punch card is found in a fascinating article by Steven Lubar, "'Do Not Fold, Spindle, or Mutilate': A Cultural History of the Punch Card," *Journal of American Culture* 15 (Winter 1992): 43–55.

A colorful introduction to the mood of the 1970s is Tom Wolfe's *Mauve Gloves & Madmen, Clutter & Vine* (New York: Farrer, Straus and Giroux, 1976). The book includes Wolfe's takes on funky chic, radical chic, and the Me Decade.

1980s

Wall Street slang is from Kathleen Odean, *High Steppers, Fallen Angels, and Lollipops* (New York: Dodd Mead & Co., 1988) and Allan H. Pessin and Joseph A. Ross, *More Words of Wall Street* (Homewood, Ill.: Dow Jones–Irwin, 1986). Yuppies are described in minute detail in Marissa Piesman and Marilee Hartley, *The Yuppie Handbook* (New York: Pocket Books, 1984).

The best historical source for hacker slang is *The New Hacker's Dictionary*, edited by Eric S. Raymond (Cambridge, Mass.: MIT Press, 1991).

A humorous look at New Age terminology is Mick Winter's "How to Talk New Age," *www.well.com/~mick/newagept.html*. A number of other lists of New Age words are also available on the Internet, for example, "A Brief Dictionary of New Age Terminology," edited by David L. Brown, *logosresourcepages.org/na-dict.html*. Other sources are "Mystics on Main Street," *U.S. News & World Report*, 9 February 1987, 67–69; "The Rocks with Good Vibrations," *Newsweek*, 12 October 1987, 78; "Ramtha, a Voice from Beyond," *Newsweek*, 15 December 1986, 42.

Sources of eighties teen slang include Charles R. Grosvenor Jr., "In the 80s," *www.inthe80s.com;* John Zinsser, "Kidspeak: The Definitive Guide to '80s Slang," *50Plus*, August 1984, 22, 63; William Safire, "Back to Tool," *The New York Times Magazine*, 22 September 1985, 14, 16; Richard Bernstein, "Youthspeak," *The New York Times Magazine*, 11 December 1988, 22, 24. Richard A. Hill offers a comprehensive look at the word *dude* in "You've Come a Long Way, Dude—A History," *American Speech* 69 (Fall 1994): 321–327.

Valspeak is chronicled in Mary Corey and Victoria Westermark, *Fur Shurr! How to Be a Valley Girl—Totally!* (New York: Bantam Books, 1982). Other sources are "It's Like Tubular!" *Newsweek*, 2 August 1982, 61, and "How Toe-dully Max Is Their Valley," *Time*, 27 September 1982, 56. *-Speak* words come from various issues of

American Speech, "Among the New Words." Examples of Haigspeak are quoted in "Haigeldygook," *Time,* 23 February 1981, 19.

Rap words are mostly from Patrick Atoon, "Unofficial Rap Dictionary," *www.rapdict.org,* Lois Stavsky, I. E. Mozeson, and Dani Reyes Mozeson, *A 2 Z: The Book of Rap and Hip-Hop Slang* (New York: The Berkley Publishing Group, 1995), and "Chilling Out on Rap Flash," *Time,* 21 March 1983, 72–73. Breakdancing moves can be found on a number of websites, including Daniel Ferro's "Bboy Neko Breakdancing," *www.bboyneko.com,* "B-Boy Breakin' Moves Dictionary," *www.b-boys.com/bboymoves.html,* and "Rap/Hip-Hop with Ifé Oshun," *www.soul.about.com/library/blbreakdancecoverpage.htm.*

1990s

Words from the Persian Gulf War are from "Terms of Bombardment," *People Weekly Extra* (Commemorative Issue), Spring/Summer 1991, 72; "Gulfspeak," *U.S. News & World Report,* 18 February 1991, 16; *American Speech*'s "Among the New Words" sections, Volume 66 (Winter 1991) and Volume 67 (Spring 1992).

Most of the Internet words are from the "Among the New Words" sections of various volumes of *American Speech* between 1994 and 1999. Another source is Kathryn Balint, "Technology and Language Results in Geek Speak," *Fairfield County Business Journal,* 7 May 2001, 4–6. Many of the business-oriented words are found in Joseph Kahn, "Between Wall Street and Silicon Valley, a New Lexicon," *The New York Times,* 1 January 2000, C1–2.

The Generation X slang comes from Vann Wesson, *Generation X: Field Guide and Lexicon* (San Diego: Orion Media, 1997). *The Random House Historical Dictionary of American Slang* offers some discussion of the prefix *Mc* and *McJob.*

Y2K words were collected from magazine articles and websites devoted to the topic, including University of Toronto at Mississauga, "Y2K Compliance at UTM," *www.erin.toronto.edu/~w3y2k/* and "Y2K Wakeup," *www.sunshicom/y2k/.* William Safire writes about the term *Y2K* in "With a Euro in Her Pouch," *The New York Times Magazine,* 7 June 1998, 28.

The verbed nouns were collected from various print sources, including magazines, newspapers, newsletters, and brochures, and from television. A few are from James Kilpatrick's column "The Writer's Art," 31 March 2002.

A copy of the Republican Contract with America is available at *www.house.gov/house/Contract/CONTRACT.html.* Many newspaper and magazine articles on the subject appeared in the last months of 1994. A thorough discussion of Ebonics, including the text of the Oakland School Board's original and amended resolutions, can be found in the *Journal of English Linguistics* for June 1998. Ebonics was also widely written about in popular magazines and newspapers during 1996 and early 1997.

Index

AA 76
AAA 48, 53
Able Grable 89
A-bomb 92, 109, 134
abortion 109
Abraham Lincoln
 Brigade 66
abrogated 60
Abyssinia 213
Acapulco gold 120,
 135
Acapulco red 135
ace 3, 16
ace a course 136
ace note 55
acid rock 130
acid washed 174
ack-ack 76
Adam and Eve on a
 raft 63
adenoid tenor 59
advertising 159
aerial assets 191, 193
aerobat 40
A.F.A. 157
affirmative 125
Affluent Society 115,
 116
African black 135
Afro 139
Afro rake 139
agent 207
AIM 128
air 145, 151
airedale 38
airhead 181, 182
airhog 40
air-minded 40
air tasking order 193
akashic record 179
Alan Laddy 89
alarm clocks 32
albatross 79

Alice blue 15
alky-cooking 36
alley-oop 7
Allies 71
alligator 27, 31
alligator bait 56
alligator shirt 169,
 174
all out 84
all-outer 84
all right 157
all that 170, 185
all the way live 182
all wet 7, 39
alpha geek 177
alreet 89
altar it 60
Altergate 146, 163
alternative 201
alternative lifestyle
 192
America Firsters 81
America—love it or
 leave it 133
Amerika 119, 126
amped 185
animal xii, 14, 136
Anzio 73
Anzio amble x, 73
Anzio Annie x, 73
Anzio anxiety x, 73
Anzio foot x, 73
Anzio walk 73
Apache 104
Apache sweater 34
aped 13
Apollonaut 141
Apollo suit 141
Apple Annie 47, 50
applejack 170, 188
applesauce 39
Aqua Velva geek 170,
 177, 182

arithmetic bug 21
Arkie 53
Armistice Day 3, 16
armored cow 79
army strawberry 71,
 79
army surplus 153
Arvin 121
ARVN 121
ascended master 170,
 179
ashtray 193
as if 183
As Really Very
 Nervous 121
assertive disarma-
 ment 193
astral body 179
astral travel 170, 179
astrodog 141
astromonk 141
Atomic Age 72, 92
at this point in time
 162
auger 157
Aunt Jane 169, 172
Aunt Mary 135
aura 169, 179
autobogophobia 177
autocamping x, 11
automat 1, 4
automatic writing 43
automobile x
automobile depot x,
 11
automobiling x, 11
automobilism 11
automobilist x, 10
automobubble x, 2,
 11
auto touring 48
auto tourist 48
Averageman's Car 13

awesome 180
axe 115
Axis 71
axle grease 20

Babbitt 25, 43
babe 13, 14
baby bomb 97
baby-bound 60
baby busters 201
baby doll dress 139
baby doll shoes 139
Baby Grand 13
back door 160
back-door furlough
 17
back number 15
back-seat mouser 198
backslide 159
backyard 159
bad ounce 134
bad vibes 120
bag 120, 130, 201
baggie 134
Baghdad Betty 191,
 193
Baghdad Biltmore
 193
bag it 182
bag on 185
bag your face 182
bag z's 120, 136, 137
bail 151
baked wind 39
Baldwin 201
bale of hay 134
ballistics 189
balloon room 134
balloon skirt 169
ballyhoo 25, 40, 44,
 151
bamboo curtain 92
banana clip 174

banana oil 39
bandwidth 204
banging 111
bank 185
bank geek 202
bank holiday 50
barbed-wire under-
    shirt 17
barefoot pilgrim 172
barf me out 183
Barney 180, 201
barneymugging 33
barnstormer 40
barrel goods 36
barrelhouse 47, 58
barrel of black mud
    61
barrel of red mud 61
basted 37
bat 14
bathtub gin 36
battery acid 79
Battle of Britain 73
Battle of the Bulge
    73
bazoo 55
b-boy 170, 185
beach 191
beanery 96, 113
bean gun 79
bear xii, 13, 14, 109,
    158
bear bait 158
bear bite 159
bear in the air 159
bear story 159
bear trap 159
beasty 182
Beat 96, 112
Beat Generation 112
Beatlemania 136
beatnik 96, 112
beaverburger 72, 81
bebop 72, 89, 90
bed-check Charlie
    102
bedpan commando
    74
beehive 139
beer goggles 180
bee's knees 28
behavior report 79
behind the eight ball
    74

beige 182
be-in 119
belch 37
belcher 59
bell-bottoms 154
bell polisher 29
Bells, man! 89
belly punch 59
belly robber 20
belly shirt 174
bend 37
bennie 96, 113, 114
Berlin airlift 72, 91
berry 39
bert 151
Bethesda gold 135
Better dead than Red
    97
Better Red than dead
    97
Betty 201
Betty Crocker 119
biddies on a raft 63
Big Bertha 17
big-boat pilot 40
big butter-and-egg
    man 27, 29, 41
big cheese 31
big enchilada 162
big eyes 72
big four 56
big John 74
big noise 3, 15
big pickle 102
Big Red 191, 193
Big Red Scare 44
big rubber 109
big thing on ice 39
big tickle 105
bigtime 201
big-time operator 74
Big Ugly 193
big up 185
Billygate 163
billys 170, 182
bimbette 180
bindle 55, 111
bindle stiff 55
binger 13
biograph 6
bird 17, 136
bird-dog 136
bird farm 119, 122
bird of passage 21

biscuit 27, 30
biscuit blast 72, 79
biscuit head 201
bit 113
bitchen 170, 182, 184
bitchin' 136, 182
bite 186
black blizzard 47, 52,
    53
black clandestine 193
black cow 48, 61
Black Crow 13
blacketeer 81
black hash 135
black is beautiful 133
black knight 171, 172
Black Monday 171
blackout girl 87
Black Panthers 126
black power 126, 127
black pride 139
black Russian 135
black stick 61
black strap 79
black stuff 111
Black Thursday 43
black time's here, ter-
    mite 105, 213
blast 134
blast furnace 102
blast off 105
blatherskite ix, 31
blind flying 79
blind pig 37
blinds 55
blind tiger 37
blink-o-roony 90
blisterfoot 73, 74
Blitz 73
blitzkrieg 71, 169, 171
blitzkrieg tender 171
blitz the cold storage
    plant 87
blond and sweet 79
blond stick 61
blot out 37
blow 115
blow in on the scene
    114
blow one's jets 113
blub 13
blubber 14
blue 7
blue-chip raider 171

blue on blue 193
blue points 81
Blunder Buss 11
blurble 13
BNF 152
BNG 122
bobatorium 25, 35
bobbysox 88
bobbysox brigade 72,
    88
bobbysoxer 88
bob-tailing 159
bodacious 180
bodacious dudette
    170
body dancing 145,
    147, 148
body slam 188
body suit 154
boffo 7, 39
bogart a joint 134
bogometer 169, 177
bogon 177
bogosity 177
bogue out 177
bogus 177, 181
boiled 37
boiler room 169, 173
bokoo 17
bolo badge 193
boloed 193
Bolshevism 25
Bolshevist 44
bomb 92, 96, 109
bomb-a-minute
    attack 193
bomb boogie 80, 81
bomber's night 193
bombing pause 122
bondage trousers 154
bone 13
Bone Crusher 11
bone dome 191, 193
bone polisher 55
bong 87, 134
boning 3
Bonus Army 66
boo 135
booboisie 26, 44
book gook 105
boomers 23
boonie rat 122
boonies xi, 119, 122,
    136, 138

bootleg 79, 82
bootlegger 36, 37, 38
boo-yah 170, 186
booze foundry 36, 37
boozehister 36
bopera 89
boss 113
bossy in a bowl 61
Boston version 7, 10
both barrels 63
boudoir 79
bovine extract 62
bow-head 180
bowlegs 17
box Brownie 3, 4
boxed 134
box tonsils 180
Boys of Baghdad 191,
    197
bozo button 191,
    198
brainiac 192, 201
brains trust 48, 51
brass 17
brass check sheet 23
brass hat 71, 74
brass looie 17
brawl 28, 32
Breadsville 113
break 159
breakdancing 185,
    187
breaker 159
breaker, breaker xiii,
    146
breaking 187
breakin' moves 170
breeze 37
breezer x, 12
brew 80
bright young thing
    26, 31
brinkmanship 95,
    99
British Invasion 120,
    136
broccoli 135
brodie 9
bronco 188
Bronxnik 101
brought to the altar
    171
brownie 74
brown paper bag 159

Brown v. the Board
    of Education
    116
brush ape 29
brusheroo 91
brush mush 89
bubble dancing 76
bubble skirt 174
buccaneers 171
bucketeer 169, 173
bucket of bolts 96,
    110
bucket shop 173
Buddha grass 134
bug 14, 21, 79
buggy 87
Bugmobile 13
bug out 102
buh-bye 213
bull 3, 13, 38
bullet 20
bull meat 20
bull nose 110
bull wool 39
bully pulpit 3, 22
bumpers 55
bump'n 201
bums 54
Bundles for Britain
    80, 81
bunion derbies 25
bunker 207
bunk fatigue 17
bunkie 74
bunk lizard 17
bunned 37
buppie 169, 175
Burma-Shave
    Company 64
burnt to a crisp 72,
    87
bush 135
bust a move 186
bust a rhyme 186
bustier 174
butter-and-egg man
    30
butt me 114
button 38
button shining 33
buy a ticket west xi
buy-in 129
buzz crusher 180
buzzing 111

Bye, bye—Buy bonds
    83
cabin camp 48, 65,
    66
cackle berries 63
Cadillac 13
Café Society 47, 67
cafeteria officing 192,
    204
cake-eater 29
cakewalk 3, 5
calaboose 55
calendar 207
California blankets
    55
Camelot 119, 142
camomail 171
camp store 66
can 17, 32, 134
can action 134
canary 47, 58, 81
can-can petticoat 95,
    104
cancelbot 198
cancelled stick 134
cancer on the presi-
    dency 146, 162
candidate for a
    plumber's
    degree 32
candy leg 29
cannon ball 55
canteen lizard 17
captain of the head
    76
caraburger 81
card reader 165
card stacker 165
careware 178
carpet bomb 193
carrying a torch 33
carrying nine hours
    and dragging six
    32
carry the banner 55
Casper 186
casual Friday 192,
    205
cat 58, 96, 112, 114,
    115
cat beer 62
cat-eye glasses 104
catsuit 154

cat's whiskers 28
CCC 53
cellar smeller 29
cemetery 96
cemetery work 105
chad box 164
chain-in 129
chair warmer 29
chakra 170, 179
changeover 209
channel 110
channeled spirit
    guides 170
channeling 43, 179
charityware 178
Charlie x, xi, 17, 111,
    119, 122, 159
charlie horse 20
chaser of Adam's ale
    62
chatter 96, 110
checkbook diplo-
    macy 193
checkbook participa-
    tion 193
checkeroo 91
check you later 157
cheese 170
cheesedog 201
Chelsea boots 139
chemise lizards 21
cherry 110
cherry Leb 135
chewed fine with a
    breath 62
Chicago Seven 142
chick 112
chicken 169
chicken in the clay 57
chicken plate 122
Chicom 102
chill 14, 185, 186
chill hard 186
chilly the most 170,
    186
chiphead 198
chiseler 38
chocolate chips 193
chocolate dust 62
choi oi xi, 122
choose off 110
chop 110
chop-chop 102
chow hound 71, 74

chuck a dummy 55
chuckle chick 89
chunk of lead 30
cinematograph 5, 6
circus bee 21
civil rightist 119, 127
civvies 17
clambake 59
clam diggers 96, 104
clanked 105
Clark Kent hippie
    120
clean bomb 97, 193
cloche hat 25, 35
closet Trekkie 152
clothesline 31
Club Kid style 205
C-note 39
cocktail 134
coconut 111
coffee cooler 74
coffin 151
Coke 63
cold meat 37
collapse 87
collateral damage
    193
collect call 159
college 207
Columbus black 135
combination stew 57
compliance 209
computer geek xii,
    169, 177
computer kit 146,
    164
computerspeak 184
con 152
concom 153
conduct a shirt hunt
    21
Coney Island 62
Coney Island chicken
    62
Congo brown 135
conk 42
consciousness-raising
    156
consciousness revolu-
    tion 169
Contract with
    America 209
convertible suit 72,
    85

convoy 159
cooking with gas 89
cool beans 201
cool dad 95, 105
cooler 17
cootie carnival 21
cootie casinos 21
cootie factory 21
cootie mill 21
cooties 21
cop out 130
copper-hearted 38
copy 160
cork-headed 3, 14
corn 58
corny 58
cosmic 130
cosmodog 120, 141
cot jockey 17
countercultural 155
counterculture 119,
    130, 131, 132
counterinsurgency
    122
counting stand 66
county mountie 146
couple dancing 147
coupon 160
Cowabunga 138
cowboy-and-Indian
    tactics 103
crab 188
crab the wind 42
cracked house 130
cracker 200
cracker box 122
cramming 96, 105
cramped 186
crash and burn 120,
    136
crate 42
C-rations 72, 79
crawk 59
credibility gap 127
creep 162
creeping 169
creeping tender 171
creep joint 37
crew 170, 186
crib 14
cricket 188
crill 183
crispy 180
crock up 17

Croix de Chair 18
crossover 9
crossover comedy 7
cross-talk 59
crosstalk act 9
crossword puzzle
    stockings 35
crown jewel defense
    169, 172
crudzine 153
crum 55
crumb hunt 76
crusheroo 91
crust 14
crystal 179
Cuban Missile Crisis
    142
cube 114
cubie 149
cubistic 96, 112, 114
curl xii, 138
curve killer 105, 106
cut in 136
cut out 114
cut the gas 105
cut the rug 47, 58
cut the scene 114
cybercafe 199
cybercapitalism 199
cybercapitalist 192
cybercast 199
cybercrime 199
cyberculture 199
cyberfare 199
cyberian 199
cyberize 199
cyberized 191
cyberjunkie 192
cyber-lifestyle 200
cyber mistress 200
Cybernetics 199
cyberpal 200
cyberpicket 200
cyberpork 200
cyberporn 200
cyberpunk 200
cyber-roadkill 192,
    200
cyberspace 199
cybersquatter 200
cybersurfer 200
cyberwonk 200

Daddy-O 96, 114

daily details 76
dai uy 122
damage assessment
    193
dance marathon 67
Dan Patch 13
darb ix, 15
dashiki 120, 139
data highway 213
data sheet 164
date bait 89
daughter track 192,
    210
dawn patrolling 71,
    76
D-Day 73
D.D.P. 105
D.D.T. 87
dead between the
    ears 47, 58
Dead Man's Corner
    18
dead tree edition
    191, 201
dead up 186
Dear Lootenant
    letter 80
Death Trail 9
Debategate 163
deck 55, 111
deck of ready-rolls
    105
deconflict 194
decruitment 204
deepie 95, 109
deep sea turkey 20
Deep Throat 162
def 170, 186
dehorn 23
dehorn committee
    23
"De Lapid 8" 11
delayed action bomb
    80
demoth 103
dep chi 122
desert cherry 194
Desert Shield 194
Desert Storm 194
designer shopper 174
De Soto 13
destroyer 87
Detroit Disaster 11
deviationism 99

devil's piano 76
devil wagon 12
dewdropper 29
dexie 96, 114
dialing and smiling
    169, 173
dialogue 192, 207
di dai xi, 122
di di 122
die for a tie 103
dig 14, 96, 114
digerati 191, 198,
    206
digital doomsday
    209
digs 115
dilly 63, 87
dim box 28, 34
dime bag 135
dime-grind palace 47
dime novel 1, 4
dimp 120, 136
dimph 109
Dinah 38
dinged 119, 122
dink 175
dinky dow 135
dip 186
dirty bop 106
dirty tricks 162
dirty tricks campaign
    146
dis 186
disco 145, 147
disco ball 145, 147
discriminate deter-
    rence 194
dode 202
Dodge City 122
doe 202
dog biscuit 20, 72, 79
dogface 71, 74
doggy xii, 32
dog out 194
dog robber 18
dog soup 62
dog tags 74
dolly 95, 106
domino theory 99
do not fold, spindle,
    or mutilate 165
don't take any
    wooden nickels
    213

don't you know
    there's a war
    on? 84
do one's own thing
    120, 133
dope 135, 186
do-rag 71, 85
dorf 137
dot-com 192, 204
dot-communists 204
dot-compost 204
do the job HE left
    behind 84
double buffalo 160
dough 103
doughboy 3, 17, 103
down chill 3
downrock 170, 188
downsizing 204
downtime 192, 204
down with 186
drag 55
drag a hoof 47
draggin' wagon 110
drag race 109, 110
drag racing 111
drag strip 96
drape shape 87
D-ration 79
dreadnought 18
dream puss 87
drooly 87
dropped front end
    109, 110
dropper 38
Dr. Scholl's 154
drug-o-reeny 90
drugstore cowboy 29
DRVN 121
dry 36
dry out 14
duck xii
duck and cover 95
duck shoes 169, 175
duck's quack 28
duck tail 104
dudd 31
dudesman 182
dudespeak 170
dudester 183
dudette 183
dudical 183
duds 182
Duesenberg 10, 13

dugout hound 18
dumb act 9
dumb dora 30, 43
dumbsizing 204
dum-dum 20
duster 12, 52
dustoff 122
dust pneumonia 52
dusty miller 48, 62
dweeb 180
dy-no-mite 157

ears 158, 159
ears are moving 115
Earth Day 146, 154,
    166
earth shoes 154
eat chain 202
eat snowballs 55
Ebonics 210
e-bouquet 201
echelon king 18
echelons beyond real-
    ity 194
e-democracy 201
Edge City 130
effort 207
egg 18, 29
egg beater 103
egg harbor 28, 29
egg heads 96, 106
egg in your beer 76
egg wagon 18
eight ball 74
eighteen-minute gap
    162
eight-minute egg 38
eight-track 145, 147
8-track 147
eighty 62
eighty-column minds
    165
eighty-one 62
eighty-seven and a
    half 64
eighty-six 62, 64
eighty-two 62
Eisenhower jacket 72,
    85
electric boogie 188
electric self-starter x,
    10, 12
electric trolley car 4
elephant bells 154

elevated 37
e-mail 201
emailingering 204
embalm 37
encounter groups
    156
end-of-file 164
end of the world as
    we know it 192
enemy ears are listen-
    ing 83
entreprenerd 205
e-postage 201
error 207
ersatz 81
Establishment 130,
    131
e-surgery 201
e-tail 191, 201
ether 48, 59
ether mail 191, 198
Eton crop 35
event horizon 192,
    209
everyman's car 2
Eve with the lid on
    62
excellent 180
exotically Edgar 106
expecting a blessed
    event 60
expletive deleted 146,
    162
eye heavy 114
e-zine 191, 201

fab 136
Fab Four 120
face time 170, 180
fade 175
fail-safe 97
fall guy 38
fall in 96, 114
fall money 38
fall out 114
fan 192, 202
fanac 153
fancon 152
fanfic 153
fanzine 152, 153
farmerette 3, 18
far out 130
fast tracker 169, 170
Father Time 31

FCA 53
feather 145, 148
fellowship 207
fellow traveler 99
fen 153
fennel 135
fer shurr 183, 184
fetish 207
F.F.F.F.T.O.Y.F.F. 87
fifth column 84
fifth generation fan
    153
finale hopper 31
finger man 38
finger of death 194
finger popper 115
finif 39
fini flight 122
fire alarm 30
fired 37
fireside chat 48, 51
firewall 205
first lady 62
fish-in 128, 129
five dollars a gear 96,
    110
fix-on-failure 192, 209
flag 120
flag a course 137
flagpole sitting 25
flag rush 14
flake 146
flake off 157
flake out 157
flak jacket 122
flame 198
flannel buzzards 21
flapper 25, 30, 31
flapper bracket 30
flapperese 30
flapperitis 30
flapperology 30
flapper vote 30
flare 154
flash 137
flash act 7, 9
flat spin 18
flattie 39
flat tire 31, 43
flat wheeler 28, 29
flavor 186
flea's eyebrows 28
flex 202
flickers 6

flinging woo 28, 34
flip a rattler 55
flip flop 160
flip out 157
Flipsville 96, 114
flivver x, 3, 12, 14,
    213
float 188
Floodgate 163
flop 'em 63
flop house 55
flopperoo 91
floppy disk 164
flower children 120,
    130, 213
flower power 119,
    130
flowstress 186
flunkenstein 137
fly 186
flying bathtub 21
flying bedstead 21
flying boxcar 21, 76
flying chicken coop
    21
flying machine 3, 4
flying the wet beam
    76
FNG 122
folding lettuce 89
foot slogger 75
forty-fours 20
fountain 207
four flusher 31
fourteen 64
four-wheeler 158,
    160
foxed 37
foxhole 18
foxhole circuit 79, 80
foxhole house 81
foxy 145, 157
fragger 194
fragging 121, 122,
    194
frame dame 87
frampton 106
frazzled 37
freak 63
freak act 10
freak out 157
Fred 201
freeboarding 138
freedom bird 123

freedom riders 125,
    127
Freedom Summer
    127
free love 120, 131
free software 178
free speech 126, 127
Free Speech
    Movement 127
freeware 178
Free World 100
frenched 96, 110
fresh 170, 185, 186
fresh bull 39
friendlies 103, 121,
    123
friendly fire 121, 123
fringe 140
'fro 120, 139
front 55
front door 160
fronter 169, 173
frontier pants 104
frost one 63
fruit salad 18
fruit tramp 54
full-race 110
funk 120, 140
funky chic 154
funsies 137
furballs 194
future shock 145, 166
fuzzy duck 106

gag me with a spoon
    170, 183
galloping dandruff
    21
galloping goose 21
galvanized gelding 76
gangster 135
ganja 135
garbage in, garbage
    out 146, 164
gas 113, 114
gas hog 81
gasolene 10, 12
gasoline gypsy 47, 51
gat 38
gate 135
Gategate 163
gatenik 163
gat up 38
gauge 135

Gay Liberation Front
    143
gayola 117
gazelleburger 72, 81
G-day 194
gear 136
geek out 177
geese 76
geet 106
geetafrate 106
geezed 37
gelatine tenor 59
Geminaut 141
Generation X 191,
    201
generic 180
generic mail 194
Gen Xers 191
George 96, 106
get faced 202
get it xi, 18
get off with your bad
    self 202
getting vertical 151
get your boogies on
    202
get your guts right
    191, 194
ghostola 117
ghost site 198
G.I. 75
G.I. Bill 72, 75
G.I. Bill of Rights 75
G.I. cocktail 75
giggle water 36
GIGO 164
G.I. haircut 75
G.I. hop 75
G.I. Jane 75
G.I. Jill 75
G.I. Jo 194
G.I. Joe 71
G.I. Josephine 75
gimme some skin 115
G.I. Moe 75
gin mill 37
gin palace 37
G.I. party 75
giraffe party 87
G.I. sky pilot 75
G.I. turkey 75
give a damn 133
give me a bell 106
give the air 33, 34

give the ozone 34
gizmo 76
Glamor Girl 47, 67
glamour boy 74, 75
glam rock 155
glided 188
glop 80
G-man 39
gnarly 183
go à la bois 106
go all out for
    America 71, 84
go ballistic 189
go by hand 55
go giver 87
go-go boots 140
go-go girls 120, 140
go-go ring 140
gohong xi, 103
goldbrick 18
gold digger 30
Golden Age of Radio
    58
golden BBs 191
Goldingate 163
gold leaf 135
gomes 146
gone 114
good buddy 146, 160
good Joe 89
gooey 20
goof 29
goofy foot 151
goon 38, 80
go on the nod 111
goon up 80
goose xii, 137
go over the falls 120,
    138
go over the hill 18, 76
go over the top xi, 18
go postal 203
go quisling 87
go rotary 96, 114
Goth 174, 176
Gothic 176
go to town 58
got to take a fast
    powder 213
goulash battery 21
governmentspeak
    184
go with the birds 55
gramophone 5

granny dress 120, 140
granny dumping 211
granny glasses 140
granny track 210
granola 180
grass 79, 135
gravel agitator 75
graveyard stew 62
gravy 145, 157
grease 38, 107, 191,
    194
Great Depression 49
great on the shindig
    31
Great Society 51, 126,
    127
great white biscuit
    120
greenmail 171
Green Moroccan 135
green stamp 158, 160
gremlin 120, 138
grind 32, 202
grind me off a hunk
    110
grobbling 202
grody 183
grody to the max 170
groove 137
groove on 137
groover 137
groovin' 137
groovy ix, 120, 137
ground ace 18
groundhog day 18
grumpies 202
grunge 137
grunge chic 205
grunge kid 213
grunger 205
grunt 119, 123
guilt 207
guiltware 178
gulf-ploitation 191,
    197
gulfspeak 194
gumby 176
gun mob 38
gun moll 38
gun opera 1, 6
guppie 175
gus 63
gutbucket 58
gut course 146, 157

gypsy look 155

hack attack 178
hacker 169, 176, 177,
    200
hacking run 178
hackishness 178
hackitude 169, 178
Haigspeak 184
hail 60
hairpin 14
half pipe 151
half portion 31
hamburgeroroony 90
Hammer pants 206
handcuff 34, 60
handcuffed 60
hand-in 129
handle 146, 159
handshaker 18
hang a dilly 63
hang a fresh 63
hang a mud 63
hang an honest 63
hangin' 202
hanging chad 164
hang one 63
hang-up 119, 131
Hanoi Hilton 119,
    123
happenin' 170, 180
happy camper 181
hard oil 21
hard roller 186
hardtop 95, 107
harem skirt 2, 15
harvest it 87
Hashbury 119, 131
have big eyes 89
have eyes for 89
have it abrogated 60
have it Reno-vated 60
have the seal shat-
    tered 60
Have you got a thing?
    111
hay 135
H-bomb 95, 97
head shop 131
health skirt 15
heater 38
heaven sent 87
heavy xii, 120, 131,
    138

heavy booking 146
heavy cream 114
heavy date 28, 30
hedgehopper 75
heelie 151
heinous 181
helicopter 188
helitrooper 103
hell buggy 76
hello sugar, are you
    rationed? 89
hello sweet, you look
    neat 89
Hell's Half-acre 18
hen fruit 63
Henry's First Go-cart
    11
hepcat 47
hep to the jive 89, 90
herd 96, 110
H-Hour 73
high ball 55
high five 186
high-gear road 48, 66
high hat 39, 42
high tech, high wreck
    205
high-top fade 176
highway of death 194
Hi good lookin',
    what's cookin'?
    89
Hi Joe, what do you
    know? 89
himbette 180
himbo 180
hip xi
hip-hop xiii, 170, 185
hipped on 27, 39
hippie 129
hippie chick 120
hipster 112, 114
Hispano-Suiza 13
hitch 18
hit the silk 76
ho 186
hobble 16
hobble skirt x, 3, 15,
    16
hobo 54
Hobohemia 55
Hobohemian 55
Ho Chi Minh trail
    123

ho-daddy 138
hog wrastle 3, 14
hokum 10
hold the hail 63
hole 18
Holy Joe 18
homeguard 23
homey 186
honcho xi, 103
hooch 36
hoochie 103
hoofer 10
hook a snake 107
Hoover blanket 47, 49
Hoover car 49
Hoover Depression 47
Hoover flag 49
Hoover flush 49
Hoover hog 49
Hooverize 3, 18
Hooverizer 18
Hoover shoes 49
Hooverville 47, 49
horsefeather 39
horseless carriage x
hoser 181
hostage crisis 166
hot 57, 58
hotdog xii
hotdogger 120, 138
hoteling 192, 205
hot gingerbread 90
hot grease 38
hot pants 155
hot patooties 47
hot plate 58
hot rodding 96
hot sketch 107
hotsy-totsy 39
hottie 186
hounds on an island 62
house around 32
house boat 62
house dog 56
household 207
H2Ogate 163
hubba-hubba x, 92
hub cap 107
huddle system 32
Hudson 13
Huey 122, 123

huff 18
huggy-bear 120
human shield 194
hump 14
Hungry Lizzie 19
hungry town 56
hunk of heartbreak 87
Hupmobile 13
huppie 175
hustle 145
hypnoid 43

I am so sure 183
ice 38
ice cream man 112
ice up 87
ickie 58
iconitis 191, 198
if it feels good, do it 120
I hear that 157
ill 186
illin' 186
I'll tell the world 19
illuminated 37
immersion foot 123
I'm outie 213
inconvenience bombing 191, 194
in country 123
incubator 205
Indian country 123
infofreak 198
infojunkie 198
information anxiety 197
information snooperhighway 200
information superhighway 191, 200
information superhypeway 200
infosize 198
insane 202
insider trading 171
instant message 192, 207
instant zen 120, 131
insult bombing 194
intense 146, 157
interfacing 180
interventionist 81

in the bag 80
in the groove 72, 137
in the money 169, 170
invert 151
iodine brigade 19
Iraqispeak 194
Iraqnophobia 194
iron curtain 72, 92
iron pony 76
iron rations 21
ish 153
It 32
it became necessary to destroy the town in order to save it 124
It Girl 25, 32
it's all good 187
it's been real 213
ivory tickler 7, 10

J 135
jacked 146, 157
Jackson 87
jake 36
James Bond 172
jams 138
jaw breakers 21
jaypee 103
jazz 26, 31
Jazz Age 25
jazz baby 27, 213
jazzbo 26
jazz hound 31
jazz ride 42
Jefferson Airplane 135
jel 183
jellybean 31
jelly tot 107
jerker 60
jerk of all trades 90
Jerry 19
Jersey green 135
jet jockey 102, 120, 141
jet set 120, 143
jetwash 102
Jheri curls 176
jib rat 197
jiggered 37
jingled 37
jink 123

jinny 37
jitney bus 1, 4
jitter 57
jitterbug 47, 57, 58, 81, 106
jitterbugger 57
jive stick 135
jive turkey 157
Joad 52
Joanie 183
Joe Brooks 32
Joe College 28
Joe Zilch 29
Johnson rod 110
John Square 114
John Wayne bar 124
join-in 119, 129
joint 135
jokeroo 72, 91
jolt 37
jonesing 202
joog house 87
journal 207
joy popper 112
juke 87
juke joint 72, 87
juking it 87
jumping the blinds 55
jungle 56
jungle juice 79
juppie 175

kangaroo meat 21
K-day 103, 194
keep America beautiful 133
keep on truckin' ix, 146, 160
keyboard plaque 198
key man 14
keynote 207
keypunching 165
keypunch machine 165
keypunch operator xii, 146, 165
kick 90
kick out 58
kicks 170, 187
Kicksville 114
kick the ballistics 187
kid 15
kill 183

killer 170, 183
killer bees 172
kill sack 194
Kilroy 78
kinetoscope xii, 1, 4, 5
king size 90
Kinsey Report 116
kip-up 188
kisseroo 91
Kit Carson scout 123
kite 76
kitten bomb 95, 97
Kitty 114
kiwi 42
knickerbockers 25, 35
knockabout 1, 10
knocked out 47
knock off the horns and drive 'em in 62
knowbie 191, 198
knowbot 198
knows her oil 28, 31
Kodak courage 202
kook 120, 138
kools 135
koon sa 135
K-plus 194
Kriegie 80
krump out 107
Krunchies 80

lacey cup 62
Lady Macbeth 59
lallygagger 29
lamb 172
lame 181
lamping 185
lapjack 198
La Salle 13
latch your lashes 90
lates 202
lava lamp 146, 147
lay a cool shift 96, 110
lay it on me 96
lay on 114
leapers 114
leaping dandruff 21
left shoulder 160
leg 194
legacy 192, 205

legger 36
leisure suit 145, 155
Lend-Lease Act 82
lend-leasing 71
let it slide 157
let me hold something 112
let's book 157
let's do what the wind does 107
letterzine 153
let the hammer down 160
let the sun shine 63
level the vibes 187
Levittown 95, 116
lexer 14
Leyte Gulf 74
liberty 3, 19
liberty bond 19
liberty cabbage 3, 19
liberty cut 85
liberty dog x
liberty pup 3, 19
liberty ship 71, 82
liberty spike 145, 148
liberty steak 3, 19
library bird 56
libspeak 184
lid 135
lie-in 119, 129
life safe 95, 96, 97
lights 62
like 182
lily 172
lindy 42
lindy hop 58
line dancing 147
line doggie 191, 194
line printer 166
lip 38
listen in 48, 59
lit 37
little bear 159
Little Bo Creep 11
Little Hollywood 191, 197
live bait 112
live in a tree 137
liver 62
Lizzie label 11
Lizzie tramp 56
lobby lizard 169, 173
lobster trap 172

LoC 152, 153
locomobile 13
loco weed 135
Lohengrin it 60
Lohengrin March 47
lollipop 169, 172
London cut 48
lone nabisco 29, 33
Lone Star 13
long count xi, 44
long hitter 120, 137
long rod 38
long underwear 58
look that needs suspenders 88
loop-the-loop 42
loose wig 115
loot-in 129
lose it 157
lounge lizard 29, 173
love beads 120, 140
love-in 120
low down 58
low five 186
low lid 31
LRRP rations 123
lubricated 37
lump lips 107
luv 136

macadocious 187
machine 96
Madame Cadenza 59
madd 202
mad minute 19
Maggie's drawers 76
magic mushroom 131
mail bomb 198
mainframe 166
main stem 56
major 181
majorly 169, 181
Ma Junk 11
make bank 192, 202
make love, not war 119, 133
make the scene 114
making whoopee 34
man 96
Manhattan Project 92
Manhattan silver 135
Manhattan white 135
manicure 135
marinate 187

maroon harpoon 107
marriage broker 171
Marshall Plan 93
Marvin-the-Arvin 121
Mary Jane 135
massive retaliation 100
max 183
maxi 120, 140
mazuma 114
McCarthyism 116
McCarthyite 95
McJob 192, 194, 202
McSalary 202
McWar 191, 194, 202
meadow dressing 14
meatlegger 72, 82
meatloaf 199
Me Decade 145, 156
media war 191, 197
mediumistic 26, 42, 43
megadeath 95, 97
megaton 97
mello-reeny 90
mellow 37
mellow man 87
mellow out 157
melted 60
Mendelssohn March it 60
mercy 160
merge 60
message 207
Methodistconated 37
Mexican brown 135
Mexican green 135
Mexican red 135
mic 187
Michigan Mistake 11
Mickey Finn 38
mickies 36
micromini 120, 140
microserf 202
middle-aisle it 60
midiskirt 140
Midnight Auto Supply 110
MiG Alley 103
milk run 76
mill 110
millennial meltdown 209

millennium bug 192, 208, 209
mince 137
mind-blowing 131
mini 120
mini-crinoline 169, 176
miniskirt 140
mint 181, 192, 202
misery index 167
missile gap 100
mission stiff 56
Mister Truman's War 103
mitt flopper 75
Model A 10
Model T 10
Mohawk 148
moll buzzer 38
Molotov breadbaskets 76
Molotov cocktail 76
mommy track 192, 210
mondo 202
mondo cool 192
mongee 21
monkey 115
monkey meat 20, 21
Monkey Trial 25, 45
mooch man 173
mood ring 145, 148
moon boots 155
moon car 141
moon jitney 141
moonlight inn 37
moonmobile 141
moonship 141
moonsuit 141
moon walk 188
moose 103
mort out 194
most excellent homey 170
Motha Higby 107
mothball 72, 88
mother of all battles 191, 196
mother of all briefings 196
mother of all corners 196
mother of all homecomings 196

mother of all journalistic changes 196
mother of all parades 196
motor 1, 3
motor ambulance 12
motor car x, 10, 12
motor chapeau 12
motor club 65
motor coat 2, 12
motor court 66
motor gypsy 65, 66
motoring goggles 12
motor truck 12
mouse 137
mousenik 101
mouse potato 198
movie palace 6
MRE 195
MTV generation 191, 202
muckraker 3, 22
mug of murk 62
mullet 107, 169, 173, 206
multiprogramming 166
multitask 166, 207
munchies 135
Munichism 82
murder 88
mushing 33, 34
mushing wave 139
mutual assured destruction 98
my bad 187
my, how sanitary 107

Nader's raiders 143
nappy 202
nastygram 198
native son 21
natural foot 151
neck 30
necker's knob 96, 110
necking 28, 34
nectar 203
negative 125
negatory 160
Nehru jacket 120, 140
neofan 153
nerf 111
nerf bar 111

nervous 109
nervous baritone 59
nervous pudding 62
Nethead 198
Netiquette 198
Netizen ix, 192, 198
Net surfer 198
Net vet 191, 198
New Age 169, 178
New Age music 179
New Ager 43, 170
newbie 191, 198
new Bohemian 112
New Deal 48, 51
New Frontier 119, 142
New Look 72, 85, 100
newsreel 7
new wave 148
New Woman 2, 22
nickel bag 135
nickel note 56
nickelodeon 1, 7
night pilot 42
ninety-eight 61, 65
ninety-five 64
ninety-nine 65
Noah's boy with Murphy carrying a wreath 62
noble experiment 35, 36
nod 135
no-hit 207
no-man's land 19
nonskid 31
nose 38
nosebleed 107
nose paint 37
nose wheelies 145, 151
notebook nabbing 198
noun plague 184
nounspeak 184
now generation 120, 131
NRA 53
nuclear club 95, 98
nuclear coffee 191, 195
nuclear furnace 98
nuclear pile 95, 98

nuclear war 172
number one 124
number ten 124
number ten thou' 124
NYA 53

oatnik 101
occupational slumming 203
October surprise 167
OD 19, 20
odd lotter 170, 173
office 208
officing 192
off the dome 187
oh, my aching back 71, 77
oil can 31
oiled 37
oil spot 124
O.J. 135
Okie x, 47, 52
old army game 19
old sexton 59
ollies 145, 151
one-digit midget 124
one-hand glide 189
one-reeler 6, 7
on ice 37
on the beam 87
on the bus 37
on the cob 58
on the hook 108
on the muscle 31
on the thumb 56
on the verge 60
oogley 88
open source 178
Operation Desert Storm 191, 192
orange crate 21
organized 37
ossified 37
Ouija board 26, 42, 43
out-of-body experience 170, 179
out of sight 131
out of this atmosphere 90
out of town 10
outsource 208
outstanding 124

over there 3, 16
over the shoulder
toss 195
Oxford bags 25, 34,
35

Packard 10, 13
packing the rigging
23
pack journalism 197
pad 113, 114
palazzo pants 155
Panama gold 135
Panama red 135
pancake turner 72,
88
panic the house 10
pank rider 145
pank riding 151
pants leg 43
pants rabbits 21
pantywaist 31
paper curtain 92
paper man 58
parachute pants 176
parapsychical 26, 43
paraspam 199
parastreaker 150
parlor snake 14
part-time papa 29
party 37
party pack 135
pashing it 60
passion pit 95, 106
Patriot baiter 197
PAVN 121
payola 115, 117
payola scandals 117
payware 178
peacenik 119, 126,
127
peace sign 127
peacherino 15
pearl 139
pearl diving 77
pearling 151
peasant skirt 155
pedal pushers 96,
104
peep 77
peerless 13
peg skirt 16
pencil 197
pencil geek 146, 157

pencil skirt 104
penny arcade 1, 4, 5,
7
Pentagon Papers 167
peppy crate 42
peter pan collar 104
pet rock 146, 149
petting 29, 34
petting pantry 34
petting party 31, 33,
34
phase shifter 192,
203
phat 187
phonograph 1, 3, 5
phonograph parlor
5
phony war 71, 83
photoplay 1, 7
pie 207
piecing 187
Pierce-Arrow 3, 13
Pierre 88
pifflicated 37
pillbox hat 120, 139,
140
pin 135
pineapple 38
ping-pong diplomacy
146, 167
pink 108
pinko 44
pinprick raid 195
pipe 32
piped 37
pipe jockey 102
pirate 171
pitching woo 33, 34
planchette 43
plant you now, dig
you later 115
platform shoes 155
player piano 1, 5
play-in 119, 128, 129
playsuit 72, 85
plucked 169
pluck the chickens
173
plug 203
plugola 117
plumbers 162, 167
plus fours 25, 35
poindexter 170, 181
polar bear 159

pompadour 3, 16,
104
pond 207
pond scum 181
poodle cut 105
poodle haircut xiii
poodle skirt 104,
105
pool journalist 197
popcorn 114
popover dress 72, 85
popping 188
poser 181
posolutely 39
posse 186
postal 203
pot 119, 135
potatoes and with-it
57
pot party 134, 135
potted 37
pour-out man 37
powder 37
power dressing 169,
176
power nap 181
power spot 169, 179
power suit 169, 176
power to the people
119, 133
PR 208
praise the Lord and
pass the ammu-
nition 84
pre-car 184
pre-car Valley Girls
170
preppie look 169
preserved 37
pretty pigeon 90
prexy 32
price-to-fantasy 205
primed 37
Prince of Wales
check 48
privilege 207
Production Code 33
Prohibition 25
project 80
psyched 145, 157
psychedelic 120, 131
psychic healer 179
psych out 157
puller 38

pull one on the city
62
punch cards 146
punch rustler 31
punk 1, 15, 57, 72,
79, 145, 148, 200
punk and gut 57
punkette 148
punkins 15
purple death 111
put in a wire 59
put on 131
put out the lights and
cry 62
puttee 19
put the cross on 37
put the hammer
down 146, 158
put the pedal to the
metal 160
putting the binger on
it 13
PWA 53

quick mixing 185
quirt counter 96, 108
quisling x, 84
quizling 116
Quonset hut 77

raccoon coat 25, 35
rack 108
rad 170
radical 181
radical chic 154
rager 203
ragged out 191, 195
ragtime 1, 5
rail job 111
rainy day woman 135
raked 96
rank on 114
rapped 170
rap session ix, 131
rare dish 87
rattler 56
rave 203, 205
raw 203
razz 173
REA 53
read one's shirt 21
Reaganaut 189
Reagan Democrat
189

Reaganesque 189
Reaganomics 189
Reagan red 189
real Bikini 88
real gone 96
real McCoy 37
rebop 90
red 14
Red China 95, 100
red dollars 124
red-hot mama 25, 31, 33
red ink 37
red lead 20, 21
red Leb 135
red marketeer 101
Red Menace 44, 101
red points 71, 83
red power 127
Reds under the bed 95, 101
reefer 56, 135
regular foot 151
rehome 208
Remington raider 124
remittance man 56
Reno-vate 47
rent party 47, 51
'rents 181
reporteress 197
reproducing punch 166
retrocognition 180
ricky tick 58
ride the pipe 103
riding the cushions 56
riff 187
riff on 187
righteous 90
rightsizing 204
rileyed 37
riot grrl 206
roach xii, 108, 135
roach clip 135
roach coach 191, 195
Road Louse 11
road rash 145, 151
road sister 56
roadster 1, 10, 12, 13
rocking chair 160
Rock of Ages 28, 31
rod 38

rog 125
ROK 103
rolfing 146, 150
rolling with 187
rollover 209
Rolls Woise 11
rooster 155
roscoe 38
Rosie the Riveter 71, 83
rotogravure 1, 6
rototilling 195
Rough Rider 11
round lot 173
routie-voutie 90
Royal Mail 13
royola 117
rubber band 188
rubber cow 43
Rubik's cube 145, 146, 149
rub out 37
rudder pouf 105
rug cut 58
rumble seat 13, 28
rum runner 36, 37
runabout 1, 13
runners 112
running board 10, 13
rush 34
rusty hen 88

sack dress 105
saddle up 125
sad sack 75
St. Vitus davenport 77
sallies 56
sal-loon, goon, alcohol you 89
salve 72, 79
Sammy 195
sample room 37
sampling 187
sand blows 53
sandwich generation xi, 210
Santa Maria gold 135
Santa Maria red 135
sao 125
sapperoo 91
sardine 31
sassy chassis 90

Saturday night massacre 163
Saudi champagne 195
sawbuck 39
scab 158
scalp box 108
scandal soup 62
scarf out 184
scat 111
scatter 37
scatter pins 105
scenic 203
schmo from Kokomo 96, 114
schnookle 108
sciencespeak 184
scissorbills 23
scope out 158
Scopes 25
Scopes Monkey Trial 45
scorched earth 172
score 192, 203
scratching 170, 185
screenager 191, 198
scrooched 37
Scud 195
Scud-a-vision 197
Scudded 195
scud in with 195
scuffle 114
scurf 14
scurve 96, 108
seam rats 21
seam squirrels 21
Sears-Roebuck xi, 20
seeing snakes 37
seeing Steve 112
seek the great white biscuit 137
see the chaplain 77
see you in the funny papers 213
see you on the flipside 158, 160, 213
self-realization 156
self-realized 145
semiballistic 189
send to the showers 34
serious 170, 181
serum 79

service the target 195
set-down 56
set me straight 112
sewer 208
sewer trout 79
sex wagon 111
sex without marriage 171
shag 155
shake 'n' bake 125
shake the leaves 161
shareware 178
shark repellent 172
sheba 31
shed 13, 158
sheik 28, 31
shellacked 37
shine 184
shiners 58
shingle 35
shirt hounds 21
shirt rabbits 21
shirt rats 21
shirt squirrels 21
shirtwaist 2, 15, 16
shiv 56
shoe 108
shoot and scoot 191, 195
shoot a western 63
shooting the Ferdinand 90
shoot one 63
shoot one from the South 63
shop-in 129
short-timer 20
shout out 187
shove in your clutch 88
showstoppers 171
shrink-in 129
shuck 187
shucking 115
side arms 79
side door Pullman 56
sidewalk surfers 151
sidewalk surfing 145
Silent Generation 105
single-parent 208
sister act 7, 10
sisterhood is powerful 133

sit-down strike 68
sit-in 119, 128
sitting in 119
six-step 170, 189
$64 question 115
$64,000 Question 96, 115
sizzle for 60
skanky 184
skategate xi, 163
skin 14
skinheads 148, 153
skin pumping 112
skins 145
skirt 38
skirtless bathing suit 16
skirt patrol 79, 80
skoshi 103
skulldragging 32
sky pilot 20
sky scout 75
slacker 192, 203
slam 145, 151
slam dancing 148
slam off 37
sleeping beauty 171
slick 123
slim 38
slimeball 170, 184
slip of a lip may sink a ship 83
slop-in 129
sloppy joe 85
slouch socks 176
slum 21
slum with the tide in 21
smackeroo 91
small rubber 109
smash 138
smear 14
smile and comb your hair 161
smoke 135
smoke-in 119, 129
Smokey 158
Smokey on rubber 159
Smokey on the ground 159
Smokey report 146, 159
Smokey with ears 159

smoking suit 35
snake's hips 28
snapperoo 91
snoop tour 80
snoozemarooed 91
snore sack 80
snozzled 37
snugglepup 29, 33
soccer mom xiii, 211
soda clerk 61
soda dispenser 60
soda jerk 60
solid 158
solid sender 87
so long, mater, see you later 89
so long pal, stay pure 96, 115
some pumpkins 15
something on the hip 37
Sophie 96, 108
sorry about that 121, 125
soso 59
source 208
space cadet 182
spacefaring 141
Spacefaring Apollonauts 120
space highway 141
spacenik 142
spacescape 120, 142
space spectacular 141
spam 199
spammee 199
spammer 199
speakeasy 27, 36, 37
speak his piece 33, 34
speed shop 96, 111
spifflicated 37
spiffy 39
spike 3, 14
spirit guide 178, 180
splash of red noise 63
spliff 135
split no-tomorrow style 114
splitters 131
spoil 'em 64
spoofnik 101
spook 111
sportspeak 184

Sputnik 95, 100
sputnikburger 101
Square Deal 3, 22
square joint 136
Squaresville 96
squid xii, 120, 138
squirrel 108
stack of bones 57
stagflation 167
standby 59
stand-in 119, 129
Stanley Steamer 13
stars and stripes 21
starter castle 205
starvation hour 32
Star Wars 189
stay in the buggy 32
stay loose 138
step to 187
step up closer to the mike 88
stereoscope 1, 6
Steve Canyon 119, 125
stick a button 14
stiff 55, 59
stiff racket 37
stinkeroo 72, 91
stinko 37
stirrup pants 176
stoke the boiler 173
Stonewall 143
stooge 80
store theater 7
stork'd 60
strafe 20
straight from the fridge 96, 114
straight, no chaser 113, 114
straight skinny ix, 138
streak 147
streaker alerts 150
Streakers Party 150
streak for impeachment 146
streaking 150
street rod 109, 111
Strekdom 153
Strekfan 153
strike breaker 31
strong bear hug 169, 171

structural integration 150
structurally integrated 146
struggle buggy 28, 34
stuccoed 37
stuck on each other 34
stud muffin 203
stupid fresh 203
STW 153
styling 187
subdeb 88
submarine 20
submarine chicken xi
subterranean 96, 114
sub-zero 88
suck around 14
sucker list 173
sucking face 180
suds 14
suedehead 148
suf 14
suffragism 22
sugar band 57, 58
sugar report 80
suitcase farmers 51
suitor 171
Summer of Love 132
Sunday school circuit 7, 10
sunflower 203
sunlight 192
sunlighting 205
super-solid 90
suppie 175
suppose they gave a war and nobody came 133
surface engagement 195
surfing 138
surfwagon 139
swabbies 20
sweater girl 71, 85
sweetheart couples 67
sweet Mary 135
swift 158
swim-in 128, 129
swinging cats 47
swinging singles 142, 143

swing out 58
swipe 189
swoony 87

table tipping 26, 43
table turning 43
taboo 208
tag 187
tagging up 187
Tailgate 146, 163
take it on the lam 37
talkie 28
tall, dark, and handy
    90
tanked 37
tapper 108
Tapsville 114
target-rich environ-
    ment 195
task 193, 208
taxi-dance hall 47
taxi dancer 47
T-bone 111
tea 135
teach-in 119, 129
tea dance 1, 6
tea gown 16
tea kettle 20
Teapot Dome 45
techno-addict 199
technoliterati 199
teddy bear pat 169,
    171
teeny bopper 132
telefraud 173
telephone number
    salary 192, 203
teleplasm 43
telepsychy 43
tell it like it is 133
ten-code 161
ten-four xiii, 146
terp team 10
terrain alteration 195
terrible 115
Tet offensive 124
that point in time
    146
that way for 60
thin ones 56
third eye 180
third force 102
thirteen 64

threatened 109
thrifting 206
thrill 32
throat 158
throw down 187
thumb 114, 136
ticket west 20
tidal wave purchase
    172
tiger meat 79
timeline 208
tin can 53
tin can shows 51
tin-can tourists 53
tin cow 21
Tin Lizzie 2, 10, 11,
    19, 53, 56
tin roof 63
titi 125
toasted 185
toast two on a slice of
    squeal 64
tobacco 80
toehold purchase 172
toes over 120, 139
Tom 106
tomato 31
Tommy gun 38
tonneau 13
tonneau cover 13
tonneau seat 13
toodle-pip 213
tool 157
toothpick village 77
toppings 57
toprock 170, 188
torpedo 38
total immersion 197
total look 174
totally 184
totally awesome 170
to the max 183
touch dancing 147
toujours la clinch 88
touring car 48, 66
town crier 59
town man 15
toy 15, 112
trackless trolley 1, 3,
    4
tramp 54
transition 192, 207,
    208

trashing 119, 128
T ration 195
treach 187
trekcon 152
trekfan 145, 153
trekfen 145, 153
Trekker 152, 153
Trekkie 153
trekzine 152, 153
trench fever 19
trench foot 19
trench mouth 19
trip 132
trip out 132
tromp it 96, 111
true-hacker 178
trufan 178
trufen 152, 153
tubular ix, 170, 181,
    184
tu dai 125
tude 184
tuff 136
tuned 37
tune in, turn on,
    drop out 119,
    133
turbo nerd 169
turkey xii, 56
turn on 132
turn turtle 13
TVA 53
twangie boy 87
twenty-something
    192
twenty-three skiddoo
    xi, 2, 213
"20-20" 87
twisted 187
twitchen 184
twitchin 184
two bits 39
two-reeler 7

ugly stick 138
uh-huh 60
undershirt butterflies
    21
unhook your ears,
    Dad 114
unisex 141
upper plate 88
upsizing 204

uptight 120, 132
uranium curtain 92
use it up, wear it out,
    make it do, or
    do without 84

Valley Forge 77
Valspeak 170, 184
vamp 30
vampire baby 30
'Varsity man 1, 15
Vatican 108
V-E Day 83
vertical 145
V-girls 83
vibes 132
victory garden 71, 80,
    83
victory girls 71
Victrola ix, 1, 6
viddle 90
viddle vops 72
video canary 191, 197
Vietnamization 119,
    121, 125
Vietvet 125
vingle 72, 85
vision 208
V-J Day 83
v-mail 83
vogue 170, 181
voguing 181
void coupon 89
Volstead Act 36
vop 90
Voutian 72, 90
vulcanized 37

wack 187
wade-in 129
waitress mom 211
wake-up 119, 125
waldo 181
Waldorf 79
wall of sound 148
wally 29
warden 108
war is not healthy for
    children and
    other living
    things 133
War of the Worlds 68
War on Poverty 127

War Time 83
war to end war 3, 20
Waste-watergate 164
water 20
waterbugger 164
waterbungler 164
waterfallout 164
Watergaters 164
waxed 125
waxes ix, 26
way 170, 181
weak sister 38
weather 80
webisode 192, 205
wedge 155
wed-in 129
weed 135
weekend hippie 120, 133
we gone 146
Welcommittee 153
Western Front 20
wet 32, 36
wet sock 32
whatever 192, 203
whatnik 101
What's buzzin', cousin? 89
What's knittin', kitten? 89
What's your story, morning glory? 89

wheel printer 166
wheels of steel 187
whip out a handcuff 33
whip over 37
whistle bait 87
white knight 169, 172
whitespeak 184
white squire 172
whizz-bang 20
whoopee 28
whoopee parlor 37
wicked 181
wig 138
wig out 114
Wilma 201
wimp 120
windmill 189
wind sucker 15
winning hearts and minds 121, 124
wipe out 139
wiper 38
wire fever 80
wireless 58, 59
with an overcoat 21
with the tide out 21
Wobblies 3, 23, 54
wolfburger stand 195
wolfess 87
wolf in Jeep's clothing 90

woman suffrage 22
women's club 22
women's lib 128
woodsies 138
word 187
word from the bird 114
word of mouse 199
wordsmith 208
word up 187
working 96
workshop 192, 207, 208
world 119, 125
WPA 48, 54
wrecked 133
wreck on a raft 64
wuss 158

yackers 173
Yanknik 101
yappie 175
yard bird 75
yegg 56
yellowjacket 112
yerba 135
yesterday, today, and forever 63
yippies 119, 126
yo 187
you can't trust anyone over thirty 133

you never had it so good 76, 77
you shred it, wheat 89
youthquake 120, 138
Y2K 208
Y2Kake 209
Y2Kaos 209
Y2K compliance 209
Y2K compliant 192
yucas 175
yuffie 204
yup 169
yuppie 169, 175
yuppieback 175
yuppie disease 175

Zacatecas purple 135
zazz girl 87
Zeppelin 20
zero dark thirty 125
'Zhappenin'? 180
zine 153
ziperoo 91
zod 184
zoning 187
zoomie 125
zoot suit 86
zorch 108
zot 138

Picture Credits

xvi	Horn and Hardart Co./New York Public Library
8	White Studio/Billy Rose Theatre Collection, The New York Public Library for the Performing Arts, Astor, Lenox and Tilden Foundations
12	Library of Congress
24	Denver Public Library
43	The Museum of Talking Boards
46	Library of Congress
50	Nat Norman/Museum of the City of New York
52	Western History Collections, University of Oklahoma Library
61	Library of Congress
70	Chicago Daily News/Chicago Historical Society
82	Picture History
86	Library of Congress
94	Picture History
99	AP/WorldWide Photos
108	Bettmann/CORBIS
118	Picture History
126	Picture History
144	Ted Streshinsky/CORBIS
147	Patrick DarbyCORBIS
168	Doug Wilson/CORBIS
188	S.I.N./CORBIS
190	Image Source/Super Stock
206	CORBIS